Gender, Nation, and the Arabic Novel

Gender, Nation, and the Arabic Novel

Egypt, 1892–2008

Hoda Elsadda

EDINBURGH
University Press

SYRACUSE UNIVERSITY PRESS

First Edition 2012
12 13 14 15 16 17 6 5 4 3 2 1

Copublished by Syracuse University Press and Edinburgh University Press.

∞ The paper used in this publication meets the minimum requirements of the American National Standard for Information Sciences—Permanence of Paper for Printed Library Materials, ANSI Z39.48-1992.

For a listing of books published and distributed by Syracuse University Press, visit our Web site at SyracuseUniversityPress.syr.edu.

ISBN: 978-0-8156-3296-2

Library of Congress Cataloging-in-Publication Data

El Sadda, Hoda.

Gender, nation, and the Arabic novel : Egypt, 1892–2008 / Hoda Elsadda. — 1st ed.
p. cm.

Includes bibliographical references and index.

ISBN 978-0-8156-3296-2 (cloth : alk. paper) 1. Arabic fiction—Egypt—History and criticism. 2. Arabic fiction—20th century—History and criticism. 3. Arabic fiction—21st century—History and criticism. 4. Masculinity in literature. 5. Women in literature. 6. Nationalism in literature. 7. Politics in literature. I. Title.

PJ8212.E53 2012

892.7'3609962—dc23 2012017586

Manufactured in the United States of America

Hoda Elsadda is professor of English and comparative literature at Cairo University. She previously held a chair in the Study of the Contemporary Arab World, in the School of Languages, Linguistics, and Cultures at the University of Manchester. She is founding member and current chair of the board of trustees of the Women and Memory Forum, a research center in Egypt, which focuses on gender issues in Arab cultural history.

Contents

Acknowledgments

This book would not have been possible without the love and support of my family. I am particularly grateful to my mother and father for always being there for me, physically and morally.

I am also deeply indebted to friends and colleagues for their support and encouragement. Special thanks go to friends who were generous with their time and edited, commented on, or read portions of the manuscript: Sahar Sobhi, Anastasia Valassopoulos, Mona Baker, Dalia Mostafa, Samia Mehrez, and Vron Ware. To my dear friend Mervat Hatem, I was enriched and inspired by our intellectual exchanges. To my friends and comrades in the Women and Memory Forum, I cherish the intellectual and human haven that has sustained me in difficult times. I particularly owe a debt of gratitude to Omaima Aboubakr, Sahar Sobhi, Hala Kamal, Rania Abdel Rahman, Amina El Bendary, Amira Sonbol, Afaf Mahfouz, and Amal Aboul Fadl.

To Professor Rasheed El-Enany, I am truly grateful for his comments and revisions of the manuscript. I also wish to thank the anonymous reviewers of the Edinburgh University Press and Syracuse University Press for their very helpful feedback.

The book could not have been completed without the financial support of the Leverhulme Trust Research Fellowship, which freed my time for research for a year, and the University of Manchester's sabbatical leave. I am grateful to both. Sections of the book were also supported by a grant from the Arab Families Working Group (AFWG). The group has been a source of intellectual stimulation for more than ten years, and I am thankful to all members of the group: Suad Joseph, Penny Johnson, Lamis Abu Nahla, Eileen Kuttab, Zeina Zaatari, Nadine Naber, Martina Rieker, Annelies Moors, Mona Khalaf, Ibrahim Elnur, Ray Juraidini, and Barbara Ibrahim.

Portions of the book appeared previously as follows: parts of chapter 1 appeared in "Imaging the 'New Man': Gender and Nation in Arab Literary Narratives in the Early Twentieth Century" in *JMEWS: Journal of Middle East Women's Studies* 3, no. 2 (Spring 2007): 31–55; "Gendered Citizenship: Discourses on Domesticity in the Second Half of the Nineteenth Century," in *Hawwa: Journal of Women of the Middle East and the Islamic World* 4, no. 1 (2006): 1–28; and "Notions of Modernity: Representations of the "Western Woman" by Female Authors in Early Twentieth-Century Egypt," in *The Arabs and Britain: Changes and Exchanges,* proceedings of a conference organized by the British Council in Cairo, the British Council, 1998, 352–66. Parts of chapter 2 appeared in "Imaging the 'New Man': Gender and Nation in Arab Literary Narratives in the Early Twentieth Century" in *JMEWS: Journal of Middle East Women's Studies* 3, no. 2 (Spring 2007): 31–55. Parts of chapter 5 appeared in "A Gender-Sensitive Reading of Latifa El-Zayyat's *Sahib Al-Bayt,*" in *Cairo Studies in English,* edited by Hoda Gindi, Department of English, Cairo University, 1995, 25–48. I am grateful to all the editors and reviewers.

Note on Transliteration and Translation

I have transliterated Arabic words and names in accordance with the system used by the *International Journal of Middle Eastern Studies.* I have omitted the use of Arabic diacritics, except for the 'ayn (') and the hamza ('). Upon their first mention, names of authors whose work has been translated into English are transliterated, and then I spell their names as they appear in English. For example: Najib Mahfuz (henceforth Naguib Mahfouz). For Arab figures whose names are known to English-speaking audiences, I use the more familiar spelling of their names, for example, Gamal Abdel Nasser. Also, for Arab critics who publish in English, I do not transliterate their names but use the same spelling that they use in English; for example Sabry Hafez instead of Sabri Hafiz. Arabic words commonly used in English, such as sheikh, are not transliterated.

All my references to novels are made to the original version published in Arabic. I use existing translations of titles of books that have been translated into English for ease of reference. Otherwise, all translations are mine.

Introduction

Gender, Nation, and the Canon of the Arabic Novel

This study engages with the national canon of Arabic literature, using gender as a category of analysis. Two basic assumptions underlie the project. The first is that the canon of Arabic literature, particularly the novelistic canon, both reflects and constructs the ideas of nation and national identity in the modern period.[1] The second is that the nation, "an imagined community," is gendered, and by extension, the canon is equally gendered. I use the concept of gender as defined by Joan Scott as "a constitutive element of social relationships based on perceived differences between the sexes, and . . . [as] a primary way of signifying relationships of power" (Scott 1986, 1067). The book sheds light on and interrogates representations of femininity and masculinity in modern Arabic fiction in order to explore their implications for the project of nation building and the imagining of subjectivities in the modern period. Representations of ideal gendered roles and characteristics not only define and shape the contours of national identity and national futures, they are also cultural interventions in ideological contestations over the image of the nation. I argue that conflicting representations of gendered roles shape and correspond to conflicting political allegiances as well as to conflicting ideologies regarding the modernity vs. tradition paradigm for explicating the modern history of the Arab world, and regarding the place of

1. My basic assumption is that national canons of literature are constructed by a specific group or elite for a specific purpose and are not natural reflections of national character. For a survey of critiques of the naturalness of the canon see Corse (1995).

the national in the context of globalization. During the *nahda* period at the turn of the twentieth century, for example, a male *nahda* elite dominated the field of literary production and shaped the nation in their own image, foregrounding their values, their ontological dilemmas, their fears and desires. The historical choice was in favor of a rupture with tradition as a condition for entry to modernity, and consequently this elite internalized many of the assumptions of a colonial discourse that instituted a value-laden binarism between the traditional and the modern.

Inevitably, and as a consequence of their dominance in the cultural field, other imaginings of the nation, other discourses that had once enjoyed credence and wide circulation and audiences were marginalized. Revisiting the modern Arab literary tradition from a gender lens interrogates the processes of inclusion and exclusion in the canon and potentially leads to the recovery of literary voices that have been marginalized because they did not fit the ideological blueprint of the dominant cultural elite. At the end of the twentieth century and into the twenty-first, we witness the rise of new writing that engages with/interrogates established dictums in the national canon, as the scene of literary production becomes more diverse and more inclusive, and as they continue to engage with neocolonial discourses in the global world order. In the book I examine selected texts and themes that are characteristic of the literary production in Egypt, starting from the late nineteenth century, until the first decade of the twenty-first century.

A Novelistic Canon

The rise and development of the modern Arabic novel ran parallel to and intersected with projects of nation building in the modern period. This is not unique to the tradition of the Arabic novel. Homi Bhabha has drawn attention to the centrality of narrative in the construction of national imaginaries, asserting that nations are narrations (1990). Benedict Anderson privileged the novel as a site for the construction of nations, or "imagined communities" (1991. Edward Said has also emphasized the role of fictional narratives, particularly the novel, as a site of colonial cultural representations in the service of empire, as well as a locus for resistance in anticolonial nationalisms (1993). The novel, as a "modern" genre, became one of the main venues/instruments for shaping the contours of the national imaginary, hence a contested site for competing ideologies and actors. It also became a critical site for the interpretation and analysis of national themes and directions.[2] Arab cultural critics have pondered the reasons for the ascendancy of the novel in the Arabic tradition and the relative decline in the status of poetry, the artistic genre that had maintained its high status until the modern period. Jabir 'Asfur, professor of Arabic literature at Cairo University and prominent cultural critic and columnist, contended that the twentieth century, particularly its second half, was the age of the novel, *zaman al-riwaya* (1999).

Recent critiques of Arab modernity have highlighted how the Arab literary establishment assimilated a Western modernist paradigm, resulting in the trivialization of traditional or popular forms of knowledge, and an acceptance of the superiority of the European forms of cultural production. Consequently, the rise of novelism in Western culture, or the institutionalization of the novel as "the characteristic expression . . . of western modernity" (Hunter 1990, 6), also became a measure of the attainment of modernity, and modern writing in both Arabic and Persian literatures, as Kamran Rastegar has argued (2007). At the same time, the privileging of the novel as the modern genre par excellence and the manifestation of the modern spirit—or world view—resulted in the marginalization of other genres and other forms of cultural expressions. Samah Selim, for example, has argued that "the national novelistic canon was predicated on the suppression and management of . . . [a] thriving contemporary field of popular fiction" (2004a, 72). The degrading of other forms of expression in favor of the novel is particularly important considering that, as Rastegar has argued, "the economy of book-printing . . . [in Iran and the Arab world] is by no means comparable to that of western European languages" (2007, 21)[3] Again more generally, Anne McClintock has questioned Benedict Anderson's insistence on the centrality of print in the formation of nations, a key factor in the propagation of the novel as the locus of cultural imaginaries, and has argued that "commodity spectacle" in

2. The literature on why the novel as a genre has been particularly relevant to the imagining of the nation is very large. See for example Timothy Brennan's account of why the novel has been identified as the genre most suited to the discursive formation of the nation (1990).

3. Rastegar makes this point with specific reference to Iran, but it applies to the Arab world as well as part of his general argument.

twentieth century nationalist projects are as important, if not more so (1995, 374). All these arguments challenge the primacy of the novel as a cultural site for the production and dissemination of ideas of nationhood and belonging and direct attention to other forms of representation.

In this book, I explore issues of canonicity and canon construction in Arabic cultural production. I have therefore chosen to focus on the novel because of the privileged status it has been accorded in cultural history, making it an ideal site for understanding the processes of inclusion and exclusion that have taken place in the cultural sphere, processes that are imbricated in the dynamics of power relations. Which novels are canonized and why, and which are marginalized, ignored, and then rediscovered, are all questions that shed light on the dynamics of cultural production in the Arab world, or on what counts as knowledge. The book also engages with issues of representation and cultural identity in national, regional, and international contexts. Muhammad Siddiq has made a case for the centrality of the genre of the novel in understanding "the major constituents of identity in modern Arab culture" (2007, xi). Furthermore, and because of the cultural status accrued by the novel through the twentieth century, not only as a genre in tune with cultural transformations but as a genre that shapes and contributes to the construction of national identities and imaginaries, it has become a locus of contestation and an ideological battlefield. Some of the battles that erupted over novels in the Arab world had serious consequences on the lives of writers, resulting either in censoring their work or, more seriously, in assaults on their lives and/or livelihoods.[4] This is an important point, as it puts in perspective the view that the limited readership of fiction in the Arab world indicates the limited influence of writers on society (Caiani 2007, 5). At the end of the day, novels do have an impact on the public sphere and are therefore sites of contestation and interrogation. Finally, I argue that many of the well-known literary debates among the Arab literati, about literary standards, artistic tastes, controversial award ceremonies, criteria for selection of texts for translation, and women's writing, are all, in the final analysis, cultural battles about the formation of the Arabic national canon and the construction of national identities.

4. See Fabio Caiani (2007, 5); Siddiq (2007, 1–22).

Canons as products of cultural processes implicated in sociopolitical transformations are necessarily subject to contestation and reformulation. A good example of a canonical literary text that has been the focus of revisionist readings and interpretations is Muhammad Husayn Haykal's (henceforth Mohammed Hussein Haikal) novel *Zaynab.* Until the last decade of the twentieth century, the widespread consensus among literary historians has been that *Zaynab* is the first Arabic novel. This is despite the fact that many Arabic novels were published and read before *Zaynab*'s appearance in 1914. Arguments for why *Zaynab* has been accorded prominence in the canon have mostly focused on technical issues, namely that it meets the criteria of the genre as specified in the Western canon, or that it is more artistically mature compared to earlier experiments. Critic 'Abd al-Muhsin Taha Badr charts the development of the modern Arabic novel in Egypt, emphasizes the formative influence of the translations of Western novels and identifies Rifa'a al-Tahtawi's *Takhliz al-'ibriz* as a text that planted the seeds of the educational novel in the nineteenth century (1963, 52). Badr's typology of the development of the genre of the novel divides the novelistic production into three categories: the educational, the entertaining, and the artistic. The nineteenth-century novels are predominantly educational and entertaining, and it is only in the twentieth century, with the publication of *Zaynab,* that we have the first artistic novel, *al-riwaya al-fanniyya* (Badr 1963).[5] On the other hand, Elliot Colla has put forward the argument that *Zaynab*'s canonical status as the first novel is based neither on chronological precedence nor on literary merit. He traces the development of the critical reception of *Zaynab* across the decades of the twentieth century and concludes that it was only in the Nasserist period with the film adaptation of the novel, as well as "the nationalization of university curricula" (2009, 214), that the novel's canonicity was enshrined. It was the convergence between the theme of the novel and Nasser's project that secured its prime position in the canon. In 1999, and in response to a rising trend in Arabic literary criticism to reconsider the status of *Zaynab* in the canon, Jabir 'Asfur argued that *Zaynab*'s prominence was justified on a number of counts. To begin with, it constituted a break with

5. For a detailed analysis of Badr's thesis see Samah Selim (2003).

traditional generic hierarchies, displacing poetry as the most elevated form of Arabic expression by the novel, a genre more expressive of the worldview of the growing middle class. 'Asfur foregrounds the feminine title of the novel, and the fact that a large number of novels written in the first half of the twentieth century carried the name of a female protagonist, because, according to him, writing about the new woman ran parallel to her liberation in society and the shaking of traditional social norms. He adds that the Arabic novel can be seen as "an agent of the modernization of the relations of literary production through [putting forward] a new kind of writing and a new kind of readership" (1999, 112). He concludes that *Zaynab* earned its status as the first Arabic novel because of its "influence, not its historical precedence, in curbing the traditional status of poetry"[6] (1999, 113). 'Asfur takes for granted the modernist idea of the necessity of a rupture with tradition as a prerequisite for modernity and, as such, espouses the view that, as *Zaynab* fulfills this requirement, it qualifies as the first proper expression of a modernist sensibility and artistic genre.

Critics of the modernist paradigm that privileges Western-style cultural production, which dominates the critical understanding of Arabic literature, have argued, for example, that Muhammed al-Muwaylihi's *Hadith 'Issa ibn Hisham* (1907) is the first Arabic novel, on account of its content and its focus on contemporary social concerns in the Arab world, in contradistinction to *Zaynab,* whose pioneering status is based on formalistic adherence to the European genre (al-Bahrawi 1996b, 45–47). Rastegar relates why *Hadith* was ignored to the view that it did not meet "the requirements of the genre" of the novel, the emblem of Western modernity, to which the literati aspired (2007, 96). In a similar vein, Radwa 'Ashur (henceforth Ashour) has made a case for Faris al-Shidyaq's *al-Saq 'ala al-saq* (Leg Over Leg), published in 1855, as the first Arabic novel. She argues that al-Shidyaq's literary project, which sought to renovate traditional forms and styles and emphasized continuity, rather than a rupture with tradition, was marginalized by the *nahda* elite because of its dissonance with their ideological choice (2009). I concur with the view that *Zaynab*'s emblematic status as the first Arabic novel is not

6. My translation.

based on artistic merit, nor on historical precedence, but on its amalgamation of important elements in the liberal national discourse about the modern nation. One of the key components at the center of the national discourse in the first half of the twentieth century is the figure of the *nahda* hero, as I call him, who represents the intellectual elite or the reformists, who led the *nahda* movement, and while doing that, shaped and defined its parameters according to their own image, interests, and ideological choices.

Feminist critics, on the other hand, have foregrounded the many narrative contributions by women writers and have interpreted their marginalization as symptomatic of a patriarchal literary establishment that ignored women writers and their concerns.[7] Novels such as Zaynab Fawwaz's *Husn al-'awaqib: Ghada al-Zahra* (Good consequences: Ghada the Radiant) published in 1899, and *Qalb al-rajul* (The heart of man) by Labiba Hashim, published in 1904, were "rediscovered" and presented as evidence of the existence of valuable literary contributions by women writers that predated the publication of *Zaynab,* hence subverting the masculine domination of the literary canon. Bouthaina Shaaban challenges what she describes as the "trivialization of Arab women's writings" and suggests that the "stifling of women's writings might well have been intentional" owing to "the novelty and seriousness" of their contribution, which was perceived as "threatening" (2009, 37). Shaaban stresses that *Husn al-'awaqib,* by Zaynab Fawwaz (1846–1914) is the first Arabic novel, as it appeared fifteen years before *Zaynab* (2009, 22). In her introduction to a new edition of Labiba Hashim's *Qalb al-rajul,* Yumna al-'Id, on the other hand, emphasizes that these pioneering women writers enjoyed high esteem among their contemporaries and that their contribution to the literary and cultural fields was appreciated and praised by male pioneers of reform. She insists that the marginalization of women writers in the twentieth century cannot be solely explained on the grounds of male prejudice because, according to her, enlightened men have always supported women, but is due to "authoritarian political thought" that counters the progress and independence of nations and that serves to sustain the dominance of men over women as a means of solidifying inequality in general (2002b, 8).

7. See Elsadda 2004 and 2008.

Shaaban's revisions are based on historical precedence and an assumption of prejudice against women writers because of the perceived threat they pose to the status quo dominated by men. Al-'Id's analysis of the reasons for the marginalization of women's writing by male critics, on the other hand, absolves the liberal elite of the charge that they wittingly or unwittingly discriminated against women's cultural production by not including their early contributions in the canon of the Arabic novel. I argue that neither historical precedence, that is, which novel was published first, nor male prejudice as such, nor the idea that women were excluded not by the liberal elite but by forces that work against progress, that is, conservative forces, offer adequate explanation of the processes of inclusion and exclusion in the literary canon. Many novels were published by women *and* men, long before *Zaynab,* as attested to by Badr (1963) and others. Also, whereas gender was certainly a factor in the exclusion of women from the canon, it was not the only one, as many literary contributions by men were also excluded. And finally, the discourse of the liberal national elite, exemplified in Qasim Amin's work, instituted a hierarchy of genders regarding both men and women that will thrive and dominate discourses on gender in the twentieth century. I argue that the processes of inclusion and exclusion in the canon were regulated by the symbolic power of a liberal national elite whose cultural imaginings shaped the literary canon so as to represent their own worldview and their ontological and cultural conflicts, as well as their aspirations for the future.

Literary canons are invariably linked to ideas of nationhood. In "The Rise of English," Terry Eagleton tells the story of how "English Literature rode to power on the back of wartime nationalism" (1983, 26). He argues that it was only after the First World War that English literature was transformed from "a subject fit for women, workers and those wishing to impress the natives" to a serious intellectual pursuit for students at Oxford and Cambridge (25). Guari Viswanathan has subsequently traced the beginnings of English literary studies to colonial India, where the study of English classics was an essential component in the cultural domination and politics of empire (1989). It follows that the canon of English literature performed a dual role, depending on different geographical and historical contexts. In post–World War I England, it bolstered a national sense of identity at a time of crisis, while in the colonies, it was a hegemonic weapon to control the minds and hearts of Indian colonial subjects, ensuring their subjugation to English values and culture. Literary canons are therefore cultural products shaped by and constitutive of the geopolitics of cultural production at a given historical moment. They can legitimize projects of conquest and domination, as well as projects of resistance and liberation.

The novelistic canon of Arabic literature has largely been constructed to reflect, indeed to comply with, a nationalist agenda, hence expressing dominant themes in national discourses and excluding other equally important themes expressed by more marginal voices and groups. "Canonical" novels written in the first half of the twentieth century that are anthologized and celebrated as expressive of Arab worldviews and concerns will inevitably address issues related to the dilemma of a protagonist, an Arab intellectual, torn between tradition and modernity, the relation between East and West, the individual and society, the woman question, all themes that occupied a central place in the national discourse (M. M. Badawi 1993; Allen 1995). These are the themes that dominated the canon in the first decades of the twentieth century. The 1950s saw the rise of commitment literature, or *'adab al-'iltizam*. Influenced by Jean-Paul Sartre's *"What Is Literature?"* (1947) and the political turmoil in the region, the term meant different things but definitely "a certain measure of nationalism" (M. M. Badawi 1993, 16). Writers felt committed to writing about social and political concerns. Many saw themselves as the spokespersons of their nations with messages to convey. Influenced by the revolutionary fervor and the rising anticolonial resistance movements in the region and elsewhere in the Third World, Halim Barakat goes a bit further and qualifies the literary production of writers who turn a blind eye to the pressing issues of their societies as "a sort of engagement in irrelevancies" (1975, 127). The avant-garde generation of the 1960s that engaged with sociopolitical issues in many ways established the view that writers, especially canonical writers, were "prophets of the nation" (Abdel Messih 2006, 22), and the view of the sociopolitical duty entrusted to them persisted and continued to exert considerable influence until the present. As Sabry Hafez puts it, "most of the novels written by the generation of the 60s gain their critical sharpness from a burning desire to change the world" (2001, 203). In the 1970s and 1980s, a sweeping wave of disillusionment created a new mood in literature that has been described as the "new sensibility," where the protagonist is no longer certain of his/her ability to decipher the outside world and resorts to techniques and artistic strategies to help him/her portray an enigmatic world. Still, writing about masculine identity in the fiction of the Arab East since 1967, Samira Aghacy qualifies the novels analyzed in the study as possessing "an underlying political awareness revealing the centrality of political life . . . and the precedence of collective over private issues" (2009, 7). Stefan Meyer identifies the political engagement in modern Arabic literature as a characteristic that distinguishes Arab modernism from Western modernism (2001, 46). In short, the consensus remains that even the most personal individual traumas are necessarily symbolic at some level of collective traumas and predicaments, that too much involvement with one's life on the part of writers is tantamount to betrayal, especially in situations of conflict (al-Jayyusi 1992).[8]

This view certainly seems to corroborate Frederic Jameson's controversial thesis that all third-world texts are necessarily "national allegories" (1986, 69), that they are always imbued with the political. Aijaz Ahmad, to give one prominent example of a critical rebuttal, argued that Jameson's "theory of cognitive aesthetics of third-world literature" essentializes the differences between civilizations, homogenizes diverse histories and trajectories of development, and, more importantly reduces third-world history and social dynamics to one experience, namely the experience of colonialism and imperialism (1987). After demonstrating that not all third-world texts need be read as national allegories, Ahmad wonders if Jameson's hypothesis institutes "the Law of the Father," that "only those texts which give us national allegories can be admitted as authentic texts of Third World literature, while the rest are excluded by definition" (12). Ahmad's Law of the Father refers to theoretical paradigms constructed by first-world critics for inclusion of works in the universal/Western canon. I argue that the canon of Arabic literature, or the Arab critical establishment, has accepted the basic premise of

8. Furthermore, scholars of Arabic literature have noted that there is no essential contradiction between experimentation and innovation on the one hand, and concern with the sociopolitical on the other, as demonstrated in the experimental fiction and innovative literary texts in Arabic literature (Meyer 2001; Caiani 2007).

Jameson's thesis, that third-world literatures/Arabic literatures are defined by their colonial and anticolonial experience, hence privileging the nationalist dimension in artistic expression, creating another Law of the Father. The main point here, however, is that this canonical dictum is not self-evident or necessarily reflective of existing Arab cultural production, but is inevitably contingent on processes of inclusion and exclusion, whereby works that do not fit the "nationalist" criteria are marginalized or undermined. Ahmad has noted that Jameson's text is "gendered," that it could not have been written by an American woman, given the tradition of feminists who have persistently challenged the opposition between the private and the public realms (24). I will argue that the pronounced nationalist character of the canon has resulted in the marginalization of cultural production that did not subscribe directly to the national edicts and has also inhibited the voices of both men and women.

Gender and Anticolonial Nationalisms

Building on Benedict Anderson's definition of nations as "imagined communities" that are socially and politically constructed, feminist and postcolonial scholars have emphasized that national imaginaries are also gendered, and moreover, sanction the "institutionalization of gender difference" (McClintock 1995, 353). Men and women have had different relationships with the nation in terms of what is expected of them and as regards perceptions of their roles and status. Invariably, women have been allocated a marginal position in the national imaginary. For although they are the designated symbols of the nation, the mothers of the nation, the bearers of traditional values and heritage, are accorded limited national agency (Yuval-Davis 1997; McClintock 1995, 354; Yuval-Davis and Anthias 1989). Anticolonial nationalisms are particularly weighed down by the burden of colonialism. Theirs is an imagined community that is taking shape in the shadow of a colonial model of what a modern nation looks like. Representations of gendered national identities are complicated by their imbrication with colonial discourses about colonized subjects. Edward Said has drawn attention to the discursive feminization of the Orient as a function of colonial domination and power over the colonized. Images of sexual domination that enforce the power hierarchies between men and women are transposed to the relationship between the colonizer and the colonized. The West is male, rational, powerful, and in control, and the East is female, irrational, weak, and dominated. Moreover, women as symbols of the modern nation in anticolonial discourses and markers of a coveted modernity are caught up in the love-hate relationship with the colonizer, a major anticolonial national dilemma. On the one hand, the improvement of their lot (read: becoming more modern and less traditional), is perceived as a prerequisite for progress and national access to modernity, but they are nevertheless expected to act as the guardians of traditional values and authentic cultural identity. Requiring women to be "modern-yet-modest" (Najmabadi 1991, 49) becomes a defining characteristic of the ambivalence of antinational discourses regarding the role of women, its "janus-faced quality" as Deniz Kandiyoti describes it (1991, 431). On the other hand, this ambivalence has been interpreted as a manifestation of a creative project of differentiation undertaken by anticolonial nationalisms "to fashion a 'modern' national community that is nevertheless not Western" (Chatterjee 1996, 217). In effect, women's bodies became the arena for the battle over identity and cultural supremacy between colonial and national forces.[9]

Feminist and postcolonial insights have informed and enriched scholarship on the Middle East and have resulted in a revision of some of the metanarratives about the history of the Arab world in general, and the history of Arab women in particular, such as: that Arab women have traditionally been oppressed and denied voice; that it was only with the advent of modernity that they were allowed access to the public sphere; that modernity necessarily meant more rights for women; that the women's liberation movement in Egypt was primarily championed by a group of enlightened male reformers. Scholarship on Qasim Amin is a good case in point. His status in history, as the father of Arab feminism, was subjected to a revisionist appraisal by feminist historians in the 1990s. Scholars drew attention to the active participation of women in shaping the discourses on liberation in the second half of

9. There is now an extensive body of literature about women's positions and roles in anticolonial nationalisms that foreground stunning similarities. See, for example, Pierson and Chaudhuri (1998) and Parker et al. (1992).

the nineteenth century in Egypt and Lebanon (Baron 1994; Badran 1995; Booth 2001b), that is, predating or simultaneously with Amin.[10] The revival of women's participation in historical events and the formulation of discourses went hand-in-hand with the discovery of early literary contributions by women, again starting from the nineteenth century. The names of 'A'isha Taymur, Zaynab Fawwaz, Labiba Hashim, and many others surfaced on the literary scene. Also, Amin's discourse about the liberation of women came under scrutiny as emblematic of the national discourse at the turn of the twentieth century. Leila Ahmed showed the intersections/overlaps between Amin's discourse about the backwardness of Egyptian women as a challenge to the development of the nation and a priority on the reform agenda, and colonial discourses that posited "the backward status" of women as a marker and proof of the backwardness of the country (Ahmed 1992 144–68). This conflation between national and colonial discourses is signaled as a feature of postcolonial modernity.

One of the main directions of the new revisionist scholarship has been a critique of the basic tenets of modernist discourses in postcolonial contexts. In a much-quoted article that looks at Egyptian discourses on gender in the post 1976 neo-liberal phase, Hatem challenges the assumptions about basic oppositions between secularist and Islamist views (1994). She argues that secular and Islamist discourses on gender are similar, in other words, that liberal positions on the woman question are not more supportive of women's empowerment and are fraught with contradictions and ambivalences, hence refuting the modernist premise that modernity brought more rights to women. This insightful thesis challenges the core of modernist histories of the Arab world, based on a binary opposition between old and new, the modern and the traditional, the secular, and the religious, and always assuming that the modern, the secular, and the new are inevitably more supportive of women's rights and are better for women. Critiques of modernist discourses

10. It is noteworthy that the groundwork that paved the way for this revisionist scholarship started much earlier in the twentieth century with studies that foregrounded the contribution of women, such as 'Ijlal Khalifa's work on women's journals (1973), al-Subki on the women's movement (1986), and other collections of writings by Arab women.

have enabled a rethinking of notions of modernity in so far as they have an impact on the location of women in national narratives, our understanding of women's agency and subjectivity, and the geopolitics of the construction of discourses.[11] To give just one example, recent research has foregrounded the nineteenth-century contribution of 'A'isha Taymur and has reevaluated her "liberation" story as well as her literary work. The feminist/modernist narratives of Taymur emphasized the role of her father as a key supporter of her literary career, blamed her mother for trying to enforce traditional roles on her daughter, disregarded the important contribution of female members of Taymur's family and female tutors to her career, and consequently abided by a male modernist narrative that glorified the role of men in leading the liberation of women in the Middle East, a narrative that expected women to abandon their feminine roles as a condition for acceptance in a male-dominated world (Hatem 1998). A new line of inquiry that contests modernist assumptions about the unsuitability of things traditional to the modern world has enabled the discovery and validation of a significant body of fictional narratives written by men and women that was previously disregarded and qualified as mediocre or not meeting the standards of modern narrative styles. 'A'isha Taymur's fictional narrative, *Nata'ij al-'ahwal fi al-'aqwal wa al-'af'al* (The consequences of circumstances in words and deeds) emerges as an important text in the development of the genre of the novel, a point which will be discussed in more detail in chapter 1.[12]

Research on gender and the Arab world gathered considerable force in the last three decades and has primarily focused on "the woman question," on representations of femininity, and on the literary production of Arab women writers.[13] In the Arab world, the advent of more women writers onto the literary scene, more women researchers and academics, and a growing

11. See Lila Abu-Lughod's *Remaking Women* (1998) and Elsadda (1993 and 1994).

12. It is beyond the scope of this introduction to review all the relevant literature, but I have particularly benefited from Lila Abu-Lughod's *Remaking Women* (1998); Leila Ahmed's *Women and Gender in Islam* (1992); Judith Tucker's *Women in Nineteenth Century Egypt* (1985); and Timothy Mitchell's *Colonizing Egypt* (1989).

13. For examples of research in Arabic on representations of women in literature and on Arab women writers, see Naji (1989) and al-Zayyat (1989).

interest in feminist and postcolonial studies in universities has led to a focus on women writers as part of academic as well as activist agendas. The 1990s saw the publication of specialized journals in women's studies in Arabic, such as *Hajar* (1993–98) in Egypt, and the establishment of women's publishing houses, such as Nur (1994) in Egypt, and Le Fennec (1987) in Morocco, as well as the founding of a large number of professional, cultural, and research organizations that focus specifically on women's issues.[14] Much of the knowledge produced by these organizations, in Arabic, is often held hostage to the grim realities of publishing and conducting research in the Arab world: limited circulation of books and journals within countries, and limited or no access to resources across the region or on the international market. Interest in women's issues, and by extension women's writing, has arguably been bolstered by undemocratic Arab states, nominally invested in creating a façade of modernity to conceal their essentially oppressive characters. The woman question in the Arab world has always been complicated by the phenomenon of an opportunistic state feminism where women's rights issues are exploited to serve state policies. The pattern of First Ladies presiding over national councils for women is a manifestation of the continuation of this phenomenon until the present.

In the West, research interest in Arab women's writing has been boosted by the increasing availability of Arabic literature in translation, as well as the growing market interest in Islam and Islamic cultures.[15] Western interest in

14. To give just two examples, the first is the Bahithat (Lebanese Association of Women Researchers founded in 1992 in Lebanon), a professional organization that consists of women researchers and academics who have organized conferences and published books as well as an annual thematic book/journal series. It is not a feminist organization, though much of the scholarship is informed by feminist theories. The second example is the Women and Memory Forum (WMF, founded in 1997 in Egypt), a research organization that promotes the production of knowledge on gender and Arab culture within the framework of a feminist/activist agenda. Among other things, WMF has focused on the revival of women's history and has republished texts by women that have gone out of circulation and been marginalized in the national memory.

15. For book-length studies focusing on Arab women's writings see, for example, Mikhail (1978); Accad (1978 and 1990); Cooke (1988); Malti-Douglas (1991); al-Ali (1994); Arebi (1994); Zeidan (1995).

Arab women is not a new phenomenon: historically, colonial aggression has been justified as a humanitarian mission to save Muslim women from Muslim men and can be understood as "part of its [the West's] interest in and hostility to Islam" (Amireh 1996, 10). More recently, the Iranian revolution in 1979 and the rise of Islam as a global power to contend with, the Gulf War in 1991, and finally the attacks on the United States on 11 September 2001, have all stimulated more interest in Islamic cultures in general, and Muslim women in particular. And although Arab women are not all Muslim, the religious diversity of the Arab region is largely ignored, as "Arab" is often synonymous with "Muslim" in the Western imaginary. This larger political context has led, as noted by many researchers and educators, to a situation where Arab women's texts are read as anthropological case studies of "other" cultures that are essentially different from the Western "self." The reception and consumption of Arab women's writing in translation in the West is inevitably tinted by the political and cultural environment of the host language, or the "horizon of expectation" as Mohja Kahf puts it, using Hans Robert Jauss's phrase. According to her, there are three stereotypes circulating about the Arab woman in the West: she is either "a victim of oppression . . . [or] an escapee of her intrinsically oppressive culture . . . [or] the pawn of Arab male power" (2000, 149). Researchers, translators, and editors of translation series directly address these stereotypes in their publications and alert readers to the potential pitfalls of ascribing to a monolithic view about gender discrimination in Arab culture and, equally, the danger of over-reading the gender dimension in women's texts. *Opening the Gates: A Century of Arab Feminist Writing* offers a very wide selection of texts and renders a much more complex picture of Arab women's interaction with their culture (Badran and Cooke 1990). Fadia Faqir, editor of the Garnet series on Arab women writers in translation, states clearly in all the introductions to the translated novels that one of the main aims of the series is to challenge or defy Western perceptions of Arab women writers by enabling their voices.[16] However, given the tug and pull between discrepant horizons of expectation of readers in the target language and readers in the source language, these efforts are far

16. See, for example, her introduction to Salwa Bakr's *Golden Chariot* (1995).

from straightforward and can lead to much controversy, as demonstrated by the "ungracious criticism" of some of the translations in the Garnet series.[17]

More recently, there has been a concerted effort to situate Arab women's literature within the canon of postcolonial studies. Arabic literature in general occupied a marginal position in postcolonial scholarship (Moore 2008, 3), relative to Indian literature for example, and as manifested in the course curricula in departments of English Language and Literature in the English speaking world as well as in the marked scarcity of scholarship on Arabic literature using postcolonial theories. Foregrounding "the complexities of the postcolonial contradictions experienced and voiced by Arab women" (Majaj et al 2002, xix) will potentially open up new pathways for the appreciation of Arab women's literary contribution in transnational as well as regional and local contexts. Anastasia Valassopoulos has argued that up to the late 1990s "most critical works on Arab women's writing centred around the feminist/nationalist debate" (2007, 13). Postcolonial approaches will not only inform the study of Arab women's writings but will also "generate fresh debates in feminist and postcolonial theory" (Valassopoulos 2007, 27). In fact, and as Wail Hassan has argued, opening up the field of postcolonial studies to pay more attention to literatures written in non-European languages will help "interrogate the limits of postcolonial theory's founding discourses from the multiple perspectives of Arabic, African, and Asian philosophies, realities, cultural worldviews, and cultural memories" (2003, 60). This new direction in scholarship on Arabic literature is clearly emerging as a vibrant field of inquiry.[18]

Critics agree that scholarship on gender and nation has primarily focused on women and the woman question to a point where gender became synonymous with women. This imbalance in the field has been recently redressed with the expansion of the field of masculinity studies and the resultant attention to representations of masculinity in both colonial and national

17. For an excellent analysis of the controversy surrounding the Garnet series, see Valassopoulos (2007).

18. There are now a significant number of book-length studies that focus on Arab women writers, using postcolonial theoretical concepts: Majaj, Sunderman, and Saliba (2002); Grace (2004); Gauch (2007); Valassopoulos (2007); Mehta (2007); Moore (2008).

narratives.[19] R. W. Connell has argued that the national narrative is dominated by "hegemonic masculinity," which "is always constructed in relation to various subordinated masculinities as well as in relation to women" (1987, 183). Men's identities are closely intertwined with that of the nation to the extent that they produce a "personalized image of the nation" (Hrock 1996, 90). Cynthia Enloe takes this a step further and contends that "nationalism typically has sprung from masculinized memory, masculinized humiliation and masculinized hope" (1989, 44). Some critics have taken issue with Connell's premise about the normality and dominance of a coherent masculine identity, arguing that identities are much more complex and that "the achievement of an absolutely unified and coherent gendered social identity, for masculinity as for femininity, is an impossibility" (Dawson 1994, 3). Hegemonic masculinity as defined by Connell, however, is not an essentialist notion but a construct that is contested and subject to change over different historical periods. Hegemonic masculinity is "normative . . . [in the sense that] it embodied the currently most honoured way of being a man, it required all other men to position themselves in relation to it, and it ideologically legitimated the global subordination of women to men" (Connell 2005, 4). "Hegemonic masculinity" qualifies unquestioned assumptions about the existence of a universal man, who in colonial contexts signified a Western, white, Christian, and heterosexual male, whose hegemonic status was sustained not only through the subordination of women, but also through the feminization of colonized territories (Said 1978), and the emasculation/effeminization of the colonized male (Krishnaswamy 1998). Frantz Fanon's insight into the assimilation and reproduction of colonial discourses by the national elite ([1961] 1967) is also valid as regards the construction of hegemonic national masculinities modeled on colonial masculinities. Inevitably, ideal national masculinities were subject to contestation as they manifested competing agendas within the national polity. For example, in the case of Egypt in the first half of the twentieth century, the ideal of national masculinity is embodied in the figure of the "*nahda* hero" in Arabic literature,

19. For a concise review of scholarship on gender and nation see Mayer 2000. For scholarship on masculinity see West and Lay (2000) and Kimmel et al. (2005).

who is invariably middle class (or espouses middle-class mores and values), literate, modern (having received a modern Western education and aspiring to a Western way of life), and ambivalent about his relationship with women (aspiring to a more egalitarian relationship with women that does not, however, compromise male dominance and control). This *nahda* hero is equally ambivalent about his relationship with the colonial West and is pithily described as having a love-hate relationship. Anticolonial nationalisms eventually construct their own brand of hegemonic masculinity, exemplified in the figures of strong national leaders, such as Gamal Abdel Nasser in Egypt, constituting "counterparts to the Western hegemonic masculinity" (Gerami 2005, 450). National hegemonic masculinities, as cultural constructs subject to historical and political contingency, are inevitably sites of contestation and negotiation. One of the aims of this study is to explore competing narratives on gendered identities as indicative of and constitutive of discourses on identity and notions of belonging, home, and exile.

Research on Arab masculinities in general, and masculinities within Arab national discourses in particular, is markedly scarce, and much of the existing research is carried out under the rubric of Islamic masculinity (Ouzgane 2003 and 2006; Wright and Rowson 1997; Murray and Roscoe 1997), African masculinity (Ouzgane and Morrell 2005) or masculinity in the Middle East (Ghoussoub and Sinclair-Webb 2000). Most of the more recent studies have benefited from the flourishing field of men's studies and subvert assumptions about the existence of a monolithic, patriarchal masculinity, shedding light on the multifaceted expressions of masculinities in Arab societies. Studies with a specifically Arab focus and that explore literary constructions of masculinities are *Desiring Arabs* by Joseph Massad (2007) and *Masculine Identity in the Fiction of the Arab East since 1967* by Samira Aghacy (2009).[20] Aghacy examines varied representations of Arab masculinities in novels written by men and women and classifies them by fictional

20. This is a fast-growing field, and the very short survey attempted here is not comprehensive. The point is to flag the fact that scholarship on masculinity is still lagging behind scholarship on femininity in gender studies. I am also privileging book-length studies focused specifically on exploring masculinities and have not attempted to list some very important articles on masculinity in Arabic literature published in the last ten years. To give just one

types, such as the virile macho, the romantic idealist, the tyrannical father, and the committed intellectual (2009, 17). Her book challenges essentialist characterizations of Arab masculinity by emphasizing the sociopolitical and historical context of production and representation. Massad traces the intellectual history of representations of same-sex desire in the Arabic tradition in the modern period, starting from the late nineteenth century and into the twentieth century. He argues that it was during this colonial phase in the history of the Arabs, where intellectuals engaged with Orientalist concepts and histories, that a radical shift took place in the ways same-sex desire was perceived and "a new sexual epistemology" was conceived (2007, 47). Massad examines selected literary representations in Egyptian fiction of same-sex desire through the twentieth century in an attempt to chronicle the phenomenon of equating homosexuality with degeneration and national defeat. The thrust of his argument is that these modern representations of same-sex masculinities as deviant are a manifestation of the collusion of colonial and national violence and not a continuation of traditional Arab thought.[21]

A number of studies on Arab masculinities published in Arabic in the Arab world are worthy of note. An early study by George Tarabishi published in Arabic in 1977 and entitled *Sharq wa gharb, rujula wa 'unutha: dirasa fi 'azmat al-jins wa al-hadara fi al-riwaya al-'arabiyya* (East and West, masculinity and femininity: a study of the crisis of sexuality and civilization in the Arabic novel), draws attention to discursive constructions of masculinity and femininity as a means of conceptualizing the relationship between human beings and the world, or the self and the other. Tarabishi notes the link between colonial expansionism and the glorification of hegemonic masculinity. He builds on Fanon's dialectic of sexual violence between the colonizer and the colonized, discussed in *Black Skin, White Masks,* to interpret Arabic fiction that engaged with the encounter between East and West, such as Tawfiq al-Hakim's *'Usfur min al-sharq* (Bird of the East), Suhayl Idris's *al-Hay al-latini* (The Latin quarter), and Tayeb Salih's

example of an excellent analysis of masculinity and imperialism in Tayeb Salih's *Season of Migration to the North,* see Wail Hassan (2003).

21. See also Khalaf and Gagnon (2006).

Mawsim al-hijra ila al-shamal (Season of migration to the North). He argues that these are civilizational novels, where the Eastern intellectual accepts the colonial premise that the unequal power relations between civilizations are gendered and are based on masculine dominance (Tarabishi 1977, 5–16). More recently, a literary study by Sawsan Naji (2006) examines images of men in short stories by women, and a study in social psychology by 'Azza Baydun explores perceptions of masculinity among Lebanese university students (2007). Two particularly important journal issues on masculinity are also published in Lebanon, and consist of multidisciplinary approaches to representations and expressions of masculinity in Arab societies and cultural traditions. The first, a special issue of *al-Ra'ida,* an online journal published by the Institute for Women's Studies in the Arab World, at the Lebanese American University, is entitled "What about Masculinity" (2004). The second is a special issue of the annual book/journal published by *al-Bahithat* and entitled *Tafkik mafhum al-dhukura al-muhaymina: al-rujula wa al-'ubuwwa al-yawm* (Deconstruction of the concept of masculinity and patriarchy in contemporary society, 2007).

Why Egypt?

This book is about gender and nation in the Arabic novel, with a focus on novels published in Egypt in the modern period. Although a case can be made for discussing the Arabic novel in general owing to the many shared characteristics, similarities, intersections, and overlaps between histories and consciousness, as well as worldview, and very important, language, I have chosen to focus on the novelistic tradition in one country. Needless to say, and notwithstanding the magnitude of what is shared, there are also significant regional and local differences that must be taken into consideration. Samira Aghacy has noted how sweeping generalizations about the Arabic novel can lead to erroneous conclusions (2009, 10). Paul Starkey has argued that "any discussion of the *nahda* must have a geographical dimension, and second (and more radically) that the concept of the *nahda* as a unified movement is almost certainly illusory" (2006, 24). It is also true that regional diversities are foregrounded more than ever in the twenty-first century. This diversity is partly a consequence of growing political divisions and ideologies in the region, partly due to the sheer volume and stunning diversity in the

Arabic literary production, and also partly due to the increase in specialization in literary studies.

Having said that, the focus on Egypt is primarily driven by two aspects of this project. This book examines the canon of the Arabic novel as a locus for the formation of a gendered national imaginary within the context of anticolonial nationalism. It is predicated on an understanding of the origins of the nationalist discourse as it was developed in the late nineteenth and first decades of the twentieth centuries. To a large extent, there is consensus among scholars of Arabic literature about the privileged status of the Egyptian novel within Arab literary production, especially in the early modern period. It has been argued that "a self-consciously modern and distinctly nationalist literature emerged first in Egypt in the 1920s" and that this literature had a marked influence on the region (Shalan 2002, 216). Roger Allen's charting of the early developments of the Arabic novel chose to foreground Egypt as a "model for the earliest phases in the development of a novelistic tradition in the Arabic-speaking world because historical, geographical, and cultural factors combined to make it the Arabic-speaking society most conducive to the advancement of the novel genre" (1995, 43–44). It follows that the Egyptian novel can act as "a matrix" for the development of other Arabic novelistic traditions, or "a microcosmic version of the macrocosm that is the Arabic novel at large" (Siddiq 2007, 7). This book attempts to address conceptual and theoretical questions about representations of gendered identities in national and global contexts. Egypt is a good starting point. It is also true that developments in the Arab world are quite diverse and that broad generalizations would not allow for an in-depth analysis of issues, especially as we move forward through the twentieth century and into the twenty-first. A country focus will allow for a more detailed and nuanced analysis of the theme. Also, the gender perspective adopted in this study lends further credence to a focus on Egypt. Egypt saw the beginnings of feminist consciousness in the region from the second half of the nineteenth century, with the publication of women's journals and women's writings, and with the establishment of the Egyptian Feminist Union in 1923. This was the background that enabled the publication of Qasim Amin's book *Tahrir al-mar'a* (1899; The liberation of women), a seminal text in Arab national history.

Scope of the Book

The overriding question in this book is: what are the implications of integrating gender as a category of analysis for Arab literary history? I focus on the representations of femininity and masculinity in Arabic novels published in Egypt, as discursive constructions of national imaginaries. Writings by women are given more focus than is usually the case in historical studies of Arabic literature. However, and in contradistinction to the majority of work on gender that limits its application to "women" and representations of femininity, I foreground representations of masculinity as an integral part of the discourse on the nation and examine literature written by male writers. I direct attention to texts that have not been accorded canonical status by critics, but I also engage with canonical texts that have been so far read by critics with a focus on how the woman question is addressed, but not the man question.

The choice of writers and texts has been primarily guided by the themes tackled in the study: representations of gendered identities as markers of ideological conflicts; the intersections between colonial and national discourses on gendered roles; the power dynamics that dictate the processes of inclusion and exclusion in national literary canons; subversive literary interventions in canonical structures. These themes are studied through textual analysis of a small number of selected texts. My aim has been to conduct an in-depth analysis of texts with the view of raising general issues pertaining to the Arabic canon from a gender-sensitive perspective. Having said that, I am very conscious of the limitations of my selection decisions and the many gaps that need to be filled. For all the gaps and omissions, I take full responsibility, but I will attempt to share the thinking process behind some.

Much work needs to be done to unearth and revisit forgotten texts by both men and women writers. In chapter 1, I shed some light on the work of 'A'isha Taymur and Labiba Hashim, while referring very briefly to Zaynab Fawwaz, three important women writers whose contribution has received critical attention only recently. It is worth noting however, that my allusions to forgotten writers are far from exhaustive, or indeed comprehensive. The early century is certainly not the only period in which literary voices were marginalized on account of the dominance of a particular national imaginary. Moreover, women's voices were not the only target of exclusion, as the work of Radwa Ashour on Faris al-Shidyaq has demonstrated. References to marginalized voices have therefore been uneven, subject mainly to thematic considerations addressed in relation to particular writers, but also prompted by whether or not the marginalized voice or text can shed a new light on a particular theme. That is why, for example, I have inserted a section on 'Asma Halim's novel *Hikayat 'Abdu 'Abd al-Rahman* in a chapter devoted to Sun'allah Ibrahim (henceforth Sonallah Ibrahim). Not only was the theme of Halim's novel very relevant to Ibrahim's artistic exploration of the emasculated national hero as a consequence of repeated defeats and disillusionments with the national dream, but also her antihero, her defeated subject, was significantly different from the canonical antihero as imagined by Ibrahim. Halim's protagonist, a working-class man, never had the luxury to own or experience the national dream of progress and prosperity, in a way that his middle-class counterpart was able to, hence undercutting the very idea of the accessibility of the national dream to large sections of society.

In a study on gender and the Arabic novel, the absence of Nawal al-Sa'dawi's fiction must be noted. Al-Sa'dawi is arguably the most famous Arab woman author in the Western world, and her novels figure prominently in women's studies programs and courses. On the other hand, her status as a novelist in the Arab world is contested and very controversial. This seemingly bizarre situation where a writer's status is radically different depending on geographical locations is pertinent to a discussion of the power relations that determine the inclusion of subversive voices in national and global canons. The decision not to include her was based on the fact that her work has been the subject of much research, and on my desire to make space for less-discussed Arabic fiction.

Moreover, a wealth of canonical texts need to be read from a gender lens. With Najib Mahfuz (henceforth Naguib Mahfouz), for example, I decided to focus on the *Trilogy* as a seminal work in the history of the realist Arabic novel, and also as it allowed me to explore the continuation of representations of the *nahda* hero, or *nahda* masculinity, and the discourses on national gendered identities. This decision was made for practical reasons, to allow for an in-depth reading of a seminal body of texts, but it meant that I did not address some important aspects of Mahfouz that certainly would have enriched my analysis. Mahfouz's prolific literary career, which spans most of the twentieth century, has gone through a number of significant mutations and developments in literary style as well as vision, a fact that rightly earned him the title of the social historian of modern Egypt. His literary oeuvre is a gold mine for understanding the historicity of discourses on Arab gendered identities. Mahfouz's oeuvre is also particularly relevant to the growing interest in Arab masculinities. A good case in point is his treatment of the figure of the *futuwwa,* who, according to Mahfouz, constituted a key force in anticolonial resistance in the early twentieth century but was gradually transformed into a derelict thug unable to abide by the rule of law in the modern nation state (Mahfouz in al-Naqqash 1998, 30).[22]

The book consists of nine chapters. The chapters are divided into three parts. Parts 1 and 2 examine canonical texts that tackle the theme of gender and nation and also draw attention to a number of significant omissions. Part 3 focuses entirely on new literature published after the 1990s.

Chapter 1 traces the beginnings of discourses on gender and nation in the second half of the nineteenth century and into the first decades of the twentieth. The chapter examines a select variety of texts by ʽA'isha Taymur, Hind Nawfal, ʽAbdallah al-Nadim, Qasim Amin, Labiba Hashim, and Malak Hifni Nasif to shed light on how discourses on gender roles in the new nation were negotiated and contested. Some of the texts, notably by Nawfal, al-Nadim, Amin, and Nasif, not necessarily "literary" in the strict sense of the word, have been chosen for their historical importance in the construction of national discourses on gender. For example, Amin's representation of the "new woman" became a major trope in national narratives and contributes to our understanding of later literary representations by Haikal, Ibrahim al-Mazini, Naguib Mahfouz, and others. Nasif's contestation of Amin's ideas about the route to progress constitutes an early critique of modernist discourses that are grounded in an oppositional logic. The year 1892 is highlighted as particularly significant in the formulation of representations of femininity and masculinity that take hold and become dominant

22. See Mahfouz's *Harafish* (1977), *'Awlad haritna* (1967), and *Hams al-junun* (1969). For a very good discussion of the historical discourse on the *futuwwa,* see Jacob (2007).

throughout the twentieth century. One of my aims is to challenge the canonical status of Qasim Amin's book *Tahrir al-mar'a,* published in 1899, by demonstrating that it was preceded by and was therefore the consequence of an already thriving public debate about the shape and future of the modern nation state. My second aim is derived from the first, which is to shed light on early literary writings by women and to address the reasons for their marginalization in the literary canon. The chapter foregrounds the contribution of women writers to cultural imaginings of the nation, particularly the work of 'A'isha Taymur, Hind Nawfal, Malak Hifni Nasif, and Labiba Hashim. I refer to the contribution of Hashim, who is of Lebanese origin, because much of her work was produced while she was in Egypt and is therefore an integral part of the Egyptian cultural scene. A third aim is to foreground representations of masculinity as essential components in discursive imaginings of the nation. Qasim Amin's imagining of a New Woman assumed the existence of a national New Man.

Chapter 2 explores the evolution of the New Man in canonical fiction as a locus of contestation and ambivalence in the national narrative. I focus on two novels, *Zaynab* by Mohammed Hussein Haikal and *Ibrahim al-Katib* by Ibrahim al-Mazini, to shed light on representations of national masculinity in fiction, epitomized in the figure of the "*nahda* hero" as I call him. The *nahda* hero is the fictional embodiment of the majority of male reformers who imagined the nation in their own masculine image, and foregrounded their ideological and ontological conflicts in fictional and nonfictional writing and ultimately succeeded in creating a prototypical national masculinity that was middle class, modern, heterosexual, and contingent on the subordination of women. I also examine short stories by Mustafa Sadiq al-Raf'i, in which he directly attacks the ideals and values espoused by the *nahda* hero. He accuses the *nahda* hero, who, for example, espouses bachelorhood as an inevitable consequence of traditional restrictions on the mixing of sexes, hence making it impossible to have a satisfactory love relationship with a woman, of being effeminate and a traitor to the nation. Al-Raf'i's stories bring to light the diversity of narratives that were negotiated in the first half of the twentieth century, as well as the gendered nature of debates on anticolonial resistance and national identity. I argue that representations of ideal masculinities in the new nation inevitably engage with, contest, or reproduce colonial discourses.

Chapter 3 examines three novels by Tawfiq al-Hakim as representative of the civilizational novel in Arabic literature. In varying degrees, all three novels depict the relationship between East and West in sexual terms and attempt a reversal of the colonial feminization of the Orient by imagining a reverse feminization of the Occident. Drawing on Frantz Fanon's characterization of the three phases in the psychological journey of the colonized national elite toward liberation, assimilation, immersion in national culture, and the fighting phase, the chapter locates al-Hakim in the second phase. I attempt a reading of *'Usfur min al-sharq* (Bird of the East) and explore its potential as a parody of colonial violence against the East, or an act of resistance, as al-Hakim's protagonist, the colonized, is male, and the colonizer is rendered female. The fact that the Eastern male protagonist has no real material power over the Western female undercuts the resistance project. I also argue that the sexual paradigm of colonial violence is inscribed onto the national narrative about ideal femininities and masculinities, leading to misogynistic views about women and the formulation of an oppressive narrative about gender equality.

Chapter 4 examines Naguib Mahfouz's *Trilogy* and its status as a national allegory, not only in the Jamesonian sense, but also in the way it encapsulates the modernist ideology of the *nahda* elite. Kamal, the protagonist, represents the crisis of an entire generation of Arab intellectuals who accepted the modernist premise about the existence of an essential opposition between traditional and modern values and ended up torn between the two poles. He is the artistically developed *nahda* hero, the embodiment of national masculinity. Within this national modernist narrative, one of the prerequisites of acceptance in modernity is a rejection of traditional, presumably irrational, values and the espousal of modern scientific values. Tradition in the *Trilogy* is berated in the figure of Sayyid Ahmad 'Abd al-Jawwad, a formidable patriarch and an icon of "traditional" masculinity in modernist discourses, and in his wife, Amina, the icon of traditional femininity and antithesis to the "new woman", who, though lovable, is superstitious, totally isolated from the affairs of the world, and hence treated with kind condescension by her children. All the other characters represent key ideas, or types, in the national narrative about the future of the modern nation.

Chapter 5 explores the literary oeuvre of Latifa al-Zayyat and raises questions about her position in the Arabic canon in the light of her interrupted literary career. Her most well-known novel, *al-Bab al-maftuh* (The open door), published in 1960, is a period piece as it typifies the revolutionary fervor and optimism of the 1950s, in the aftermath of the 1952 revolution by the Free Officers, the evacuation of British forces, and the mobilization of resistance to the Tripartite Assault on Egypt in 1956. With the change of mood in the 1960s and the overwhelming sense of frustration and disillusionment in the wake of the 1967 defeat, al-Zayyat went through a phase of artistic silence, which lasted until 1986, with the appearance of a collection of short stories, *al-Shaykhukha* (Old age), followed by more writing in the 1990s. This silence has been interpreted in many different ways, and specifically by al-Zayyat as a form of self-inflicted "political censorship." I argue that one of the main reasons for her silence is her disillusionment with a national discourse that was ambivalent and contradictory vis à vis the position of women in the national struggle. I focus on the novel *Sahib al-bayt,* (The owner of the house) and argue that it is a powerful feminist critique of third-world nationalist politics toward gender equality.

Chapter 6 examines the antithesis of national masculinity, the anti-national defeated male, focusing on novels by Sonallah Ibrahim. Ibrahim's first novel, *Tilka al-ra'iha* (The smell of it), published in 1967, ushered in the theme of the emasculation of the national male as a direct consequence of political oppression in the newly independent nation state. In *al-Lajna* (The committee) and *Sharaf,* the protagonist's sexual violation is symbolic of the moral and national defeat experienced by third-world citizens. Women are no longer the sole guardians of national honor, as male honor becomes a primary target of aggression by the combined powers of national and global forces, or glocalization. Only female protagonists are capable of showing a certain resilience vis à vis the deluge of the glocal, as manifested in the novel *Dhat.* In *Amrikanli* and *al-Qanun al-faransi* (French Law), Ibrahim tackles the impact of colonial and neocolonial violence on both the colonizer and the colonized, and the disempowerment experienced by individuals on both sides of the colonial/national divide. The chapter also sheds light on a forgotten novel by 'Asma Halim, *Hikayat 'Abdu 'Abd al-Rahman* (The story of Abdu Abd al-Rahman), published in 1977. The novel offers an interesting variation on the theme of impotence and emasculation of the national male. The defeated male in the novel is not the disillusioned national middle-class intellectual, or the intellectual political prisoner, but a poor working-class man. This nominal target of Nasser's reform continues to be disempowered as he is locked into a life of dire poverty.

The last three chapters examine novels published in the 1990s and after. Chapter 7 begins with a discussion of two debates that took place in the 1990s about the literary production of a new generation of writers. The first debate centered on an accusation leveled against young writers, that their work was not committed to *al-qadaya al-kubra,* the larger sociopolitical concerns that characterized the opus of earlier generations. The second was about *kitabat al-banat* (girls' writing), a dismissive label used to describe the literary production of young women writers, and again characterizing their work as apolitical and too focused on their personal lives. I argue that these debates constitute ideologically motivated cultural battles about the national canon of literature. I attempt a reading of two novels, *Qamis wardi farigh* (An empty pink shirt), by Nura Amin, and *Dunyazad,* by Mayy al-Tilmisani (henceforth May Telmissani), and argue that their focus on the very personal is political, rendering them enactments of the famous feminist dictum.

Chapter 8 explores narratives of estrangement and exile in Sumayya Ramadan's (henceforth Somaya Ramadan) *'Awraq al-narjis* (Leaves of narcissus) and Husam Fakhr's fiction. I argue that their fiction can be interpreted under the rubric of the postcolonial nomadic novel, where identities are undetermined by fixed points of reference. Ramadan moves between Ireland and Egypt in search of an identity unmarked by cultural fault lines. Her quest leads to madness, a space outside conventional routes, and binaries. Fakhr's novels address exilic experience and the possibility or impossibility of simultaneously belonging to two places.

Chapter 9 examines three novels all published in the first decade of the twenty-first century: *Lusus Mutaqa'idun* (Thieves in retirement) by Hamdi Abu Julayyil (henceforth Hamdi Abu Golayyel), *'An Takun 'Abbas al-'Abd* by Ahmad al-'Aydi (henceforth Ahmed Alaidy), and *'Injil Adam* (The gospel according to Adam) by Muhammed 'Ala' al-Din. The first is set in one of the many *'ashawa'iyyat,* or informal housing settlements, scattered around and inside Cairo and portrays the lives of men and women living in marginalized spaces, unrecognized, even rejected by the national center. The second explores the emergence of another manifestation of nonnational individuals, alienated and living on the edges of society. The third, is an existential search of a new subjectivity amid chaos and the dissolution of certainties. All three novels depict men and women living in liminal spaces, undefined and unlimited by national, ideological, or physical boundaries.

All the texts discussed in part 3 were published not by the more established state-owned publishers, but by new, independent publishing houses. Most of them have had a mixed reception when they first appeared. And most have also been awarded prizes that have been contested. The novels have been chosen to shed light on some of the shifts in taste and direction currently taking place in the Egyptian cultural scene and the emergence of new cultural imaginaries, particularly as they impact representations of gendered identities.

PART ONE

1

Beginnings

Discourses on Ideal Manhood and Ideal Womanhood

The second half of the nineteenth century in Egypt was a crucial period in the formation of discourses about the shape and directions of the modern nation in the making, and about the characteristics and identities of future citizens and their expected roles. The era raged with debates between various parties and factions in the media, in literary and cultural salons, in essays and articles published in magazines and journals, and in dedicated treatises and publications, as well as in fiction. More critical attention was given to the discussion of the role of women and their status in the new nation, though invariably, either implicitly or explicitly, there were equally intense debates going on about men and their expected roles as well. This overemphasis on women, or "the woman question," is largely due to the theoretical lens used to study gender dynamics of nation building in postcolonial contexts, discussed in the introduction, but also partly due to the prominence given to Qasim Amin's contribution to these debates: his two books, *Tahrir al-mar'a* (1899; *The Liberation of Women,* 1992) and *al-Mar'a al-jadida* (1900; *The New Woman,* 1995), were regarded by both his contemporaries and later cultural commentators as seminal texts in the formation of discourses on gender in Egypt and beyond. Amin established the idea that the betterment of the status of women was a prerequisite for progress, and that the nation required a "New Woman" to secure access to modernity. The "New Woman" became a central trope in nationalist narratives and an ideological indicator of attitudes regarding progress, anticolonialism, and modernization. Yet despite the widespread use of the term, there was no agreed clear-cut definition of what it actually meant to be a New Woman in turn–of-the-century

Egypt. Scholars have pointed out the various ambivalences that the term carried, which in turn reflected the ambivalence of the nationalist project toward "the woman question." Unlike the "traditional woman," her cultural sister, she was educated, made good use of her time, did not languish in laziness, and was not prey to superstition and irrational ideas. She was also an excellent wife and mother who perfected her household duties, creating an idyllic environment for her husband and children. The New Woman was insistently compared to her European sister, who very often became a measuring rod for assessing how far the Egyptian woman managed to gain entry to the modern world (Elsadda 1998). Notwithstanding, she was expected to be "modern-yet-modest," as her access to modernity was conditional on the preservation of her distinct cultural identity (Najmabadi 1991, 49). Mona Russell has shown how the New Woman was an "urban phenomenon" shaped by education and the new consumer culture that accompanied the spreading of print media. She warns, however, against simply equating her with the Westernized woman and explores the various layers of meaning that were brought to bear when using this label (2004, 2–3).

Debates about new gendered roles for men and women in the modern nation were well underway through the second half of the nineteenth century. In this chapter, I will look at the beginnings of cultural imaginings of gender and nation in a number of early texts, some more widely recognized than others. As early as 1888, 'A'isha Taymur published her fictional narrative *Nata'ij al-'ahwal fi al-'aqwal wa al-'af'al* (The consequences of circumstances in words and deeds), a largely ignored text, in which she explores the question of manhood through the journey of a modern prince to self-discovery. In 1892 three seminal publications appeared: 'A'isha Taymur's *Mira'at al-ta'amul fi al-'umur* (Mirror for reflection on affairs, a short treatise about the changing roles of men and women and the implications of these changes on their relationship; Hind Nawfal's *al-Fatah* (1892–94, The young woman), the first women's journal in Egypt; and 'Abdallah al-Nadim's *al-Ustadh* (1892–93, The professor), an educational and political journal. The publication of Qasim Amin's *Tahrir al-mar'a* in 1899 initiated a stream of responses that ranged from unadulterated praise to vicious vitriol. I will also shed light on the contribution of Malak Hifni Nasif, whose powerful critique of the *nahda* narrative was marginalized and forgotten for many decades but was revived in the 1990s in feminist revisionist histories. Nasif's representations of ideal womanhood and manhood clashed with many of the givens in the dominant discourse, which resulted in her occupying an ambivalent position in national memory.[1] I will then conclude with reference to a novel by Labiba Hashim, *Qalb al-rajul* (The heart of man), published in 1904, almost ten years before the appearance of Mohamed Husayn Haikal's *Zaynab,* and posit that it was not acknowledged as an important contribution to the beginnings of the Arabic novel because of its divergence from the *nahda* narrative about ideal modern masculinity. My main point is that the modernity vs. tradition conflict also manifested itself as a conflict between different paradigms of masculinity and femininity. I have chosen to focus on these early texts because they shape as well as anticipate competing constructions of ideal manhood and womanhood in the modern Arabic novel.

'A'isha Taymur

'A'isha Taymur (1840–1902), or al-Taymuriyya, as she is widely known, addressed "the man question" in the modern nation, a project she began in her fictional narrative *Nata'ij al-'ahwal fi al-'aqwal wa al-'af'al,* then in *Mir'at al-ta'amul fi al-'umur.* Taymur belonged to an aristocratic family and wrote poetry in Arabic, Persian, and Turkish. She was schooled at home and had women teachers who taught her Arabic grammar and prosody. *Nata'ij* is about the importance of a sound education for the making of a strong, modern prince.[2] Prince Mamduh's undisciplined upbringing results in his falling under the corrupting influence of the ministers of defense and finance, who, upon the death of the king, usurp his throne. Mamduh survives a plot against his life and embarks on a journey of self-discovery that brings him face-to-face with his own failings and eventually closer to his people. He meets up with one of his father's faithful companions, who guides him on his journey and educates him by telling stories that help illuminate his path.

1. See Elsadda (1994).

2. Zeidan maintains that Taymur benefited from early translations of Western fiction in Arabic, particularly Rifa'a Rafi' al-Tahtawi's translation of Fenelon's *Les Aventures de Telemaque* in 1867. He adds that we can trace parallels in subject matter as well as characterization (1995, 63).

Mamduh succeeds, with the help of faithful supporters, in acquiring wisdom and knowledge that enable him to return to his kingdom and regain his throne. True manhood, as characterized by Taymur through the voice of the prince at the end of the story, means "piety, patience, contentment, and acceptance of the workings of fate" (Taymur 1888 [2003], 277). Taymur emphasizes the importance of *tarbiyya* (good upbringing) in instilling proper norms of conduct, following the tradition of *adab* in the Arabic tradition. Omnia Shakry has pointed out how the new discourses on motherhood and the education of the modern woman drew on the indigenous concepts of *adab* and *tarbiyya* in order to "reconstitute motherhood along middle-class lines of rational-economic and scientific-hygienic domesticity and child rearing" (Shakry 1998, 127). In other words, dominant discourses, which focused on the construction of the ideal woman, sought to blend new modernist concepts about modern child rearing methods with old *adab*. Taymur diverted from this trajectory in two significant ways: first, she focused on men and not women; second, she foregrounded the Islamic dimension in education. According to Mervat Hatem, Taymur did not consider modern education theories as "a source for modern new values, but rather as tools for an inner *jihad* for the Muslim community" (2003, 13) in order to produce ideal manhood. In *Nata'ij*, a good upbringing and a sound education are key elements for ideal manhood.

Taymur's adoption of an Islamic frame of reference in her work, her integration of modern and traditional styles, and her focus on the reformation of men rather than women, put her at odds with the dominant trends in national discourses.[3] This approach certainly resulted in a mixed reception to her work and her marginalization in the literary canon. Her collection of poetry *Hilyat al-tiraz* (1884, Decorative embroidery) gained her recognition by her contemporaries, and also later, in the twentieth century, by prominent writers, such as 'Abbas al-'Aqqad, Mayy Ziyada, and 'A'isha 'Abd al-Rahman.

3. My argument in this section on Taymur is deeply indebted to Mervat Hatem's work, particularly regarding the arguments she made about the adherence of Taymur to an Islamic frame of reference and her emphasis on masculinity. Also, for a detailed analysis of Taymur's works and era see Hatem 2011.

Al-'Aqqad praised her poetry for attaining "the highest level reached by writers in Egypt in mid-nineteenth century till the 'Urabi revolution." 'Abbas al-'Aqqad's tribute to 'A'isha, however, was not free of prejudice against women writers in general. He considered Taymur an exceptional woman poet because women do not excel in poetry in general. He particularly lauded her elegies and argued that Arab women can only master this particular genre (1965, 153). His literary judgment of Taymur was challenged by 'A'isha 'Abd al-Rahman, who argued that Taymur excelled in *ghazal,* or love poetry, and that her poetry, which was "liberated from emotional smothering *wa'd,* had encouraged future generations of women to express their feelings with unrestrained freedom" (1962, 19). Hatem pointed out that Taymur subverted the predominantly masculinist canon of Arabic poetry by placing female figures of her family at the center of her poetry (2008, 250).[4]

Nata'ij was met with a more guarded reception because of a perceived archaic quality that detracted from its credentials for inclusion in the canon of modern Arabic literature. According to Mayy Ziyada, *Nata'ij,* is the *bariqat al-fan al-qasasi al-hadith* (an early example of modern prose fiction) ([1926] 1975, 206). However, she found the narrative lacking and limited in vision because of Taymur's imitation of old styles, a judgment that was repeated by subsequent critics. Mervat Hatem has argued that a modernist approach to Arab women's history as well as to literary history has resulted in the dismissal of Taymur's significant contribution by paying lip service to her pioneering status, while characterizing its style and content as reflecting obsolete traditional styles that are at odds with the dominant literary aspirations to emulate modern sensibilities as exemplified in Western genres and styles (1998). In an introduction to a reprint of *Nata'ij* in 2003, Hatem invites the readers to disregard the "caricaturist gaze" that is directed at the literary language in this period and characterizes it as excessively preoccupied with matters of formalistic styles at the expense of meaning. She argues that

4. Hatem refers to a conversation with the late Magda al-Nowaihi, who criticized "the masculinist construction of the Arabic canon" manifested in the status given to al-Khansa''s elegies of her brothers, that their praise of al-Khansa' was based on "its affirmation of Arab masculinity" (2008, 229–30).

this gaze results in a reading that does not pay attention to the content, in this case an exploration of the meaning of responsible manhood.

Mir'at al-ta'amul fi al-'umur (1892) is an important text that directly engages with the debate on gender roles in society. In this short treatise, Taymur situates herself within an Islamic paradigm and broaches one of the most sensitive issues regarding the relationship between men and women, namely *al-qiwama.* She poses the question: what are the consequences of a reversal of gender roles, that is, what if men do not perform the duties expected of them, and women find themselves obliged to step in and take over? She uses a parable about a lazy lion who stops hunting, so his wife takes over the responsibility of providing food for both of them. When crossed, he tries to regain his control and authority, but his wife laughs and says: "This [claim to authority] was when you were you, and I was I. Now, however, our roles have been reversed, and I have become you [the man] and you have become me [the woman]. Therefore, you are now entitled to what I owed you, and I am entitled to what you owed me." The lion is dumbfounded and only has himself to blame (Taymur [1892] 2002, 7). Although she paints a scene of chaos and promiscuity as the inevitable result of the reversal of roles, she nevertheless makes a case for a woman's obedience to her husband as conditional on his financial support and good character. In her discussion of marital duties and responsibilities, she defines the qualities of a good wife and a good husband and specifies the jobs that are expected of both. Hatem points out that her definition was not restricted to the modern notion of "the management of the household," but that instead, she posited that a good Muslim wife was "to become an active agent in the reformulation of the very important Islamic injunction (to give up bad habits and to command reform) in her relations with her husband" (2001a, 6).

It is noteworthy that 'Abdallah al-Nadim announces the publication of Taymur's treatise in his magazine *al-Ustadh* and commends the author because "she denounces many of the customs followed by women and exposes the disastrous consequences of their leaving their homes."[5] Al-Nadim either completely misses the point of Taymur's treatise or deliberately sends out a

5. al-Nadim, "*Mir'at al-ta'amul fi al'umur,*" *al-Ustadh* 33 (4 April 1893): 775.

distorted message. She does criticize many of the accepted customs of her times, but the overall point is a very different one. The point, in fact, was picked up by a conservative cleric, Sheikh 'Abdallah al-Fayyumi, who swiftly responds in a book called *Lisan al-jumhur fi mir'at al-ta'amul fi al-'umur* (The voice of the people on the mirror of contemplation).[6] The main thrust of al-Fayyumi's argument is that it is a wife's duty to obey her husband unconditionally, whether or not he fulfills his responsibilities toward her.

al-Fatah

Al-Fatah (1892–1894), the first women's magazine to be published in Egypt, established an important precedence and certainly paved the way for an increase in women's involvement in the cultural field. The first issue appeared in Alexandria on 20 November 1892. Its editor, Hind Nawfal, was among the Syrians who came to Egypt to escape political upheaval and Ottoman censorship in Syria. Her family moved to Egypt when she was a child, and she went to school in Alexandria. Her mother, Maryam al-Nahhas, wrote *Ma'rad al-hasna' fi tarajim mashahir al-nisa'*, a biographical dictionary of both Eastern and Western women. Her father was a writer and helped manage the office of the magazine. The last issue of the magazine appeared on 16 March 1894. It ceased when the editor married and decided to devote herself to her new role. In spite of its short life, the magazine initiated an impetus that continued in the following years, as more women's journals appeared in Egypt and more women were encouraged to write and participate in public debates.

The subtitle of *al-Fatah* describes it as "scientific, historical, literary, and humorous."[7] Nawfal also maintained that it was a specialized publication that did not tackle political or religious topics. A brief description of the contents of the first issue is fairly representative of the magazine's overall direction and goals. In the opening address, the editor declares that it is not a magazine that will be involved in political or religious disputes, but that it will focus on defending the rights of women and draw attention to their

6. 1892; reprinted with 'A'isha Taymur's *Mir'at al ta'amul fi al-'umur* ([1892] 2002).

7. Hind Nawfal, "'Idah wa iltimas wa istismah" (A clarification, an appeal and an apology), *al-Fatah* ([1892–93] 2007, 21).

responsibilities and duties. She urges women readers to consider the magazine a forum for their opinions and their affairs and encourages them to write and participate. She also makes a case for the legitimacy and respectability of women's writing in magazines and refers to women writers in Europe and the United States whose writing has earned them respect and has not compromised their status in society. She draws up a list of the increasing number of women's magazines all over the world and includes numbers of women writers in various countries. The remaining articles and news are as follows: biographies of prominent Western women with particular emphasis on Queen Victoria; an article about women's rights and duties; an article that compares different customs and traditions, focusing on different standards of beauty in various countries; more comparisons between customs and rituals in marriage and celebrations; miscellaneous news of women (for example, 252 women students of medicine in France, 50 women lawyers in Chicago); news of a women's section in an exhibition in Chicago; marriage announcements and news of royal celebrations; some strange and humorous news; and a letter in praise of *al-Fatah.* In the following issues, we come across more biographies of Western and Eastern women; more letters of encouragement for *al-Fatah;* many more articles on women's rights, responsibilities, and history; and many articles and news Arabized or translated from European and American magazines.

The magazine propagated a domestic ideology premised on a division of gender roles and an acceptance of essential differences between men and women. Hind Nawfal states very clearly that women will only achieve equality with men by providing a good example and doing good work, *bil fadl wa mahasin al-a'maal.*[8] She adds that the work that women can and should do has nothing to do with what men do. Women's work is what women are meant to do and only women can do, that is, their work inside their homes. She elaborates the principles of good housekeeping, such as cleanliness, orderliness, and responsible child care. The responsibility of improving women's status

8. Hind Nawfal, "Fi al-mar'a wa wajibatiha wa huquqiha" (About women's duties and rights), *al-Fatah,* part 1 ([1892–93] 2007, 34).

in Egypt is put on the shoulders of women and is made conditional on their willingness and ability to become modern managers of their homes. Domestic ideology is posited as a strategy to ensure worth and status for women. In the fifth issue, the magazine offers a summary of a book on housekeeping. In customary fashion, the book denounces ignorant women who are unable to manage their homes and raise their children according to the modern principles of child care and good housekeeping.[9] At the same time, the book places the management of the home on equal footing with the management of a kingdom. The writer argues that men's power and control over political affairs in the public sphere is supported by women's control and good rule over their homes. Household duties are given high status, comparable to the status usually accorded to the duties and responsibilities of political leaders and prominent members of society. In addition, women are admonished to give equal attention to raising their daughters and educating them. The writer argues that with proper education, women can eventually assume responsibilities in the public sphere, and reference is made to women's struggle to obtain political rights in the United States.[10] It can be argued that women's glorification of their "natural" roles has been a strategic decision to gain ground. It is also true that domesticity was not the only message disseminated by *al-Fatah.* In fact, all the biographies of prominent women, and all the news, are about women who have participated in the public sphere and who have excelled in professions that are assumed to be exclusively male. Nawfal's magazine enabled women's voices, encouraging them to write and participate in debates. It also succeeded in drawing around it a significant group of contributors and readers who made a point of supporting publicly the overall venture and idea. It is fair to say that the dissemination of the cult of domesticity was paralleled or went hand-in-hand with the propagation of ideas and information that supported women's aspiration to further integration in the public sphere.

9. Hind Nawfal, "Fi al-mar'a wa wajibatiha wa huquqiha: fi tadbir al-manzil" (About women's duties and rights: on house management) *al-Fatah,* part 5 ([1893–94] 2007, 210–13).

10. Hind Nawfal, "Fi al-mar'a wa huquqiha wa wajibatiha: fi tadbir al-manzil," *al-Fatah,* part 6 ([1893–94] 2007, 269–72).

al-Ustadh

An important party to this debate on gender roles in society was 'Abdallah al-Nadim (1845–1896), a leading nationalist figure in the struggle against British occupation and the orator of the 'Urabi revolution. Born in Alexandria to a poor, working-class family, he soon became a student of Jamal al-Din al-Afghani and began writing articles and delivering speeches at an early age. In 1881, he published a magazine, *al-Tankit wa al-tabkit* (Banter and rebuke), "a nationalist, literary, and humorous weekly magazine,"[11] in which he voiced his nationalist views and supported Ahmad 'Urabi. In response to a request by 'Urabi, who wanted the magazine to have a title and tone that was more appropriate to the challenges facing the nation, al-Nadim changed the title and the approach of the magazine and called it *al-Ta'if* (The wanderer):

> The time for jest and censure has passed: the time now is for freedom and the knowledge of rights. This is what made us change the name of the magazine and its direction and have transformed it into an overtly political magazine, instead of integrating politics in debates and lessons. We have made it a magazine that advocates for the rights of the nation and defends the rights of the government. (quoted in al-Jimi'i 1994, 24–25)

After the defeat of 'Urabi in 1882, he was exiled by the British to Jaffa. In 1892, he was granted a pardon by Khedive 'Abbas II and returned to Egypt on the condition that he stayed away from politics. In the same year, he managed to resume his vocation as a journalist and a main participant in public debates on sociopolitical issues. Through his brother, he succeeded in obtaining a license to publish *al-Ustadh.* He described his magazine as "scientific, educational, and humorous"[12] and indicated that it did not address political or religious issues. Al-Nadim honored his deal with 'Abbas and stayed away from matters of state, but he inevitably touched upon the larger political issues that were integral to all debates on Egypt's future. His magazine was banned after ten months; the last issue appeared on 13 June 1893.

11. This is the subtitle of the magazine.
12. al-Nadim, *al-Ustadh* 1, no. 1 (24 August 1892): 1–2.

Al-Nadim is noted in history for a number of things. In addition to his nationalist anti-British struggles, he was one of the first reformers to use colloquial Egyptian Arabic in newspapers. His reasons were that he wanted to reach the uneducated masses who did not understand classical Arabic and were hence excluded from national debates about the future. From another angle, his magazines are considered rare forums for the voices of the masses to be heard. Accordingly, he is regarded as one of the most original writers to play a role in narrowing the gap between classical Arabic and spoken Arabic, and he created a language that was compatible with the spirit of the age. He drew upon the tradition of *adab* (proper behavior manuals) and used short dialogues between two or more characters for the discussion of social issues (Metcalf 1984, 4–11). These short dialogues are regarded by literary critics as "embryonic narrative discourse" (Hafez 1993, 125).

Al-Nadim meant to guide and to instruct, hence the title of the magazine, which means "the professor." One can argue that his lifelong project has been to educate the nation. He left "a lasting legacy on Egyptian educational and associational life" when he founded the first Islamic Benevolent Society in Alexandria, which eventually opened *madrasat al-jam'iyya al-khayriyya al-islamiyya bi al-askandariyya* (Islamic Benevolent Society School of Alexandria) (Herrera 2002, 5). In 1881–82, he was associated with a political society in Alexandria called *jam'iyyat al-shubban* (The Young Men's Association) where he "gave stirring speeches" (Cole 1993, 244). He dealt with the topical issues that were discussed at the end of the nineteenth century, such as the relation between tradition and modernity, what to take or leave from Western civilization, and the position of women in society. He harshly criticized blind imitation of Western ways and ideas, argued for blending modern and traditional religious education, discussed the principles of modern education, advocated the establishment of Egyptian schools and warned of the dangers of missionary schools, and called for supporting local industries and crafts and the boycott of foreign goods, to give a few examples. He also dealt with the woman question and discussed the education of women, women's role in society, and the definitions of masculinity and femininity in the modern nation.

Al-Nadim sets the tone for a modernist domestic ideology that aims at confining middle-class women to their homes. He argued that, unlike peasant women who worked hard beside their menfolk, middle-class women, *rabbat al-rafaha,* lived a life of comfort, hence rendering their "fraudulent claims . . . for equality with men . . . unacceptable to people with wisdom and experience."[13] He blamed middle-class women for their perceived laziness and denounced the efforts of contemporary women to gain access to the public sphere. What is striking about al-Nadim's position is that despite his closeness to the working classes, he nevertheless, and very much in line with mainstream nationalists who only address the middle classes, preached a middle-class ideology regarding the relations between the sexes. This ideology is contrary to a dominant view of al-Nadim as a man of the people who went beyond the elitism of the nationalist discourse and founded "a new cultural paradigm" that involved the populace.[14] On the one hand, a domestic ideology that glorifies women's roles in the private sphere is premised on a class of women who have the choice of staying at home and ignores the realities of working-class women. On the other hand, even though the peasant woman is spared the stigma of laziness bestowed on middle-class women, she does not feature as the role model to be emulated, nor does her acknowledged labor grant her status and worth. Al-Nadim's ideal woman remains middle class and espouses a domestic ideology as a creed to be disseminated and preached to other women.

In al-Nadim's social dialogues, it is always the middle-class woman who is sought out by poor or peasant women for help and guidance. When a group of poor women convened to discuss possible solutions to their husbands' drinking problems, they agreed to seek the advice of Sit Najiyya because she reads and writes and has connections with upper-class women, "al-hawanim al-kibar."[15] In another dialogue, Bahana, who is originally a peasant woman but has settled in the city, advises Sit al-Balad, a newcomer to the city, about how to behave and gain respect. Bahana chides Sit al-Balad for lack of cleanliness, for unseemly behavior, and even advises her on how to

13. al-Nadim, "'An al-rajul wa al-mar'a" (About men and women), *al-Ustadh* 1, no. 7 (4 October 1892): 161.

14. Hawwas (1997, 129–33). Also Madiha Doss maintains that "al-Nadim did not adopt colloquial Arabic as a substitute for Classical Arabic, but regarded it as a tool for reaching the masses" (1997, 291–92).

15. al-Nadim, "Latifa wa dimyana," *al-Ustadh* 1, no. 7 (4 October 1892): 157.

treat her husband. As for Bahana's relation to the world outside her home, Sit al-Balad warns her not to be seen outside the door of her house, nor should she rush outside and run her errands unveiled the way she is used to doing in the countryside. She adds that women in the city are considered virtuous and respectable only when they hide behind closed doors. "This is because our men are very jealous, and religion prohibits a woman to be seen by a stranger, or to speak to anyone but her husband. So, keep your door locked and do not open it except for your husband."[16] Bahana is teaching Sit al-Balad a middle-class morality and way of life.

In another dialogue in the series "School for Girls," Sharifa (the virtuous one) lectures Bahiyya on the perils of going out behind her husband's back to visit shrines and participate in a *zar.* She supports her contention by consulting a renowned sheikh who backs her up. Bahiyya is seen to have erred on two counts. First, she went out of her house without her husband's permission. This mistake is described as *haram,* or against the teachings of religion. The second error is her thinking that visiting a holy shrine, or going to a *zar,* is a legitimate reason for leaving her house. The dialogue can best be understood against the background of a nationalist discourse that reprimanded women for partaking of traditional customs or rituals that are deemed irrational and superstitious, or not an integral part of "true" religion. The other crucial aspect of this dialogue is its emphasis on the necessity of women's total obedience of their husbands, regardless of the reasons or circumstances that may have led to their acting on their own initiative. This was an issue that was widely debated at the end of the nineteenth century and can only be interpreted as a corollary to the rising demands of women for more freedoms and less restrictions on their participation in the public sphere. The following words by the sheikh about the religious duties of women toward their husbands are symptomatic:

> A woman's leaving her house behind her husband's back is a grave sin. It can only be forgiven if she tells her husband that she left on such and such a day without his permission, have looked at a man at a particular place,

16. al-Nadim, "Madrasat al-banat" (Girls' school), *al-Ustadh* 1, no. 16 (6 December 1892): 371–72.

> talked to another on this corner. If her husband forgives her, then God will forgive her. If he does not then God will punish her because [she has trespassed on] her husband's rights . . . not God's rights, so God cannot forgive her if she has not secured her husband's permission.[17]

Also, in a series of dialogues about girls' education, urban middle-class life, with its values and morals, is offered as the prescribed norm and valued way of life. In one of the dialogues, a mother gives advice to her daughter on household management, principles of hygiene, and the orderly behavior of the ideal housewife. These are posited as suitable topics for the education of girls. In a revealing dialogue, which is still part of the series on girls' education, Zakiyya and Nafisa discuss their views on what constitutes a useful education for girls. Here, the issue of women's work is brought to the fore. Zakiyya ridicules Nafisa because she is studying French, piano, and dancing besides Arabic and religion. French is useless, she maintains, because she will never mingle with foreigners, as she is confined to her home.

> Men are entitled to learn foreign languages because they deal with foreigners and need to understand their conversations and read their books. As for us women, we are not going to deliver any public talks, nor are we going to write in magazines, nor work as translators, nor travel abroad. So, what good would French do us anyway?[18]

As for piano, it can only lead to promiscuity because music inspires women with love and will encourage them to pursue their passion with more men.

This conversation is particularly revealing of the ambivalences and contradictions in nationalist discourses on women's role in society. On the issue of the piano, al-Nadim does not suggest, for example, that, whereas the piano is a good instrument in its own right, it would be worthwhile for women to study the *oud*,[19] an Oriental instrument, so that they do not lose touch

17. al-Nadim," Madarasat al-banat," *al-Ustadh* 1, no. 17 (13 December 1892): 398.

18. al-Nadim, "Madrasat al-banat," *al-Ustadh* 1, no. 11 (1 November 1892): 247.

19. It is noteworthy that Malak Hifni Nasif uses the piano versus *oud* distinction to argue a different point. She criticizes the tendency to teach women the piano not because music is subversive or not good for women, which is al-Nadim's point, but because she finds

with their music tradition. Instead, in his zeal to denounce anything foreign, he discards music for women altogether. This pattern is repeated insistently. Music and the West become conflated, suggesting that Egyptian women never enjoyed music before the piano was introduced to them. Second, his dismissal of the study of languages for girls is another form of manipulation of the weapon of accusing advocates for women's rights of Westernization to undermine their credibility and to defeat their cause. Also, al-Nadim's suggestion that women will never be translators or writers in magazines, or public orators, can only be described as a blatant attempt to ignore the contributions of contemporary women in the public sphere. Women already had been publishing articles and speaking in public meetings.

In addition to his "School for Girls," al-Nadim wrote four dialogues under the title "School for Boys," as part of his larger project to educate the nation and shape the new citizens who would lead the progress of the country. The idea for a school for boys was tentatively launched by al-Nadim in *al-Tankit wa al-tabkit* in a few sketches between him and a young schoolboy. The lessons first begin in the form of advice given by Nadim to "one of his sons," in which he charts two paths for the young boy, the path of servitude, hypocrisy, and civic apathy on the one hand, and the path of freedom, civic responsibility, and active participation on the other.[20] The pupil vows to follow the "law of humanity." The next lesson consists of a lecture on duties, the duties of the pupil toward his educator followed by his duties toward his nation and the ruler.[21] In the third lesson, the pupil reports to Nadim, a journalist and a persona of al-Nadim, that he and his fellow students took the initiative to help serve their school, and he seeks his advice on the best approach to managing school governance. Al-Nadim's lesson, in response to this question, is a political manifesto on how to encourage people's participation in politics, bearing in mind their lack of experience. The student's initiative

---

it a clear example of the dominant and uncritical preference for everything European in the national discourse ([1910] 1998, 129).

20. al-Nadim, "Nadim's Advice to One of His Sons," *al-Tankit wa al-tabkit,* 21 August 1881, 179–81.

21. al-Nadim, "Dars tahthibi," *al-Tankit,* 18 September 1881, 219–25.

demonstrates the valuable influence of al-Nadim, and by extension, the crucial role played by education and educators in the progress of the nation. The idea is foregrounded in the magazine by a juxtaposition between al-Nadim's student and another "student of old wives' tales" (*tilmidh al-'aja'iz*), a man who is guided by silly superstitious beliefs and practices.[22]

In *al-Ustadh,* al-Nadim's educational aim is more pronounced and direct. In his school for boys, the first three dialogues are between Nadim and a young boy called Hafiz. The fourth dialogue takes place between Hafiz and Kamil, a friend who went to a foreign school. Al-Nadim lectures Hafiz about personal hygiene, healthy habits, how to perform ablutions to prepare for prayer, and some basic guidelines for performing Muslim religious rituals. He also lectures him on the meaning of civil rights, and duties:

> You must treat people with the attitude of someone who is aware of civil rights and who is keen on preserving national characteristics. . . . Do not be silent and give advice to your fellows and teach them what you have learned from me and from your teachers. . . . Make sure that you gain the approval of your parents. . . . Consult your parents. . . . Disregard their failures and mistakes. . . . Always tell the truth.[23]

In the fourth dialogue, Hafiz is approached by Kamil, a student in a foreign school, who asks Hafiz to teach him how to say his prayers. When asked why he does not know, he explains that students at his school are only taught Christianity and not Islam. Al-Nadim is then careful to point out that this is not just a problem for Muslim students but is also an issue for Coptic students, who are encouraged to change their sect and follow the school denomination. The lesson here is about the dangers of foreign schools and their role in obliterating the religious traditions of Egyptians. In this lesson, the student, Hafiz, becomes the teacher as he follows al-Nadim's advice in passing on his knowledge to his friends and community.

Al-Nadim's idea of education for boys differs quite significantly from education for girls. To begin with, the characters involved in the dialogues

22. al-Nadim, "Tilmiz al-'aja'iz," *al-Tankit,* 4 September 1881, 193–94.

23. al-Nadim, "Madrasat al-banin" al-Ustadh 1, no. 16 (6 December 1892): 364–69.

are very different: in the "School for Boys" we have a journalist, an educator, and young school boys seeking advice. In the "School for Girls," the dialogues take place between mothers and daughters, or between a schoolgirl and an illiterate woman: there is no educator posing as a figure of authority and credible knowledge. Indeed, for young girls, the figure of authority is the mother or the old wise woman. This is different from the figure of the old but unwise mother who appears in *al-Tankit wa al-tabkit,* and becomes the source of senseless superstitious beliefs, or old wives tales, that misguide men. It appears that for al-Nadim, "traditional" women are better educators of young girls compared to modern schools, who teach them music and French and "useless" pursuits. These same "traditional" women are, however, inappropriate educators for young men, who are told to seek knowledge in schools. Furthermore, whereas the education of girls is all about taking care of all members of their family, washing their clothes, keeping the house, and providing them with clean food, boys are shown how to achieve personal and moral excellence. For al-Nadim, the ideal woman is the modern domestic woman, who puts her education in the service of her immediate family. Boys, on the other hand, are groomed to become the model citizens of the new nation. It is significant that the dialogues entitled "School for Boys" are written in standard classical Arabic, whereas the "School for Girls" dialogues are written in colloquial Arabic. The gender distinction here suggests that he consciously or unconsciously believed in a hierarchy of linguistic styles that corresponded to his belief in a certain hierarchy between genders.

For al-Nadim, ideal manhood is congruent with the concept of citizenship, informed and participatory citizenship. Like all reformers, his ideal citizen was a project in the making, an imagined male citizen who would rise with the rise of the new nation. As a follower of the 'Urabi project of independence, a popular movement, his target audience is the masses, the *sha'b* of Egypt. In his work, his publications, he addresses the masses, the poor, the *fallahin,* the future citizens who will join the revolution against British and foreign exploitation. He was particularly critical of the Westernized elite who, according to al-Nadim, have lost touch with their roots and national character and have joined forces with the British imperialists. On the other hand, and like other reformers and nationalist leaders at the turn of the century, he was acutely aware of the challenges faced by the urban and rural poor, the *fallahin,* who constituted the majority of the population of Egypt: they suffered from illiteracy and years of exploitation and abuse. In colonial literature, the *fallah* was a symbol of authentic Egyptian manhood in all its failings and strengths. Like the Egyptian woman, he was represented as the symbol of failure and backwardness that hindered national progress. Like her, though, in a different way, he became the object of the national reform projects.

Despite the many similarities between the representations of the *fallah* and the representations of traditional womanhood, the figure of the *fallah,* the object of change, was more complicated and ambivalent, as it was conflated at a more basic level with the identity of the educated reformer, the agent of change. Samah Selim has argued that "the *fallah* begins to appear as a recognizable literary figure in the late-nineteenth-century drama and journalism of Ya'qub Sannu' and 'Abdallah al-Nadim. . . . Sannu' created his *fallah* in the image of the oppressed and rebellious 'son of the soil,' while Nadim developed a more ambiguous peasant character that both embodied the backwardness and ignorance of the Egyptian national character and acted as a kind of proto-nationalist foil to the corrupt, Europeanized bourgeois" (2004b, 17). In al-Nadim's writings, the *fallah* is both the target of rebuke and harsh vilification and the model of inspiration and guidance. In *al-Tankit wa al-tabkit* in particular, we meet a number of *fallahin* who are gullible, victims of illiteracy and silly superstitions, and who are also morally lacking. Al-Nadim's criticism is harsh and unequivocal; the backward status of the *fallah* is a reality that must be taken into account and faced in order to change it. At the same time, he is very critical of a *fallah* who receives an education but loses his identity. In "'Arabi tafarnaj" he mocks the son of a *fallah* who is given an opportunity to obtain a modern education and is sent to Europe for four years, only to come back having forgotten his Arabic and rudely dismissive of his native customs and habits. He concludes that the problem with this *fallah* is that he was not educated properly at a young age to understand the rights of his nation and his language, nor did he appreciate the honor of his country and the value of patriotism.[24]

24. al-Nadim, "'Arabi tafarnaj," *al-Tankit,* 6 June 1881, 7–8.

In another article addressed to "the civilized man" *'ayyuha al-mutamaddin,* the *fallah* emerges as a symbol of indigenous Egyptianness, and the main resource for the progress of the country. Al-Nadim blames the civilized city dweller for his disdainful neglect of the *fallah.* He tells him that the *fallah* is "the ladder to higher realms, the substance of your life, the source of wealth . . . he is the light that guides you to preserve your health from the darkness of hunger . . . if you are fair, you would have mercy on him, wipe the mud off his body with your expensive gown."[25] The *fallah* is the authentic antithesis to the Westernized elite who have lost touch with their identity and their roots. He is also the indigenous Egyptian man who is in need of education to become a citizen of the modern nation, hence the main target of al-Nadim's educational project for the reform and construction of the new modern citizen.

Qasim Amin

Much has been written about the role of Qasim Amin (1863–1908) in forging a liberatory discourse about women in the modern period. Widely acclaimed as the "liberator of women," Amin's seminal texts *Tahrir al-mar'a* (1899) and *al-Mar'a al-jadida* (1900), are credited as two of the most controversial and debated texts in modern times. I have already demonstrated that Amin was not the first to render "the woman question" a central concern in national narratives. He did, however, play a prominent role in establishing the link between the position of women in society and the level of development of a nation on the ladder of progress. He also contributed to the construction of the concept of the New Woman and to its consolidation in the national imaginary as a correlative of modernity. Amin believed that the improvement of the status of women lay at the heart of the project of social and political reformation. He blamed women for the backwardness of the nation and believed that their bad habits, their useless pursuits, and their belief in superstitions were detrimental to all members of the family. Education was a necessity for the improvement of the lot of women and the future of the nation. Amin's paragon of ideal womanhood was an urban middle-class

25. al-Nadim, "La 'anta 'anta wa la al-mathil mathil," *al-Tankit,* 15 August 1881, 155–57.

woman who was confined to her home and afforded the luxury of servants to run her errands. This focus on the middle-class woman and resultant oblivion to the lived reality of the majority of Egyptian women, who were productive and not secluded, becomes a feature of national debates on the woman question. His denunciation of women's unemployment was meant as a severe criticism of their assumed laziness. His aim was not to argue for their participation in public life or the labor force. He wanted them to be better citizens by performing their assigned domestic roles in society. What is key to his project for the improvement of the status of women is that he wanted them to become fit and worthy partners to their husbands. The modern Egyptian man, or the New Man, he argued, was at a loss finding a woman who could share his life in a meaningful and fulfilling way. With this theme in mind, we can read Amin's comments on the woman question as a covert exposition of his representations of modern Egyptian masculinity.

Amin's writings on the woman question went through phases that are worth noting. In 1894, he published a book called *al-Misriyyun* (The Egyptians) in response to a book published in 1893 by the Duc d'Harcourt called *L'Egypte et les Egyptiens,* in which the duke maligned Egyptians and Egypt. In his book, Amin goes through pains to refute the duke's contentions but agrees with his derogatory description and demeaning judgment of women in Egypt.

> Physically, the Egyptian woman seems to be closer to ugliness than to beauty; mentally she is a lazy creature with a meditative nature that lacks agency; she laughs and chats a great deal; she loves her religion but does not practice it; she has no ideal role model and always adapts to everyday life. She is a perfect wife and an affectionate mother, but she has very limited talents when it comes to household management. Yet, and this will come as a surprise to my readers, she will be content with very little love. . . . She spends her life sewing and managing her home to the best of her ability, though she rarely does so with very high standards. ([1894] 1989, 246–47)[26]

He makes sure that he is not advocating that Egyptian women follow on the footsteps of their European sisters, expresses his distaste for women

26. All quotations from Qasim Amin's works are taken from this edition.

pretenders who imitate men, and questions the femininity of women politicians or writers. He then declares that he despises women pedants and holds that he is only advocating that women receive some education to lift them from their state of ignorance (Amin [1894] 1989, 249). Five years later, in 1899, he published his famous book, *Tahrir al-mar'a* (The liberation of women) in which he presented a very strong argument for women's liberation. In this second book, Amin became one of the main defenders of the women's cause in the modern period. The story is that his attack on Egyptian women in his first book drew the attention of Princess Nazli Fadil, a member of the royal family and a woman intellectual who hosted a literary salon in her palace. She invited Amin to her salon and succeeded in showing him the wisdom and higher status of Egyptian women when they are allowed access to education. In his second book, Amin put forward the contention that the position of women is an indicator of the level of development of any nation. He analyzed the condition of Egyptian families and society and came to the conclusion that most of the problems faced in society or within families were caused by the backwardness of its women. For the sake of the nation, he called for the education of women as a prerequisite for progress and freedom. He advocated primary education because that was what they needed to improve their minds and acquire the basics of household management. In other words, women were to be educated in order to appreciate their husbands and provide them with worthy companions, and to become better household managers and better mothers to their children. The book contained a section that proposed some legal reform in the personal status laws regarding issues of divorce and polygamy. It also advocated unveiling, that is, uncovering the face and hands, a custom that was observed by urban middle-class women in Egypt. The authorship of the book has been the subject of study and speculation. Although mainstream historians credited Amin with authorship, many believed that the section on Shari'a laws was written by Sheikh Muhammad 'Abdu, and that Ahmed Lutfi al-Sayyid also had significant input into the ideas and style. In this sense, *Tahrir al-mar'a* is the national manifesto of a *nahda* elite on debates on "the woman question" that had raged in newspapers and magazines between men and women for approximately two decades.

In 1900, Amin published his third book, *al-Mar'a al-jadida* (The new woman), which offered a more "Westernized" view than the one presented in *Tahrir al-mar'a*. In the latter, his eyes were focused on Egyptian society: he analyzed its ills and attempted a prescriptive remedy from within Islamic culture and tradition when he resorted to Muhammad 'Abdu's reformist interpretations of Islamic doctrine. He allied himself with 'Abdu's project, which attempted to demonstrate the compatibility between modernity and tradition. Nevertheless, the book triggered one of the most violent waves of antagonism and rebuttal against Amin. In the third book, Amin obviously decided to take sides on the modernity-versus-tradition divide and made a very strong case for the Western model of progress. Amin posits the New Woman, an ideal representation of some European women, as the model for emulation and guidance for Egyptian women in the modern world. The primary role of this New Woman is still to be carried out within her home, but she needs to be equipped with the necessary training to shoulder heavier tasks if the need arises. There is no hope for a nation or a society, or a family, unless "its women are reared to be able to share with men their ideas, their hopes, their pains, let alone all their endeavors" ([1899] 1989, 512).

In addition to his much-discussed blueprint on the New Woman, Amin also writes about his own perceptions of the New Man. According to Amin, this man already exists, and he devotes a section in his book, which has largely gone unnoticed, to delineating his characteristics. According to Amin, the New Man is miserable in his marriage and feels totally isolated because of the cultural and emotional gap that exists between him and his wife:

> An educated man likes to have a well-presented and ordered home. He has good taste and is inclined to admire pleasant structures, fine feelings, and tender gestures. These things could mean so much to him to the extent that would lead to his neglecting of material concerns. To understand a situation he only needs a word and would even prefer to have a sign. Sometimes he is silent, other times he speaks and sometimes he laughs. He has ideas, which he cherishes, a cause which occupies him, a society which he serves and a nation which he holds dear. He has mental pleasures and pains. He weeps with the poor, sympathizes with the wrongly charged innocent, and rejoices for any good that befalls others. With every thought he develops a feeling that affects his nerves and he wishes to find someone else beside him to explain his feelings and share the moment. This is a

> normal inclination in all of us. However, if this man's wife is ignorant, he will hide his joys and pains from her. ([1899] 1989, 334)

This man suffers because his sensitivity and moral and intellectual pursuits cannot be shared with his ignorant wife. In his view, the characteristics of an ideal wife will include "a delicate taste," "an astuteness of mind," "good management," "an ability to maintain order," "a warm heart," "an honest tongue," and "sincere loyalty" (334). He then goes on to talk about the importance of love in marriage and concludes that it is impossible for most Egyptian marriages to be based on love because of the lower status of the wife in comparison with her husband. From the husband's point of view, love cannot exist "because his wife is totally behind him as far as their intellect and education *tarbiyya* are concerned" (336). Looking at the matter from the wife's side, she will find herself incapable of loving her husband because love is linked to respect "and respect is contingent on our knowing and appreciating the worth of those we respect, and an ignorant woman cannot appreciate her husband's worth" (337). He adds that a woman's judgment of a man's worth is dependent on her own intellectual level. She will probably know nothing about him except his physical appearance and will be oblivious to her husband's "intellectual and moral worth, his honest reputation, his sensitivity of feelings, the scope of his knowledge, his work and his goals in life" (337). In the same vein, Amin links a woman's ignorance with her ability to be a good mother and household manager. Amin's views on the incompatibility between the New Man of modern Egypt and the majority of Egyptian women who needed to become New Women became a common theme in discussions on gender relations in the early twentieth century.

Malak Hifni Nasif: A Counternarrative

An important participant in debates on gender and nation, and one who forged an alternative discourse, is Malak Hifni Nasif (1886–1918). She is famously known for her rejection of Qasim Amin's call for the unveiling of women as a point of entry into the modern period and a prerequisite for the advancement of society as a whole. Her writings can be read as an early critique of nationalist discourses on gender in the Arab world. Although she died young, she succeeded in her short career in making an impression on the cultural scene in Egypt in the first decades of the twentieth century. Nasif was among the first class of women to get a degree from a government school in 1900. In 1903, she obtained a teaching diploma from al-Saniyya school. In 1910, she addressed the Egyptian parliament with a list of demands. Nasif wrote regularly in journals and magazines and had a column in *al-Jarida,* the newspaper of the nationalist *'Umma* party, called *Nisa'iyyat* (Pieces dealing with women's issues). In her articles, she engaged in topical debates about gender issues, modernity and tradition, education for women, and the dangers of polygamy, to give some examples. Her articles initiated heated debates among writers and early reformers. The popularity of *Nisa'iyyat* encouraged her to give public lectures: the first was delivered at the offices of *al-Jarida,* and the second was at the Egyptian University. Nasif inspired other women to lecture in public. At Nasif's memorial service, held at the Egyptian University, Huda Sha'rawi, prominent leader of the women's movement, delivered her first public lecture.

Nasif was held in high regard by her contemporaries.[27] This is worth mentioning because the memory of her faded away for most of the twentieth century and was only revived in the 1990s.[28] *Al-Nisa'iyyat,* published in 1910, was endorsed and introduced by Ahmad Lutfi al-Sayyid (1872–1963), editor of *al-Jarida,* who lauds her moderate approach to women's rights, which, according to him, was different from that of radical feminists whose demands for absolute equality were unreasonable.[29] Al-Sayyid was known as the "Professor of a Generation" in acknowledgment of the role he played in supporting social and educational initiatives. Nasif's memorial service was a large gathering of some of the most noted figures in Egyptian public life. Among the most distinguished figures were Sheikh Mustafa 'Abd al-Razik, head of the Department of Islamic Philosophy and later minister of 'Awqaf and grand sheikh of al-Azhar, who delivered a eulogy in her honor, and the

27. For a critique of Nasif's representation in biographical entries in the early twentieth century, see Booth (2001a). Also, for an analysis of Nasif's reception in the twentieth century see Hatem (2001b).

28. See Ahmed (1992) and Elsadda (1994).

29. Ahmed Lutfi al-Sayyid, "Introduction" to *al-Nisa'iyyat* by Malak Hifni Nasif ([1910] 1998, 42–46).

poets Hafiz Ibrahim and Khalil Mutran, who wrote elegies praising her virtues. In another commemoration held seven years after her death and organized by women, she was acknowledged by Mayy Ziyada, Huda Shaʿrawi, Nabawiyya Musa, Alexandra Averino, and many others.[30] Added to this, journals and magazines published in the early century testify to her involvement in lively debates with prominent figures of different political and ideological allegiances. References to Nasif continue to be made by later writers, critics, and analysts in journals and magazines such as *al-Hilal* and women's magazines such as *Hawwa'*. Mayy Ziyada wrote a full-length biography of her (1920; one of three biographies she wrote about women). In 1976, ʿAbd al-Mitʿal al-Jabri published a full-length book about Nasif, identifying her as a worthy role model for the modern Muslim woman.

Still, unlike Mayy Ziyada or Huda Shaʿrawi, several historians have noted that Nasif was wronged by history and that her name has not been adequately incorporated in Egyptian memory.[31] That is certainly true despite the few scattered references to her achievement.[32] It is my contention that the reason for her marginalization in mainstream cultural memory is her early critique of the dominant nationalist discourse on gender. Her counternarrative was situated on the edges of two warring modernist narratives, commonly referred to as liberal and Islamist, not quite fitting in either. Al-Jabiri (1976), for example, hails her as a committed and devout Muslim woman who set a path to be followed by other women in this century. Unlike other "Westernized" leaders of the women's movement in Egypt, he holds, Nasif is distinguished by her adherence to the right path as prescribed by Islamic teachings. A large section of his book, however, is devoted to correcting some of her errant ideas that do not conform to an orthodox reading of Islam. Hence, though she is claimed by Islamist voices, her views always require some correction, as her discourse seems to "err" on the secular side. His position is an extension of the views of some of Nasif's Islamist contemporaries,

30. The texts are published in Nasif's *Nisa'iyyat* ([1910] 1998, 217–46).

31. See for example ʿAbd al-Halim (1982).

32. For a discussion of Nasif's legacy in Egyptian cultural history, see my introduction to *al-Nisa'iyyat* (Elsadda 1998, 13–19).

such as Sheikh 'Abd al-'Aziz Jawish and Sheikh Husayn Wali. Both men claimed her as a supporter of their views on ideal gendered roles, but not quite, hence warranting some clarification and correction.[33] The other point of view is well-expressed by Suhayr al-Qalamawi, prominent writer and professor of Arabic studies at Cairo University. In her 1962 introduction to *'Athar Bahithat al-Badiya,* a reprint of *al-Nisa'iyyat* with some additional material, al-Qalamawi sums up the representation of Nasif in the liberal nationalist narrative. She acknowledges Nasif's contribution in creating a space for women to express themselves and takes a step further and puts her on par with prominent reformers such as Qasim Amin. She concludes, however, that Nasif's goals were "more short term and modest." For, according to Qalamawi, despite the fact that those goals were as worthy and as noble as Amin's, they were not as comprehensive and holistic, nor were they as particular and deep (1962, 11). As late as 1995, Joseph Zeidan, in his survey of Arab women writers, characterizes their entry into the public sphere as "apologetic and hesitant" and maintains that writers such as Nasif who addressed controversial issues were "far more conservative even than the men" (1995, 88). Zeidan reiterates the dominant view of the secular elite, who mistook Nasif's critique of unqualified embrace of European modernity as an indication of a conservative, or less liberal, temperament.[34]

Nasif admired "European women" for their house management skills, efficiency, and care of their children. She also praised them for their participation in the public sphere and their success in some of the professions that are assumed to be the domain of men. On the other hand, she criticized perceived failings of Egyptian women and argued for the necessity of education as the means for improving their lot. Yet her approach to the comparison between the "European woman" as an icon of modernity and

33. The two commentaries on Nasif's articles were published in her *al-Nisa'iyyat* in 1910 (see Nasif [1910] 1998, 177–78, 181–90).

34. It is worth noting that Mayy Ziyada's commemorative biography of Malak Hifni Nasif also subscribed to the view that she was more conservative compared to Qasim Amin. And, on the basis of Ziyada's critique of Malak's "conservatism," 'Ulfat al-Rubi, in an article about Ziyada's biography of Malak Hifni Nasif, argues that Ziyada's feminist awareness "surpassed that of Malak" ("mujawizan li wa'y Malak") (2001, 54).

the "Egyptian woman," as the representative of tradition differs distinctly from mainstream nationalist voices.[35] First, Nasif challenges the essentialist dichotomies at the heart of these comparisons. In a speech delivered at the Egyptian University entitled "A Comparison Between the Egyptian Woman and the Western Woman" she adds a subtitle to clarify her aim: "About their habits with the purpose of deducing some salient points to be used as guidelines for action."[36] Nasif follows the lives of both Egyptian and Western women from the moment of birth to maturity in an attempt to reach some objective observations, not about essential differences, but about reasons and causes for these differences. Most important, she notes that stereotypical representations of both groups of women have only produced unsubstantiated generalizations that were not very useful. For example, Nasif tackles

35. While male representations of European woman evinced an internalization and reproduction of modernist colonial assumptions about the essential backwardness and inadequacy of Eastern women, representations by some women authors questioned a number of the basic tenets of modernity by testing them against their lived experiences. I am not suggesting that all women questioned modernity because, as is expected, many of them internalized male discourses and reproduced them. In an important article on this issue, Mervat Hatem discusses "the writings of European Orientalist and Egyptian nationalist women . . . [and how they] presented idealized and partial images of one another" (1992, 36). She distinguishes between Egyptian and Levantine-Egyptian women and describes the three Egyptian women she chooses, Huda Sha'rawi, Malak Hifni Nasif, and Nabawiyya Musa, as nationalists, hence aligning them with their male nationalist allies. She argues that they "envied European women's unrestricted freedom" (36) defended Islam against colonial charges that held it responsible for women's backwardness, and marked colonial presence as the main enemy of women. (Musa angrily criticized British adverse interference in implementing educational reform for the benefit of women.) What distinguished women's nationalist discourse from male nationalist discourse was their bitter criticism of the phenomenon of mixed marriages, primarily between Egyptian men and European women. From their perspective, European women were perceived as competitors. While I agree with the general thrust of Hatem's analysis, I argue that women's perception of and reaction to the modernization process, of which the European woman was a symbol, was more complex and varied than that of their male, nationalist supporters. They had the advantage of testing the principles of modernity against their own lived experiences and perceptions of their own identities.

36. Nasif ([1910] 1998, 148–67). All quotations from *al-Nisa'iyyat* are taken from this edition.

a dominant stereotype used to distinguish Egyptian women from Western women, namely that Egyptian women are prey to superstitious beliefs and practices because of their limited education, while Western women are modern and hence rational and not superstitious. Nasif is severely critical of any superstitious practices in the lives of Egyptian women but draws attention to the fact that Western women can also hold superstitious beliefs "though some of us believe that she is irreproachable" (163). In short, Nasif critiqued the nationalist modernist discourse that blamed women for "backwardness" and hence made the improvement of their lot a prerequisite for progress. She also exposed the latent prejudices in a discourse that laid the burden of blame on women's shoulders while absolving men. In her articles and speeches, she often addressed men and called upon them to recognize their role and responsibility in the challenges facing the nation.

A good example of Nasif's critical rethinking of modernist concepts can be found in her treatment of the issue of Western modes of dress or Western fashions. Again, she is arguing against a dominant liberal espousal of Western styles as symbolic of the modern (read: practical and beautiful) and Eastern styles as symbolic of tradition (read: impractical and ugly). In a comparison between Western and Egyptian women, Nasif refutes claims about the ugliness, impracticality, and unsuitability of "traditional" modes of dress as opposed to the superior taste and beauty of Western dress. She points out that "Eastern modes of dress are lighter, less expensive and more suited to our hot weather than Western dress." As for Western fashion, it consists of "an array of complex, multiple pieces that are difficult to wear and remove." She highlights the suffocating effect of high collars, which obstruct the movement of the neck, and tight corsets, which squeeze the abdomen and the lungs and impede breathing. She marvels at the weight of hats armed with pins and "birds and their feathers and branches with flowers and fruits," and the time wasted on tying and untying these elaborate items of clothing (133). Her views on dress throw light on Nasif's rejection of dominant representations of European and Egyptian women as occupying opposites sides on the tradition/modernity paradigm. It is worth noting that she did not try to undermine the achievements of Western women, as she praised their independence and contribution to professions. She also adopted modern ideas about child rearing in her criticism of Egyptian women for their lax approach to raising their children. However, she strove to avoid the trappings of a discourse that posited Eastern women, Egyptian women, as traditional and backward. Nasif rejected the famous "east is east and west is west" opposition and resorted to history as "a fair judge as it contains numerous examples of Eastern women who had reached heights of knowledge and renown at times when Western women were totally unknown" (146).

Nasif challenged dominant liberal representations of ideal manhood and womanhood. In an article entitled "My Views on Marriage: (The Reasons Behind Women's Complaints)"[37] she responds to the article written by Ahmad Lutfi al-Sayyid entitled "Our Sons and Daughters," published in *al-Jarida* in 1908.[38] Al-Sayyid begins with a comparison of the Egyptian family in the past with that of the present. He comes to the conclusion that the family in the past was much happier: there was compatibility between the spouses at the level of education, which led to an agreement on what it meant to have a happy marriage. And although these marriages were often polygamous, the wife used to accept the situation as long as the husband treated all of his wives fairly and provided for their material needs. Al-Sayyid expresses his bewilderment at this harmony, *wifaq,* in the Egyptian family in the past despite the practice of polygamy, and the lack of harmony in the present, even though there are fewer polygamous marriages. This observation prompts him to contemplate the changes that have befallen the new family in order to understand the reasons behind the discord between the married couple and the marked increase in the complaints and criticism of marriage by young men. He depicts the modern Egyptian young man in the best of lights: he is educated; his understanding of marital happiness is in accordance with the latest prescriptions of "modern wise men"; he admires the delicate slim woman who wears simple tasteful clothes; he loves pale colors and prefers natural beauty to artificial beauty; he feels that real love resides in mutual trust, so he expects his wife to believe him when he assures her that he will not marry another; he is convinced that "a good marriage

37. Nasif, "Ra'yi fi al-zawaj wa shakwa al-nisa' minhu: radd 'ala ma katabahu hadrat mudir al-jarida fi al-'adad 383 bi 'unwan banatuna wa 'abna'una," in *al-Nisa'iyyat* 383:57–60.

38. "Banatuna wa 'abna'una."

should last a lifetime." This young man, who appreciates art and beauty, finds himself trapped in a relationship with an ignorant wife who believes that it is beautiful to be white and fat[39] and who wears layers and layers of clothes, "overburdening her body, then leaves her arms without gloves" (al-Sayyid [1908] 1937, 170). Moreover, this wife does not believe him when he promises his devotion and loyalty. As Amin does in his representations of the New Man, al-Sayyid paints a picture of a highly sophisticated and modern sensitive young man in search of a companionate marriage with an equal partner.

In her response to al-Sayyid, Nasif first acknowledges his point about women's dissatisfaction with contemporary marriage arrangements, but then disagrees with his analysis and his conclusions. More important, she disputes his representation of the modern New Man. From her point of view, "traditional" men were more pious and better husbands than modern men. The New Man, on the other hand, is too Westernized in the sense that he has relinquished the good qualities in his traditional upbringing and imitated the worse aspects of Western societies. This New Man makes a virtue of drinking and promiscuous behavior, qualities that are not conducive to a healthy marriage. In this respect, she echoes 'A'isha Taymur's criticism of modern men in *Mir'at al-ta'amul fi al-'umur.* Nasif then admonishes men to assume responsibility for their actions and stop laying the blame on women's doorsteps. She adds that if men really wanted marital happiness, they should choose the right woman and not follow obsolete customs. She also advises them to approach life seriously and to stop trivial pursuits that have allowed other countries to colonize the nation. She concludes that if men are rational, their wives will be rational too, and that it is the man who has the responsibility of setting the example. Nasif's intervention in this debate attempts to redress the balance that was heavily tipped in directing criticism and advice to women while appearing to absolve men of their responsibilities.

Nasif's critique was primarily directed at the *nahda* elite who led the reformation movement and sought to create a nation in their own image. She rebuts their attempt to lay the burden of blame on the shoulders of women ("What is the excuse of our enlightened and educated men for leaving the

39. This is a reference to traditional Egyptian standards of female beauty.

upbringing of their daughters to nature, not following any proper rules?" [1910] 1998, 110). She exposes their double standards and ambivalence regarding gender equality, for whereas they treat a foreign women with courtesy, "carry her bag and raise their tarbushes in respect . . . none of them would ride in the same carriage with his wife" (105). More important, she rejects their patriarchal hold over the approach to women's issues.

> We want men to let us scrutinize their views and choose the wisest. We do not want them to dominate our liberation, the way they ruled over our enslavement. We are tired of their domineering. We are not afraid of the air or the sun, but we are afraid of their eyes and tongues. If they promise to avert their gazes as instructed by religion, and guard their tongues as advised by propriety, we will consider our affairs and theirs. (202)

The above quote addresses the masculine domination of the *nahda* discourse and its marginalization of women's voices. Nasif's challenge to the male-centric liberal discourse about women's liberation is exemplified in her famous refutation of Qasim Amin's call for the unveiling of women. Amin accepted the colonial representation of veiling as an indicator of the oppression of women and proof of the backwardness of the East and therefore argued for the unveiling of women as a prerequisite of women's emancipation and the modernization of the nation.[40] Nasif did not defend the veil because it was a sign of authentic cultural values or because she believed it was intrinsically good or that it protected morals and virtues. Her argument was that unveiling should not take precedence over education, which was a priority that would enable women to make informed choices about their lives and in their own best interest rather than get lost trying to suit the interests of men: "Give girls an education then let them choose for themselves" (51). Nasif expressed her frustration at the "pseudo *nahda*" hailed by reformers (1962, 318).

Labiba Hashim's *Qalb al-rajul*

Women's literary contributions to the rise in the fortunes of the novel as a modern genre in the nineteenth century is yet to be fully explored and

40. See Ahmed's critique of Amin's assimilation of colonial discourse (1992).

evaluated. They certainly participated in the translation of Western novels and short stories that filled the magazines at the turn of the century, as well as wrote early experiments of novels that have largely been ignored. Reference must be made here to Zaynab Fawwaz's remarkable oeuvre. Fawwaz (1846–1914) published essays on social, political, religious, and cultural issues, which were collected and published in 1906 under the title *al-Rasa'il al-Zaynabiyya* (Zaynab's epistles). She drew on the traditional forms of biographical dictionaries (*tarajim*) and produced *Kitab al-durr al-manthur fi tabaqat rabbat al-khudur* (1894; Scattered pearls in the lives of secluded women), which consisted of short biographies of Eastern and Western women and highlighted their participation in public life. She included 'A'isha Taymur and other contemporary women, hence pioneering the tradition of women writing about women, notably followed by Mayy Ziyada (Booth 1991, 1995; al-Rubi 1999). Fawwaz indirectly challenged the modernist veneration of domesticity and subverted the binary opposition between a backward past and a progressive present. Her book emphasized continuity and synthesis between old and new, rather than a rupture with the past. She also wrote *al-Hawa wa al-wafa* (1893; Love and fidelity), a play in four acts about a love story in Iraq; *Husn al-'awaqib or Ghadat al-Zahra* (1899; Good consequences or Ghada the Radiant) a historical novel with a moral message; and *al-Malik Qurash* (1905; King Qurash), a historical romance full of intrigues.

Labiba Hashim (1882–1952) belonged to one of the many families of Syrian/Lebanese origin who moved to Cairo in the second half of the nineteenth century in search of a more liberal political and cultural environment. She attended the literary salon of Warda al-Yaziji and was quickly integrated into Cairene cultural circles. She started writing at an early age and penned three novels, *Hasna' al-jasad* (1898), *Qalb al-rajul* (1904), and *Shirin* (1907) (al-'Id 2002b, 12). In 1899, she published a story in the magazine, *al-Diya'* entitled *Hasanat al-hub* (Love's good aspects), which she described as "a literary story and an economic sermon." Hashim wrote numerous essays and translations of stories and novels. She also delivered lectures at Fu'ad I University (now Cairo University) in 1911 and 1912. In 1906, she published *Fatat al-sharq* (Eastern young woman), a women's journal that continued until 1952.[41] In the opening editorial of the journal, she emphasizes the importance of enabling women's voices in sociopolitical and cultural discussions because, compared to men, their views are grounded in their real-life experiences, which makes them better able to understand women's needs and aspirations (1906).

Hashim's *Qalb al-rajul* (1904; The heart of man) contributed to debates on representations of masculinity and femininity in the modern nation. The novel is set between Syria/Lebanon, Egypt, and Paris and depicts the lives of Syrian exiles, whose lives were disrupted by the outbreaks of sectarian fighting in the Levant. The opening paragraph refers to the massacres that took place in Mount Lebanon in 1860 and that led to the fleeing of many Christian families in search of safer circumstances. The plot revolves around stories of love, survival, and betrayal, as it follows the fortunes of two families who end up in Egypt at the turn of the nineteenth century. At the center of the novel is a love story between Rosa, a young woman of Syrian origin who is brought up in Egypt, and Aziz, another migrant to Egypt of Syrian origin. It depicts the development of their love and their subsequent parting on account of Aziz's infidelity and his inability to keep the promises he made to Rosa. Aziz's fickleness is sympathetically portrayed as the writer finds excuses for weaknesses that led to his infidelity. Rosa, on the other hand, is the epitome of fidelity and steadfastness, as she continues to love and help Aziz despite his treacherous behavior toward her and her father. She fulfills her father's dying wish and marries Farid, who is devoted to her, while Aziz ends up single and vows never to marry as a form of penance for his sins.

With so much being said and written about women and their attributes, their strengths and weaknesses, the title of the novel reveals an attempt by Hashim to engage with modern manhood and directs the reader to contemplate the various directions taken by male characters in search of love. Although all the women in the novel are faithful and true, most male characters are also

41. The publication of *Fatat al-sharq* was interrupted by Hashim's migration to Chile in 1921, where she established another journal, *East and West.* She returned to Cairo in 1924 and resumed the publication of her journal, until her death in 1952.

portrayed as virtuous and as devoted to love as women, with the exception of Aziz. However, he is not portrayed as a scoundrel with no saving grace, but as a weak man who struggles with feelings of guilt. At one level, however, Hashim reverses gender stereotypes, where women are represented as less constant, or more emotionally unstable. She also ascribes traditional male attributes to women characters and describes, for example, Rosa's insistence on bailing out Aziz from bearing the consequences of his theft as "a woman's chivalry." This was not lost on her audience, as is demonstrated in a review of her novel. The reviewer praises the novel but calls upon men to write about "a woman's heart, so that we can decipher whose heart is closer to a branch that bends and to the wind that changes direction, and who is more faithful and true" (Sarkis 1904, 1794). He further challenges Hashim by saying that even if a man possesses a foul temperament, he would still never sink to low conduct, whereas women do not possess men's higher morals and are more likely to be envious and vengeful. He concludes that Rosa's faithfulness is the exception that proves the rule (1794). The review highlights Hashim's subversive intervention in a debate that had implications for representations of women and their access to the public sphere.

Conclusion

The woman question as a central concern in the imagining of the new nation has been the subject of much discussion and analysis. I have tried to show that a similar concern about manhood, or the "man question" also prevailed, though was not necessarily named and foregrounded as such. Most of al-Nadim's writings are as concerned with the making of the modern man as they are with women, even in texts that are manifestly about women. Amin's construction of the New Woman was always in service of his imagining of a new modern man who is the ideal citizen of the new nation. Amin's New Man is educated, middle class, and speaks a foreign language, which he has learned at school or because of an educational visit to a European country. He is every male reformer who embraces a Western modernity as the path to progress. He is also the *nahda* hero who dominates the fiction of the early generation of male writers in Egypt, the founding fathers of the Arabic novel.

On the other hand, discourses on domesticity and women's position in society were not the only existing discourses circulating in the late nineteenth century. Although *al-Fatah* propagated a domestic ideology to its readers, in line with many women's magazines and with the emerging national discourse on womanhood, it also disseminated another message about women's potential in the future. Moreover, Malak Hifni Nasif put forward an early critique of *nahda* discourses and insisted on women's right to chart their own paths to freedom. I foregrounded the literary contributions of 'A'isha Taymur and Labiba Hashim, two women writers whose cultural interventions were marginalized for much of the twentieth century. Taymur's writing did not meet the criteria of a Western-centric Arab literary establishment that accepted the modernist evaluation of traditional forms and styles as obsolete and unfit for modern sensibilities. Within this framework, writers, who drew on traditional genres such as *al-maqama* and styles such as rhymed prose, were not recognized as pioneers of modern prose fiction. Taymur's work is one example, and so is Muhammad al-Muwaylihi's *Hadith 'Issa ibn Hisham,* a text that had a late resurrection at the end of the twentieth century. Taymur contributed to discussions about the ideal characteristics of the citizens of the new nation and the pathways for reform. In *Nata'ij,* she focused on issues of good rule and leadership, thus reflecting the interests of her class and her desire to improve the performance of the ruling family following both modern and Islamic principles of *tarbiyya* (Hatem 2003, 17). In *Mir'at al-ta'amul,* she directly addresses the qualities of manhood that legitimize male leadership roles within the family. Labiba Hashim wrote about the experience of her community of migrants from the Levant and explored male/female relationships and characteristics. In her novel, love is a supreme value that conquered sectarian friction and divisions. Her subject matter was topical and representative of a significant minority community in the Egyptian cultural field. She also attempted to explore men's psyche and challenged stereotypical representations of the sexes. It is fair to say that her work was not representative of the interests and ideas of the dominant intellectual elite that led the *nahda* and imagined it in their own image, hence her marginalization in the canon.

2

The New Man

Conflicting Masculinities in the Fiction of Haikal, al-Mazini, and al-Rafi'i

In the previous chapter, I argued that discursive representations of the New Man were not just a subtext in representations of the New Woman, but that he was very much a construct that was overtly debated and contested. Mona Russell has suggested that the New Man emerged during the 'Urabi Revolt of 1881–82, before the appearance of the New Woman and "the resulting occupation brought about his emasculation" (2004, 88). Yet her definition of the New Man is restricted to his political role and is contrasted to the personal or family demands initiated by the New Woman (166). Lisa Pollard, on the other hand, has argued, with reference to Amin, that the New Man will be created by the New Woman; in fact, he is her responsibility. If she succeeds in instilling "order in her home" she will shape a new man who is monogamous and can enjoy new "partnerships with women" and "a new relationship with a just ruler" (2005, 161). However, in my reading of Amin, I have tried to show that the New Man was seen to have emerged well before the New Woman and that the formation of Amin's New Woman was a prerequisite both for nation building and for providing a worthy partner to the New Man. Her role was then to ensure that the characteristics of the New Man became national characteristics for all citizens of the nation. The new masculine identity was imaged in the narratives of the early male reformers and writers as representations of the "self" in search for meaning in a changing world. Many of the writers saw themselves as representatives of a new generation of Egyptian men whose identities were reshaped in accordance with new aspirations and pursuits.[1]

However, whereas the New Woman has been extensively researched, her logical counterpart, the New Man, has not received sufficient attention. Why? The first answer that presents itself is that the phrase *al-rajul al-jadid* was not coined and given prominence in early modern discourses on nation building in the same way that the term *al-mar'a al-jadida* was coined and propagated. In fact, there is hardly any reference to *al-rajul al-jadid.* Writers discussed the identity and characteristics of *al-rajul al-'asri,* or *al-rajul al-masri,* or *al-rajul al-'arabi,* or *al-rajul al-muslim.* References to male roles and characteristics predominantly assumed the existence of a universal man who was a member of the modern world.[2] There was certainly a debate on the preferred characteristics of this "modern man," or the citizen of the new nation-state, which raged sometimes quite heatedly between different parties. Distinctions were made among men from different classes or men adhering to different ideologies, or between old and new generations of men, but the term "New Man" did not gain currency and did not become a prerequisite for the success of the new nation-state. In short, on the semantic level there was no counterpart to the New Woman. This absence raises the issue of the politics of naming and the implications of introducing new coinages at a particular moment in history for a particular group. However, the fact that the term was not coined in early national discourses does not necessarily explain its absence as a critical concept in the scholarship on gender in the Middle East. This lacuna is partly an effect of the theoretical lens that has been used to study the gender dynamics of nation building in postcolonial contexts, as has been discussed earlier.

1. It is worth noting that the New Man as a cultural construct intersects and overlaps at many levels with the *effendi* or the class of the new *effendiyya.* The *effendi* is more grounded historically, and the connotations of the term have changed over time as Lucie Ryzova argues. For a detailed discussion of the term see Ryzova (2005).

2. In Naguib Mahfouz's *al-Sukkariyya,* published in 1956, the grandson of Ahmad Abdel-Jawwad works for a magazine called *al-Insan al-jadid* (The new human being, [1957] 1984, 104). Again, the adjective "new" is not applied to men, but to the universal generic human being.

Representations of the New Man within the Egyptian nationalist narrative on nation building and modernity have yet to be explored. As early as 1994, Deniz Kandiyoti wondered about the motives of "those 'enlightened,' pro-feminist men" (1994, 197) who championed the cause of women in Turkey, Egypt, and other parts of the Middle East and suggested that their representations of women can be construed as reverse images of themselves. She examined some institutions where masculine identities were produced and looked at male narratives of the self and concluded that "behind the enduring façade of male privilege lie profound ambiguities which may give rise to both defensive masculinist discourse and genuine desire for contestation and change" (1994, 212). In fact, representations of the New Man have always been a subtext in representations of the New Woman.[3] Debates about ideal manhood ran in tandem with discussions on ideal womanhood. They might not have dominated the cultural scene in the same way as did the debates on "the woman question," but they nevertheless were very significant and revealing of the complexities of gender politics.

In this chapter, I will examine literary narratives published in the first three decades of the twentieth century, by Mohammed Hussein Haikal, Ibrahim 'Abd al-Qadir al-Mazini, and Mustafa Sadiq al-Rafi'i. I focus on their treatment of a common theme in national narratives about the difficulties encountered by middle-class men in finding a fit partner to marry among Egyptian women. I argue that the dilemma of the New Man of the modern nation, the "hero of the *nahda* narratives" (Elsadda 2000),[4] emerged as the logical outcome of the liberal nationalist discourse on "the woman question" in Egypt. While advocating for women's rights and education, women were made to carry the burden of the "backwardness" of Egyptian society. Reformers bemoaned their inability to have fulfilling relationships with their wives because of the assumed discrepancy between their levels of education and culture. Also, the segregation of the sexes was signaled as

3. Looking at journals published by men but classified as part of the women's press, Marilyn Booth also questions "what men's writing on women and femininity has to say about men's gendered identities" (Booth 2001c, 174).

4. An early version of my argument in this chapter about the *nahda* hero was published in an article in Arabic (2000).

another impediment to the possibility of aspiring to a marriage based on love and understanding. Men's failed quests to find an equal partner in marriage led to a celebration and justification of bachelorhood: men were forced to remain unmarried because of the "lower status" of Egyptian women. Alternatively, these same men opted for marrying "foreign women" who were perceived as being more compatible.[5] Debates on the marriage crisis in the early twentieth century bring to the fore the centrality of gender in imaging the new nation, rendering the relationship between the sexes a vibrant locus of contestation and negotiation.[6] I have chosen to explore texts written by prominent members of the *nahda* generation, men who, in many ways, have had a marked impact on the ongoing debates.

Mohammed Hussein Haikal

The novel *Zaynab* (1914; English translation, *Zainab* 1990) by Mohammed Hussein Haikal (1888–1956) occupies a special status in the history of the Arabic novel, for being "ahead of its time" (Badr 1968, 169), an early contribution to a "national literature" (Khulayf 1993), an autobiographical novel (Badr 1968, 323), with Hamid, the protagonist, as a "prototype of the young men of his generation" (Haqqi 1986, 164). Most important, it has been identified as the first Arabic novel. It was published in 1914, first under a pseudonym, *misri fallah* (an Egyptian and a peasant), then later in 1929 under Haikal's own name. In his introduction to the third edition of the novel, Haikal justifies using a pseudonym on the grounds that his reputation as a young lawyer would be overshadowed by his identity as a writer of fiction, at a time when fiction had not yet attained social status and due respect ([1914] 1992, 7).[7] Haikal then proceeded to have a distinguished career as a university lecturer, a member of parliament, editor of *al-Siyasa* in 1922 and al-*Siyasa al-usbu'iyya* in 1926. Haikal is credited in mainstream history for

5. Marrying foreign women or mixed marriages was a hotly debated issue in the early modern period. In Egypt, it was closely linked to comparisons between Egyptian women and Western women, a point that I refer to in my discussion of the woman question.

6. Hanan Kholoussy uses marriage "as the central lens for studying anti-colonial nationalism" (2010, 10).

7. All quotations are taken from this edition. All translations are mine.

his role in building bridges between East and West, and in defending secular thought and freedom of expression. He famously contributed to the cultural battles that erupted around the publication of 'Ali 'Abd al-Raziq's book *al-Islam wa usul al-hukm* in 1925 and Taha Husayn's *Fi al-shi'r al-jahili* in 1926, where he defended the right of writers to *ijtihad* ('Asfur 1996).

Zaynab was actually written in 1910 and 1911 in Paris, London, and Geneva, while Haikal was still a doctorate student in Europe. His motivation for writing the novel was his feeling of nostalgia for his homeland while in Europe, but also his discovery of and great admiration for French literature (Haikal [1914] 1992). His nostalgia explains his romanticization of the countryside in Egypt and the idealization of the life of peasants. His admiration for French literature as an emblem of French identity and national pride brings to the fore an important dimension in Haikal's literary project: his awareness of the vital role of national literature in the consolidation of national identity, and, hence, his desire to contribute to the creation of an Egyptian national literature that would represent the new nation. The French connection also foregrounds his modernist worldview where the West was a model for inspiration and emulation for his generation of *nahda* elite. Haikal sheds light on the intention behind the choice of a pseudonym, *misri fallah:* it was meant to emphasize his pride in being an Egyptian and the son of a peasant, an act of defiance and affirmation of national pride (7–8). Haikal, however, was not a *fallah* in the strict meaning of the term, but the son of a wealthy landowner, and neither was Hamid, his persona in the novel, who clearly belonged to an affluent family. Pierre Cachia has suggested that the *fallah* in this case indicates someone of Egyptian lineage to be distinguished from an upper-class elite of Turkish descent (1990, 113). This is a valid point and certainly sheds light on Haikal's motivation for emphasizing his identity as a *fallah.* His identification as a *fallah* not only counters upper-class Turkish sense of superiority vis à vis local inhabitants, but also is an act of defiance against colonial denigration of colonized masculinity in the figure of the *fallah* as the native and authentic representative of Egypt. The *fallah* and his lifestyle are romanticized in Haikal as part of his larger project to forge a new national masculinity that superseded traditional models of masculinity, but with roots in a 'purer' more 'authentic' Egypt. A new edition published in 1929 triggered another wave of critical reception and appreciation, a fact that revitalized the literary scene and paved the way for the appearance of more novels in the 1930s.

Zaynab is about Hamid, a typical *nahda* hero who is torn between two cultures. He is on vacation from his studies abroad, which he spends in his parents' house in the Egyptian countryside. He is very critical of the social customs that do not permit the development of love relationships, particularly between the men and women of his class. This is because middle-class women are isolated in their homes, and their movement is restricted by tradition. As for peasant women, though they have more freedom of movement, and hence more possibilities for mixing and interacting with men, he finds that the class chasm is too wide to bridge. In the novel, Hamid meets a woman of each type. The first, Zaynab, is a beautiful peasant girl who spends happy times with him and responds to his kisses and flirtatious advances. Nothing, however, comes out of this affair. The second is Aziza, his cousin and childhood sweetheart. She, however, is out of reach and can only communicate with him by writing letters. Eventually, she breaks up with him and informs him that she has been promised in marriage to someone else. Zaynab also enters into a loveless marriage, as the man she loves, Ibrahim, is too poor. Hamid ends up alone, miserable and alienated.

Hamid's dilemma in the novel can be ascribed to his inability to contract a marriage based on love, given the social and cultural restraints imposed on middle-class men and women. This is how Haikal presents his protagonist's inner conflict:

> Where would a young man find such pleasure in Egypt? Where would he find joy? He is a miserable and unfortunate man. He finds himself torn between two evils: he will either continue with his deathlike existence, which is the inevitable outcome of the inherited life and all the rules imposed on him by the older generation, or, he will throw himself in the arms of the rotten leftovers hurled at his poor country from the happy but criminal West. (189)

Hamid expresses his rebellion against the chains of the East and finds himself unable to embrace the ways of the "criminal West." Yet, this West seems to hold the keys to the happiness for which Hamid is searching. It is a happiness derived from having the opportunities that would allow for the development of love relationships between men and women. According to Hamid, inherited social customs that restricted the interaction between the sexes and led to the isolation of women and the limitation of their abilities constituted obstacles to love relationships, and hence could only result in loveless marriages. Marriage based on love and companionship was impossible in the Egyptian context because of traditional rules of segregation. He fails to attain happiness with Aziza not only because she is married off to someone else, but also because he feels that they are miles apart, for he "was soaring high in the sky and she was hidden in her corner" (249). As for Zaynab, the class barrier is too high for their relationship to continue. That is ultimately the case despite Hamid's obvious attraction to Zaynab, and certainly in spite of his laborious attempts to justify the possibility of such a union. Hamid's conclusion is that the real culprit responsible for the misery of young men like him is a society that watches over its members "with an unmoving, rigid eye and a cold heart that is impervious to beauty."

Zaynab's story parallels and consolidates Hamid's crisis. Unlike Aziza, she is not shackled by middle-class rules, which force women into seclusion and restrict their interaction with men. She has the freedom to roam in the fields and to have the opportunity to fall in love with Ibrahim. She is also less constrained by a middle-class morality that condemns premarital sexual contact and actually accepts Hamid's flirtatious advances spontaneously and without remorse. Zaynab, however, is also the victim of oppressive customs. She is married off without her consent, after her father strikes a bargain over her dowry with the groom's family. Chained to a loveless marriage, she is unable to forget her lover and eventually dies, as her abject state makes her an easy prey to tuberculosis.

Aziza, Zaynab's middle-class counterpart, is equally destined to unhappiness, again on account of oppressive traditions. Compared to Zaynab, she is literate and has access to some of the privileges of modernity. But, unlike Zaynab, her life behind walls deprives her of simple pleasures, like going for a walk alone in the countryside, a situation that negatively affects her physical and mental well-being. Her voice is expressed in an exchange of letters with Hamid at the end of the novel, where she articulates her despair and misery every time she remembers the moment when she reaches puberty and is forced into seclusion:

> Do you think, brother Hamid ,that us young women are happy in this old prison? You think we are always content, but only God knows the poison in this bitter existence. . . . What girl does not remember the last day of her freedom . . . the last hour of my free and virtuous life as I say good-bye to my cousins here in the village and return to the city, only to find the cloth of my veil ready and waiting for me at home! This black garment, the garment of sorrow and pain. (192)

Aziza's seclusion destroys her chances for happiness as she becomes incapable of reciprocating Hamid's love. She resigns herself to her fate, accepts a loveless arranged marriage, and appeals to Hamid to forgive her.

Hamid, according to Haikal, is a different kind of man, a New Man who is the citizen of the modern world. He stands apart as he rebels against the customs and traditions that result in his alienation and unhappiness. He lives in the world of reason and freedom and does not always adhere to the dictates of custom. His mind usually triumphs over his traditional convictions as "he thinks with absolute freedom and laughs at the obstacles that would restrain him" (257). However, Hamid also carries the scars of an oppressive social order. He vents his anger and frustration in a letter addressed to his family, in which he tries to explain to them the reasons for his obvious unhappiness. At the center of his letter and his dilemma is his conviction that "a life without love is pale and worthless" (249). His search for love is thwarted by obsolete traditions and values. Hamid's rebellion, however, is futile and ineffective, as he makes no attempt to change the status quo (al-Ra'i 1964, 34). He is critical of women's seclusion but seems to accept all the trappings of middle-class morality that consolidate this seclusion. Similarly, he criticizes the exploitation of the *fallah* by rich landowners and colonial rulers but, again, accepts the advantages of his class without interrogating their legitimacy or ethicality. In effect, he sets himself up for a miserable situation: he detests a social order that bestows on him privileges on the basis of his gender and class but limits his chances of happiness, but, at the same time, he is not yet willing or prepared to relinquish his privileges and change the foundational principles of a discriminatory social order.

Haikal uses the adjective "wretched" to describe Hamid many times in the novel. This epithet is also used to describe a friend of Hamid's who is about to get married. From Hamid's point of view, his friend is a wretched fellow because he will never find the happiness he is looking for in marriage. On the other hand, another view of marriage is expressed by ʻAli Effendi. He disagrees with Hamid's desire for a marriage based on love and insists that his friend is only following a mirage: "Say what you will about the wife you all desire. Make her into the paragon of beauty and perfection! . . . She will end up being a woman like all other women" ([1914] 1992, 131). In rural areas, continues ʻAli Effendi, men get married every day, not to attain happiness, but to find women who can help them carry the burdens of life, and the same is true for all men of all classes (131). Hamid's quest for love seems untenable in a traditional setting, but it remains a desire and a goal.

Ibrahim al-Mazini

Ibrahim al-katib (1931; English translation: *Ibrahim the Writer,* 1976) was written by Ibrahim ʻAbd al-Qadir al-Mazini (1889–1949)[8] and published in 1931. Al-Mazini tells the story of how he decided to embark on this project, suggesting that it came as a pure coincidence. Having encountered an Austrian woman who shared with him the details of her problem-ridden life, he decided to reciprocate the gesture by recounting a story that is allegedly about his own life. There is a consensus among critics and literary historians that the novel is autobiographical.[9] The protagonist of the novel is the same *nahda* hero, torn between two cultures and suffering accordingly. It is about Ibrahim, who embarks on a quest for meaning for his life, which he hopes to find in a romantic love relationship. Ibrahim is a talented writer who is deeply involved in the larger questions about existence but totally unable to lead a productive and successful life. Al-Mazini portrays him as a man who believes in the power of reason, who is proud without being conceited, "who gazes inwards to understand himself," and who is excessively shy and cautious with

8. His date of birth has been the subject of speculation. See Ahmad al-Sayyid ʻAwadayn (1998).

9. Mohamed Mandour has argued that, in general, al-Mazini has written about every little detail of his life (1954, 22). Niʻmat Fu'ad also recounts that al-Mazini's son confirmed that the family recognized some of the events of the novel and some knew some of the characters (1978).

women (al-Mazini 1931, 24). About Ibrahim's views on women, al-Mazini points out that

> he did not hold them in high esteem, though he did not despise them either. From his point of view, a woman was primarily a means for the preservation of the species and her beauty was merely a trap set up by life and was best avoided. He also believed that, in general, a man was more beautiful than a woman, because the attraction [*fitna*] of a beautiful man, unlike that of a woman, does not rely on basic instincts. His behavior around women manifested his opinion of them: he considered a woman to be a creature worthy of compassion and playful consideration. This did not preclude a man's strength to ensure his mastery and control over women. (24)

In another scene, Ibrahim watches the difference in behavior between men and women who need to go through a door that is still wet with paint. Most men pushed the door with their feet and avoided contact with it, as they were all able to assess the risk and act intelligently.

> As for the women, their approaches were more varied. The first one came . . . in her black dress that swept the floor behind her, her arms bent and parallel to her chest and her palms open as if she is trying to ward something off with them. She pushes the door with her hands, which become sticky with wet paint, but failing to understand what has happened, she seeks the nearest man to explain what has happened to her. As for the second, she pushes the door with her shoulder and goes on her way totally oblivious to what has happened to her clothes. (41)

Ibrahim has three love encounters with women in the novel: Shushu, his cousin, who is a graduate of a French school and is enslaved by obsolete tradition; Mary, a Syrian nurse, whom he loves but considers her beneath him socially; and finally Layla, a liberated girl who represents the model of the Western woman. Ibrahim's feelings toward the three women are characterized by confusion and ambivalence. In his words, "I remember Mary and I feel the might of power. . . . I imagine Shushu and I feel the dignity of experience . . . and when I am with Layla, I find myself learning the story of life following the rhythm of youth" (226). About Layla, he adds that she "does not move the Eastern side in him . . . but was always in his eyes a symbol of pleasant, tender devilry [*shaytaniyya*]—and other qualities acquired from the West" (294). Comparing Western and Egyptian marriages, Ibrahim maintains that most of the latter are not based on love. In the West, many men try to win the love of one woman,

> and the matter is resolved by her choosing one of them after examining her feelings and emotions. She could make the wrong choice . . . but she will have passed the test anyway. For, if she falls in love, there will be no doubt that its object will be one special person. As for her Egyptian sister, she rarely has the chance to pass that test. (303)

In 1943, Al-Mazini wrote another novel, entitled *Ibrahim al-thani* (Ibrahim the second) following the life of his protagonist Ibrahim the writer. In the second novel, he is older and married to Tahiyya, a woman he loves and who understands him, but he is still searching for fulfillment and for romantic love. He has two affairs, the first with 'Ayda, who dies young, and the second with Mimi, whom he eventually encourages to marry Sadiq, a relative who is in love with her. The protagonist is older and is able to look back on his life, but as one critic has suggested, "it is the same experience, or even the same novel" (al-Bardi 2001, 116).

In his introduction to *Ibrahim al-katib,* al-Mazini addresses the issue of whether the position of women in society had an adverse effect on creative writing. Discussions of the woman question in the early twentieth century had implications for the literary field, as writers debated whether the restricted position of women in society undermined the creative literary process itself. Many, including Haikal, have argued that the isolation of women constituted a major impediment to the development of the genre of the novel as it restricted the exploration of relationships between men and women, a key theme in the modern novel. In his introduction to *Ibrahim al-katib,* al-Mazini addresses this issue directly and disagrees with proponents of the view that "Egyptian life is not conducive to the emergence and advancement of the novel . . . and that the veil that is still imposed on women—to some degree—is an obstacle that impedes creative writing" (1931, 9–10). He argues that the theme of love is not a prerequisite for writing a novel and wonders: "Don't people in this world have pursuits other than love, other aims than for a man to win a woman's love or vice versa? This limited view is nothing but hysterical" (10). Al-Mazini's position seemingly goes against the contention that the restricted status of women disrupts not only marital happiness but also the creative process. Nevertheless, this particular view is not borne out in his novels, all of which deal with love, or the quest for love, in the midst of social restrictions on the interaction between men and women.

Furthermore, and in light of the consensus on the autobiographical dimension in his novels, particularly in *Ibrahim al-katib,* al-Mazini makes an effort to distance himself from his protagonist. He admits that physically there are some similarities—they are both short and physically weak. Al-Mazini emphasizes his character's preference for the world of ideas and for philosophical contemplation and his excellent taste. His strength resides in his eyes rather than in his body. Needless to say, all of these are qualities that might very well be common to both writer and character. But al-Mazini goes on to say that he does not respect his protagonist very much, that is, he does not think much of him as a man. This disrespect for his protagonist's expression of manhood is best understood in the light of the heated debates that raged about the meaning of modern masculinity and its relation to nation building in nationalist discourses. Al-Mazini's views reveal the contested nature of the liberal representations of national masculinity, even among liberal writers. It is also indicative of how the debate developed, becoming even more polarized in the 1930s. His novel, as well as the views expressed in the introduction, are a significant intervention in the ongoing debate about the New Man who was going to lead the nation to prosperity. This New Man, as I have argued, is refraining from marriage because he is unable to have a fulfilling relationship with a woman because of traditional restrictions and segregation between the sexes. He is Hamid and Ibrahim. He is the young man described by al-Sayyid in his essay and the husband in Amin's work. He is also the modern man criticized by Malak Hifni Nasif in her articles. All of these writers are redefining masculinity and charting new horizons for the New Man of the nation. The last writer I have chosen to discuss takes the debate to a new level, highlighting the gravity of the issue and the high stakes involved.

Mustafa Sadiq al-Rafi'i

Mustafa Sadiq al-Rafi'i (1880–1937) is classified as conservative and traditional. His famous battle with Taha Husayn over the latter's book, *Fi-al-shi'r al-jahili* (On pre-Islamic poetry), published as a book, significantly entitled *Tahta rayat al-Qur'an* (Under the banner of the Qur'an), secured him the reputation of being a hard-core conservative and made him the target of attack by representatives of liberal thought such as 'Abbas al-'Aqqad, and many others. Also in the cultural battles that raged between conservatives and innovators, *al-muhafizun wa al mujaddidun,*[10] he was firmly in the conservative camp. These battles ranged from disagreements on literary innovation, the relationship between colloquial Arabic and classical Arabic, and the desired or undesired changes in language styles and literary genres to different points of view that reflected sociopolitical forces at work in society. According to Sabry Hafez, al-Rafi'i "wrote mainly to teach and to impress his reader," but his narrative "displays hackneyed and reactionary views" (1993, 146–47).[11] In all his writings, he was vehemently critical of the lifestyle and values of the European woman. He denounced what he perceived to be the moral laxity and promiscuity of the West and called for the protection and preservation of the moral superiority of the Islamic family and the Muslim woman. He repeatedly referred to the woes and disasters inflicted upon the nation by marriages between Egyptian men and European women. In his short stories, written in the last few years of his life and published in *al-Risala,* al-Rafi'i set out to define the parameters of masculinity and femininity in the modern nation.[12] His stories can be read as counternarratives that contested the nationalist constructions of gendered identities as manifested in the work of Haikal and al-Mazini.

It is worthwhile pausing to consider *al-Risala* (1933–1953), the forum in which al-Rafi'i published his short stories. It was owned and edited by Ahmad Hasan al-Zayyat (1885–1968), a prominent intellectual, columnist, short-story writer, translator, and editor of a literary magazine—*al-Riwaya.* He studied in al-Azhar University, then traveled to France and encountered French culture and literature. He believed in building bridges between East

10. For an account of cultural battles in the first half of the twentieth century in Egypt, see Anwar al-Jindi (1966).

11. Also see Ni'mat Fu'ad's critique of al-Rafi'i (1953).

12. It is worth noting here that according to al-Rafi'i's biographer, al-'Aryan, al-Rafi'i considered the short story to be an article or an essay to express his views (al-'Aryan 1939, 206).

and West and devoted his life to reviving the Islamic cultural tradition and making it accessible to the modern reader. The title of the magazine, *al-Risala,* which means "the message," immediately brings to mind the message of God delivered by the prophet Mohamed. *Al-Risala* succeeded in becoming a vibrant forum for the discussion of topical cultural, social, and political debates about the future shape and character of the modern nation. It encouraged experimentation with new literary forms and schools of thought. It also contributed to the revival and dissemination of Islamic themes by publishing *islamiyyat* literature, and by making accessible old manuscripts and texts from the Islamic tradition. *Al-Risala* was controversial and elicited conflicting views. It brought together writers from left and right, Islamists and secularists. It was described as "a liberal open university" that played a seminal role in the education of generations of Egyptians and Arabs (Shalash 1988, 147). On the other hand, the overall direction it opted for was described as a "retreat" (Safran 1961, 165–80) from the gains of liberal thought propagated by the first generation of reformers. In many ways, *al-Risala* provided an appropriate space for the expression of contested views on masculinity and the modern nation.

Al-Rafi'i particularly targeted the representations of the New Man as someone who is incapable of finding a fit partner in marriage because of societal restrictions on relations between the sexes. These representations only encouraged a celebration of bachelorhood, a condition that according to al-Rafi'i was detrimental to the advancement of the nation, as well as a violation of an Islamic directive about marriage constituting the fulfillment of a religious obligation, being *nisf al-din.* Al-Rafi'i ridicules and attempts to discredit those he describes as the Westernized elite and questions their manhood. Marriage, he maintains, is the cornerstone of manhood and a principle of national allegiance. A man who does not marry is like a deserter from the army: both betray their responsibility and duty to their nation. Manhood can only be attained through marriage and by assuming the responsibility of a family. He lashes out at the educated elite for mimicking Western ways and style of life. Their pursuit of love, or their desire to secure a love relationship with their future spouses, is characterized as an indication of Western infiltration in Egyptian society, and as a disruption of authentic cultural values. He writes sweepingly: "Europe colonizes through ideology and military prowess. It conquers with the army, the navy, the book and the teacher, pleasure and enjoyment, women and love" (*Istanwaqa al-jamal* [He mistook the he-camel for a she-camel] 1934c, 1563). In al-Rafi'i's view, marriage is clearly distinguishable from love, or the pursuit of love. The first is a national duty and a prerequisite of true manhood; the second is proof of the perverse infiltration of Western influence. Al-Rafi'i goes a step further and accuses bachelors of effeminacy. They inhabit this unruly space of the in-between, neither men nor women, neither Westerners nor Egyptians. He warns bachelors of the gravity of their failure: "Be warned that men will have proceeded while you retreat, will have shown strength and stamina while you cried out in pain . . . will have acted like men, while you acted like a woman" (*Armalat al-hukuma* [Widow of the nation] 1934, 1644). He compares these men unfavorably to camels: "If a camel behaves like a she-camel, it becomes effeminate, it softens and succumbs, but it continues to carry its burden. As for these men, when they behave like a she-camel (like women) they become effeminate, then soften and succumb, and refuse to carry their burdens" (1934c, 1564).

Al-Rafi'i identifies two reasons for the deterioration in the state of the nation. The first is the weakness in religious education. The second, he explains, is the "the effeminization of the male temperament, the exaggerated inclination to comfort and meekness, and the retreat from shouldering responsibilities" (1934c, 1565). He proposes that the government dismiss all unmarried men who are eligible for marriage. Until this moment comes, he calls upon the people of the nation to punish them by calling them "widows of the nation," meaning that their single status inevitably leads to its demise. To drive the insult home, al-Rafi'i coins the phrase "widow of the nation" to describe a bachelor. He explains in a footnote that the added feminine suffix *al-ta'* to the word for widower, *armal,* is not meant to connote the feminine gender *al-ta'nith* in Arabic. Rather, it is a new suffix in the Arabic language the function of which is to ridicule, *ta' al-huzu'*. He continues to say that if all married men and women agree on calling any bachelor "widow of the nation," it will function as "a linguistic purifier" (1934a, 1643) that will help rid the nation of a decadent and immoral phenomenon.

Having demarcated a clear-cut distinction between love and marriage, marriage being a national duty and a manly responsibility, the ideal man, according to al-Rafi'i, is capable of resisting the temptations offered by love. Love in the writings of al-Rafi'i is a very complex concept. A great deal of his writings and poetry are attempts to construct definitions of love, secular love, spiritual love, the disappointments of love, the pains of love. In the introduction to his book *'Awraq al-ward rasa'iluha wa rasa'iluhu* (1931; Rose petals: her epistles and his epistles), which deals with the philosophy of love and beauty, al-Rafi'i points out that there is a rich Arab tradition about the philosophy of love and claims that his book is a significant contribution to this tradition. Nevertheless, he represents love between a man and a woman, which is the favored theme of modern novels and short stories (romantic love based on admiration, understanding, and a meeting of the souls) as a source of temptation, which he often conflates with the pervasive presence of alien Western ideas in Egyptian society. Men who seek love are consciously or unconsciously promoting a Westernized worldview that is in conflict with the national agenda. Again, the background here is the theme of the frustrated search for love by the *nahda* hero, who bemoans the segregation of the sexes in Egyptian society and considers it a major obstacle in his quest for happiness.

After distinguishing between love and marriage, marriage being the only ultimate expression of committed national manhood, al-Rafi'i prescribes the virtuous national attitude to temptations of love. In a story entitled "al-Qalb al-miskiyn" (The wretched heart), he tells the story of a friend of his who falls in love with a beautiful singer. Not only is she desirable, but she is also available and willing. The friend, who is a "real" man, deals with this experience as a test, a trial that he has to go through to attain virtue and purity of soul. Manhood here is synonymous with virtue, with the strength of mind and soul to resist temptation. The friend takes a vow of celibacy toward this woman. He abstains from indulging himself in the worldly pleasures offered by love, a love that is equated by al-Rafi'i with a Westernized worldview.

The third cornerstone of manhood, according to al-Rafi'I, is dominance and control over women. To counter the liberal fascination with the model of the educated, outgoing European woman, al-Rafi'i insists on the looseness of the Westernized woman and the virtuous religiosity of the uneducated Egyptian woman. In his fervor to make clear-cut distinctions between Egyptian and European women, he summarily condemns educated Egyptian women who are capable of expressing their opinions forcefully, hence vying with men on equal footing. If the education of women leads to their breaking away from the control of men, then education is not a good idea. Ideal womanhood is synonymous with virtue, and motherhood is constructed as virtue incarnate. In a story entitled "al-Ta'isha" (1935; A reckless woman), he describes the free, educated woman as a disaster. In another short story, and along the same vein, he posits that women's easy access to the public sphere leads to the corruption of the norms of nature ("Zawjat imam" 1935, 282). A woman's education can be virtuous if it is directed and controlled by her male relatives. The logical conclusion to his views on ideal womanhood boils down to the religious and natural necessity of women's total acquiescence to their husbands, even if these husbands are not worthy.

In his short story "Fi al-lahab wa la tahtariq" (1934b; In the flames and she does not burn), he tells the story of a dancer who, after finishing her performance at a nightclub, goes home and prays. Al-Rafi'i begins his story with a question, "Is this possible?" He expresses his bewilderment at the coexistence of two seemingly incompatible elements from his point of view. Dancing was used by critics of Western influence, al-Rafi'i included, as a symbol of a Western way of life that threatened Egyptian values and promoted moral laxity. Women who danced at parties with men, or dancers in nightclubs, like the heroine of this story, were all condemned for relinquishing their tradition and cultural heritage. Hence this dancer, who on principle is seen to be violating a grave prerequisite of Islamic identity and culture, has another side to her character, as a devout Muslim who regularly performs an essential ritual of Islam. Al-Rafi'i wonders: Is this possible?

Al-Rafi'i's narrator is clearly intrigued by the woman. He uses a language that reveals his fascination and admiration for the girl, whether she is dancing or praying.

> She was a beauty. If the moonlight were to shine on anything on earth, it would shine on her face. Everyday you see her, she appears even better than before. You would think that the sun adds magical beams every hour to her face, and that each dawn leaves her dew-drops and splendor in the morning. When I saw her, my heart witnessed the light of beauty and ablution on her face. (1934b, 1283)

He proceeds to explore this puzzle and argues that all women were born with a religious instinct, which he describes as their "natural ruby," which they can either hold onto or relinquish. In this case, this dancer has managed to preserve her "natural ruby" despite her promiscuous job. Al-Rafi'i allows his character to tell the story of how she became a dancer. It was out of necessity, not choice, because the other options that were open to her were limited to domestic service or becoming a trader in the market. She argues that as a dancer she has more control over her life. She then reverses the writer's question to her, about the incompatibility between virtue and dancing and says:

> There are veiled women with naked souls, and unveiled women with veiled souls. If you do not know this, it is time you did. The real question is not the one you posed, but rather: do you only see my clothes, or do you see me, and my clothes? Here you are looking deeply into my eyes, searching for distant meanings. Do you see the eyes of a dancer?" I answered: "No by God. I do not see the eye of a dancer, but the eye of a fighter in the name of God." She laughed and said: "Rather say, the eye of a fighter who conquers a devil or many devils every day. (1934b, 1284–85)

The dancer challenges another dominant marker of identity, namely the veil. Defenders of the veil presented themselves as the guardians of Arab and Muslim cultural heritage; critics of the veil saw the seclusion of women as the main reason behind the backwardness of Arab societies. Heated debates raged between the *muhajjibun* (advocates of the veil) and the *sufuriyyun* (advocates of unveiling). Here, the question posed by the dancer to al-Rafi'i subverts the dominant equation and puts forward a view that goes beyond fetishized symbols and calls for a reconsideration of rigid dichotomies and politico-cultural biases. Al-Rafi'i concludes:

> She chokes with dancing and is refreshed with prayer. Everyday, she chokes and is refreshed.
>
> But I still say: is this possible?
>
> Can the following words be synonymous from an Islamic point view: she danced and prayed? (1934b, 1285)

The story ends with the same bewildered question. It is noteworthy that the narrator does not condemn the dancer, but presents her very sympathetically and emphasizes her higher qualities throughout the story. He gives her the chance to justify her position and accepts her arguments. When she asks him to look deeply into her soul, he sees a positive image of a woman warrior, rather than a whore. In this sense, his repetition of the question at the end of the story can be read as an invitation to the reader to reconsider some of the prejudices and biased judgments.

The second point of ambivalence in his narrative is revealed in his conclusion to the series of stories called *al-Qalb al-miskiyn* (1936; The wretched heart), about a married man who falls in love with a dancer but takes a vow of celibacy and resists temptation. The narrator of the story dreams that his heart is on trial for committing the sin of love. He chooses the dancer herself to act as his lawyer and defend him in court. The story presents two conflicting points of view expressed by the prosecutor and the lawyer. They engage in a witty repartee where the lawyer/dancer succeeds in defeating the prosecutor's arguments using her wit, intellectual superiority, and feminine wiles. She even defends the occupation of the dancer by presenting her as a woman who makes a living using one of the few alternatives available to women in a patriarchal society. Her rendering of the story brings tears to the judge's eyes. Although the prosecutor denounces the lawyer/dancer, drawing upon the conservative dogma that we find in al-Rafi'i's other narratives, al-Rafi'i's portrayal of the lawyer's eloquence, wit, and strong arguments, renders her both fascinating and threatening. Al-Rafi'i declines to offer the reader a conclusion to the debate between the two opposites, choosing instead to leave his story open-ended. The narrator wakes up from his dream before the judges render the verdict. Al-Rafi'i then calls upon readers to participate in a contest, where they are expected to imagine the verdict in the case, and the best written verdict will win a copy of one of the writer's books. It is noteworthy that al-Rafi'i does not condemn the lawyer/dancer. On the contrary, she shines in a very appealing light and emerges triumphant in her debate with the prosecutor. The fact that she overpowers him completely by her presence and wit tells of the hidden fear of, yet fascination with, the powerful woman in misogynist discourses. Al-Rafi'i's ambivalent attitude is certainly revealed in his unwillingness to make up his mind and pass a verdict. Her representation combines fascination and awe.

Conclusion

Representations of new national masculine identities were constantly interrogated and contested, very often by the writers themselves. A good case in point is al-Mazini's expressed disdain for his protagonist. His remarks in the introduction to *Ibrahim al-katib,* in which he distances himself from Ibrahim and insists that they are not the same person, raise the question: why would he say that? One possible answer can be gleaned from the kind of attack that targeted the masculine prototype of the liberal elites imaged in figures such as Hamid and Ibrahim al-Katib. Al-Rafi'i has attached the label "effeminate" to the *nahda* heroes who espoused the ideals of bachelorhood because of their failed pursuit of romantic love. They have given up their manly attributes and have celebrated qualities that are traditionally female and unmanly. They have set themselves on a futile path searching for a relationship with women that was bound to alienate them from their culture and their national duties. However, his sympathetic admiration for the dancer subverts his views and signals his wavering between the two extreme positions. Al-Mazini's reluctance to identify himself with his protagonist reveals his ambivalence toward conflicting definitions of masculinity. Yet his insistence on exploring the horizons of romantic love in most of his fiction indicates how this pursuit is conceived as an act of resistance against dominant patriarchal and colonial challenges to new emerging national masculinities.

Edward Said has shown how the Orient was feminized to establish an unequal power relation between East and West. Revathi Krishnaswamy has added that the "real goal of feminization is effeminization, a process in which colonizing men use women/womanhood to delegitimize, discredit and disempower colonized men" (1998, 3). Mrinalini Sinha has demonstrated how the concept of effeminacy was used by the British colonizers to describe the Bengali elite who imitated Western ways, to maintain a distinction between them and the "manly Englishman" (Sinha 1995). In Egypt, Cromer despised what he described as the class of "Europeanised Egyptians" who were "demoslimised Moslems and invertebrate Europeans" (Cromer 1908, 228). The objects of his disdain were al-Rafi'i's "Westernized elite" who shunned their traditional way and sought to create a new litany of norms and mores. In both views, these men dared trespass on the fixed borders between cultures and merited disdain for their in-between status. They could therefore be dismissed as effeminate, an in-between state that is neither here nor there. But we need to be careful in equating colonial constructions of masculinity in different historical and geographical contexts.[13] And I would like to focus on the ambivalences inherent in literary discourses on masculinity. Al-Rafi'i's dismissal of romantic love and glorification of loveless marriages as a national duty can only be fully understood in the context of his philosophical reflections on love and beauty as part of a rich Arab tradition. His fascination with the dancer who also says her prayers sheds light on the contested nature of many of the markers of identity, making them subject to interrogation. In a study of representations of masculinity in the interwar period in Egypt, Wilson Jacob has argued that "the tarbush was simultaneously a sign of the modern and the traditional, the national and the foreign, the masculine and the effeminate" (2004, 24). His work sheds light on the dynamic exchanges that took place between men and new definitions of masculinity against the backdrop of colonial and national discourses.

It would be too easy to come to the conclusion that new constructions of masculinity as embodied in the New Man were championed by the "secularists" and rejected by the "traditionalists." That would reaffirm the modernist opposition between tradition and modernity that has dominated mainstream analyses of the history of the modern nation. Both sides had their own ambivalences and contradictions that, very often, indicated commonalities rather than divergences, particularly on gender issues. The New Man was certainly a modern construct, and his advent heralded a shift in representations of Arab masculinity. Like the New Woman, he was caught up in ideological warfare and was the contested subject of conflicting views and cultural imaginings.

13. Connell noted that the "British in India constructed different images of masculinity for different peoples under their rule, for instance, contrasting effeminate Bengalis with fierce Pathans and Sikhs" (2002, 254).

3

Tawfiq al-Hakim and the Civilizational Novel

Tawfiq al-Hakim (1898–1987) occupies a prominent place in the cultural history of the Arab world. His fictional as well as nonfictional writings have been at the center of the Arabic national canon. His literary oeuvre addressed key issues that occupied his generation, particularly the East/West agon and its imbrications with national projects of liberation and resistance. Like other members of the *nahda* literati, al-Hakim wrote novels that are autobiographical or semiautobiographical, where the protagonist is often his persona or mouthpiece, experiencing the dilemmas and challenges of a colonial encounter with Western civilization. Two of al-Hakim's novels are based on his early life as a young student, trying to figure out his place in the world against the background of colonial aggression against his country and identity. Muhsin, the young student in Cairo in *'Awdat al-ruh* (1933; English translation, *The Return of the Spirit,* 1990), and then in Paris in *'Usfur min al-sharq* (1938; English translation, *A Bird of the East,* 1966), is widely recognized as al-Hakim. Like Muhsin, al-Hakim lived with his relatives in Cairo in order to go to high school. He studied law in Egypt and learned French. In 1925, his father, a judge from a rural background, sent him to obtain a law degree in France. There, al-Hakim pursued his literary interests, and he returned in 1928 without a law degree. A later novel, *al-Ribat al-muqaddas* (1944 The sacred bond) is also semiautobiographical and is described by Ghali Shukri as the next sequel in the trilogy, which records the development of al-Hakim's life and views (1966, 199).

In this chapter, I attempt a reading of al-Hakim's trilogy from a postcolonial gendered perspective. I argue that his anticolonial discursive resistance is caught up in the violence of the colonial Manichean world (JanMohamed 1983), a violence that is ultimately projected onto his relationships with women and his definition of postcolonial masculinity in contradistinction to femininity. The trilogy is a postcolonial bildungsroman that charts the journey of a young man, Muhsin, from childhood to adulthood, highlighting his inner conflicts as he deals with colonial violence. It is also a psychological account of anticolonial consciousness. Like many Arab intellectuals of his generation, al-Hakim was torn between two powerful feelings: a deep admiration for Western modernity and civilization as beacons of progress and cultural excellence, on the one hand, and a visceral hatred of the ugly face of Western colonialism, on the other. Frantz Fanon divided the typical psychological journey of the colonized national elite toward liberation into three phases: first, "unqualified assimilation"; second, an immersion in national culture as the intellectual remembers who he is; and third, "the fighting phase" (1967, 179), which produces revolutionary literature that rids itself of colonial paradigms and logic. Al-Hakim's oeuvre is located in the second phase, attempting an immersion in national culture as the writer resists colonial erasure by extolling the values and achievements of his culture. Nevertheless, the boundaries between the phases as charted by Fanon are not clear-cut, as many national writers, while resisting colonial violence, remain trapped in its binary Manichean logic. In the following reading of the trilogy, the colonial "homology between sexual and political dominance" (Nandy 1983, 63) is assimilated by al-Hakim and becomes constitutive of his representations of ideal masculinity and femininity in the modern nation. His trilogy is first and foremost about the evolution of modern national masculinity in a postcolonial context.

'Awdat al-ruh was written in Paris and, like Haikal's *Zaynab,* tells the story of an Arab intellectual's attempt to come to terms with what he perceives to be the essential opposition between East and West. Muhsin, the protagonist and al-Hakim's persona, is a teenager who lives with his cousins in Cairo in order to go to school. The bulk of the novel depicts Muhsin's infatuation with and adolescent attachment to his neighbor, Saniyya, whose attention is directed elsewhere, resulting in dramas of unrequited love and frustration. In the last two chapters, the 1919 revolution breaks out. Muhsin and two of his uncles join a secret resistance cell. The police raid their apartment and arrest

all the men, including the manservant, Mabruk. This final incident encapsulates the gist of the novel: when a leader emerges, the spirit of Egypt, buried in the consciousness of the people, rises and gives them strength to change reality. It is also this final episode that reveals al-Hakim's larger project: the deeper meaning of the novel, many have argued, is inspired by the Pharaonic myth about the murder of Osiris and the journey of his sister Isis all over Egypt to collect the scattered pieces of his body. In this sense, Saniyya symbolizes Isis, a figure who unites the torn pieces of Egypt (al-Ra'i 1964, 107). Critics have also noted the absence of balance or artistic integration between the surface meaning of the novel and the symbolic, but nevertheless, many agree that it is a great novel that must be appreciated for its progressive politics and larger goals (al-Ra'i 1964, 117; Haqqi 1986, 133).[1]

The novel starts with the premise that there are distinct differences between the civilizations of the East and the West. People in the East, like Muhsin's family, share a deep sense of community and belonging to one another. They fall ill together and convalesce in the same small room; they are arrested together and share the same cell; they rise together when the right leader appears. Although seemingly bound by obsolete traditions and customs, they are capable of doing the right thing and taking active measures in the face of crisis. The theme of the hidden strength of the people is further developed in the middle of the novel, when Muhsin takes a trip to the countryside to visit his parents. There he observes the life of the Egyptian peasant, the *fallah,* and is filled with admiration and awe, for, in spite of the stark hardship and poverty, the *fallah* lives in harmony with the universe, hence possessing a deep wisdom that he inherits by virtue of being heir to an ancient civilization. Like Muhsin, the *fallah* awaits the return of the spirit, which eventually comes about at the end of the novel with the outbreak of the 1919 revolution led by Sa'ad Zaghlul. In fact, one can read his idyllic rural interlude as a conscious effort to rebut colonialist claims about the backwardness of the East, of Egypt in this particular case, claims that are

1. It is noteworthy that many noted critics have found the symbolism lacking, especially Saniyya as a symbol of Isis. 'Abd al-Qadir al-Qut for example maintained that the "intellectual design of the novel undermined its artistic structure" 1982, 19–23.

reinforced with reference to the life and customs of peasants who constitute the majority of the population. Consequently, extolling the *fallah* and identifying points of strength and value in his life is a validation of national identity, of Egyptianness and Egyptians, at a moment in history when their national identity is threatened by erosion or annihilation.

Al-Hakim's project is spelled out in a conversation between an English irrigation inspector, Mr. Black, and a French archaeologist, Monsieur Fouquet, who are invited to dinner at Muhsin's parents' house in the countryside. The Englishman, who appropriately voices British colonial views and interests in Egypt, speaks disdainfully and disrespectfully about the *fallahin.* His discourse is the logical extension of Lord Cromer's views about Egyptians and their inability and unpreparedness to assume the responsibility of self-rule and to succeed in modernizing their country. The Frenchman, on the other hand, is able to discern the hidden strength and wisdom of the *fallah.* Faced with the total incredulity of the Englishman, who is incapable of accepting or understanding the point being made, the Frenchman proclaims: "This is the truth that Europe is ignorant of. Yes, these people (*sha'b*) whom you consider ignorant know many things, but they know them with their hearts, not with their minds. There is sublime wisdom in their blood and they do not know it. And there is strength in their souls and they do not know it. . . . The only difference between us [Europeans] and them is that they are not aware of the treasures they possess!" ([1933] 2005, 274–75).[2] The fact that it is the Frenchman, a colonial aggressor, who refutes the colonial discourse of the English administrator is indicative of al-Hakim's insecurity and vulnerability vis à vis colonial violence. He resorts to the authority of the Frenchman, a European, to vindicate his culture and identity, hence demonstrating his own lack of discursive power and authority in dismantling colonial assaults. Al-Hakim uses the same technique in his later novel, *'Usfur min al-sharq,* when he uses the voice of Ivan, a Russian, to vilify Western materialism and modernity.

Al-Hakim's portrayal of the Egyptian countryside and the life of the *fallah* is idyllic and highly romanticized. It is vaguely reminiscent of the work of

2. All quotations are taken from this edition. All translations are mine.

eighteenth-century pastoral poets, who idealized the life of the countryside to criticize and expose the materiality of life in the city. Al-Hakim's glorification of rural Egypt bears some similarities, but also key differences. The countryside is extolled for its simplicity and purity of existence. The *fallah,* the inhabitant of rural Egypt, is also extolled, "almost to mystical heights," as he achieves unity with nature in ways that are not possible for urban dwellers (Starkey 1987, 120). On the other hand, the country/city opposition is replaced by the East/West conflict. However, unlike the English poets who glossed over signs of hardship or misery of pastoral life, al-Hakim is acutely aware of the problems and limitations of rural life. His awareness is largely due to a colonial discourse that posited the *fallah* as the "authentic" male, the true inhabitant of the land, who is uneducated and unfit for modern life. For the anticolonial intellectual, the *fallah* becomes the object of reform projects but is also the original "self" of the observer, the postcolonial reformer, who cannot be denigrated. From his position as a member of the national educated elite, al-Hakim recognizes the limitations of the *fallah* but is ontologically compelled to credit him with some saving grace.[3]

Al-Hakim's vindication of the *fallah* against colonial attacks does not only serve the purpose of an affirmation of national identity: more important, it is a validation of national masculinity. Muhsin, like Haikal's Hamid and al-Mazini's Ibrahim, is another *nahda* hero, torn between his admiration of the West and its cultural and scientific achievements and his sense of belonging to his roots. Shukri 'Ayyad has pointed out that Muhsin was not the persona of al-Hakim alone, but that he represented "the role-model of an entire generation" (1971, 53). He too belongs to a cultural elite that is

3. See Samah Selim's discussion of the romanticization of the *fallah* by *nahda* intellectuals. She posits that the literary *fallah* was created in 1910–20 by a liberal elite who made it their business to educate the masses in order to reform their society. Samah Selim describes Ahmad Lutfi al-Sayyid as a "classic liberal" (Selim 2004b, 9) who believed that he was entrusted with the role of educating the masses and raising them to his level. "This elite vanguard did not properly belong to the defective 'society' imagined by [Fathi] Zaghlul, al-Sayyid and their contemporaries. Rather as a class, they stood over and above the teeming, chaotic, dissipated mass of Egyptians in urgent need of correction. It analyzed them, represented them and spoke on their behalf" (2004b, 9).

influenced by Western thought and culture and is acutely conscious of the social and cultural challenges, especially when seen through the distorted mirror of Western imperialism. Having internalized colonial representations of the backwardness of the *fallah,* and by extension the backwardness of the original Egyptian man, al-Hakim, directly addresses the question: what happened to the *fallah,* or what are the factors that resulted in this dire state of affairs? Al-Hakim lays the blame at the door of foreign influences that corrupted Egyptian life. These are Western influences, Turkish influences, and also Arab influences.[4] Muhsin is painfully ashamed of his mother, who flouts her Turkish ancestry as a marker of distinction and superior status and is cruel and discourteous to all the peasants, simply because they are peasants. Muhsin's father is portrayed as a weak man who suffers from an inferiority complex vis à vis his wife and hence allows her to have her way. This caricature representation of his own family is a commentary on a social order in which foreign influences and views have become so ingrained in the psyche as to hinder the revival of the spirit of Egypt.

Al-Hakim's exaltation of Egyptian national masculinity is premised on a hierarchical opposition between men and women. The gender hierarchy is at the heart of the discourse of the *nahda* elite. Like Qasim Amin, who responds to the duke's attack on Egypt and Egyptians by defending the peasant and condemning women, al-Hakim follows in the same tracks. Contemplating the ugly and dirty face of the countryside in his philosophical *Himar al-Hakim* (1976; al-Hakim's donkey), he consoles himself with his awareness of the "innocent spirit of the countryside and the *fallah*'s tolerant and generous soul" (52) but then holds the peasant woman, the *fallaha,* responsible for the "filthy" life of the peasant (103). The Egyptian woman, he posits, is still heir to white slavery (101). Unlike the European woman who earns the title of mistress, who supports the master and performs duties that he cannot

4. In a debate between al-Hakim and Taha Husayn published in *al-Risala* in 1933, al-Hakim argues for the necessity of discovering the spirit of Egypt. He argues that this spirit is distinct from what is Arab or Greek. He says: "I have no doubt that Egypt and the Arabs are radically opposed on this: Egypt is the spirit; it is tranquility; it is settlement; it is construction. The Arab is the material body; it is speed . . . it is ornament" (quoted in al-Jindi 1966, 562).

perform, the Egyptian woman is still lagging behind (101–15). His glorification of the inner spirit of the peasant, as the indigenous face of the inhabitants of the land of Egypt, is juxtaposed to his condemnation of the peasant woman who bears the responsibility of the manifest problems of the peasants and the countryside. This condemnation is consistent with al-Hakim's overall attitude toward Egyptian women[5] and consistent with *nahda* writers who blame women for the ills of society.

'Usfur min al-sharq (1938) is the second novel in the trilogy and the one most directly engaged with the relationship between East and West.[6] Muhsin is now a student in Paris. He is infatuated with a Parisian woman, Susie Dupont, who works as a ticket salesgirl in a cinema house. He spends long days and nights watching her from a distance and idealizing her as a goddess. Asked who she is, his description of her is so unrealistic that his friends wonder: "Does this woman live in Paris? Or in the Thousand and One Nights?" (1938, 37).[7] Encouraged by his friends, he finally approaches her and establishes a relationship. He gives her a parrot, whom he trains to respond to the name Muhsin, and he is happy being her parrot. He then discovers that she has a boyfriend and is devastated. Al-Hakim put this woman on a pedestal, only to accentuate her fall from grace.

This failed love affair is an allegorical tale that symbolizes the main theme of the novel, which is a comparison of East and West. As part of his journey to self-discovery, Muhsin is so infatuated with Western civilization that he is content to become a parrot that mindlessly mimics its sounds, just like the parrot he gave to Susie Dupont. However, this bird from the East has another side to him, one that is incompatible with the West he reveres and aspires to emulate. His main interest lies in spiritual pursuits, in union with the sky, in abstract ideas about love and beauty, and in art and music. Gradually, and with the help of Ivan, a Russian worker, Muhsin encounters

5. Also see al-Hakim's *Tahta shams al-fikr* (1938, 48).

6. Tarabishi maintains that it is the first Arabic novel that tackles the relationship between the East and the West ([1977] 1997, 18).

7. al-Hakim, *'Usfur min al-Sharq* (1938; 1966). All quotations are taken from the 1966 edition.

the harsh reality of a West that represents materiality and the pursuit of worldly pleasures. Ivan, who is disillusioned with Western materialism and with Marxist ideology, admires the East because of its spirituality, which gives people hope for a better future in a better life, and denounces the West for renouncing heaven and the afterworld. As a product of a civilization that has relegated all religions to the status of myth, he has no illusions about Eastern faiths, but he nevertheless envies Muhsin for maintaining his belief in a better world. He admires the prophets of the East for giving people hope, hence improving the quality of their lives on earth. He also regards all modern Western achievements as a mirage, in which people are trapped while the quality of their lives is deteriorating.

Al-Hakim's invective against the West on the premise of an essentialist opposition between the spirituality of the East and the materiality of the West has been noted as one of the weaknesses of his fiction. Ghali Shukri comments on al-Hakim's use of Ivan's voice to "expose" the shortcomings of the West and the moral bankruptcy of Marxist materialism and points out that Ivan is not a well-rounded character but another voice for al-Hakim in his condemnation of the West and vindication of the East.[8] Rasheed El-Enany compares *'Usfur min al-sharq*'s depiction of the theme of East meets West to Yahya Haqqi's (1905–92) treatment of the same theme in his *Qindil Umm Hashim* (1944; English translation, *The Saint's Lamp and Other Stories,* 1973) and finds Haqqi's vision more realistic and balanced: "While al-Hakim indulged in nationalist-motivated, self-deluding idealization of Eastern civilization and denigration of Western civilization, Haqqi readily diagnosed the ailment of his country, prescribed the medicine . . . [and] was able to make a more sober approach to the cultural question" (El-Enany 2006, 73).[9] Al-Musawi, on the other hand, has argued that Muhsin's dis-

8. Ghali Shukri finds this to be a failing in the novel (1966, 210).

9. Many critics have pointed out the artistic failings in *'Awdat al-ruh, 'Usfur min al-sharq,* and *al-Ribat al-muqaddas.* See also Starkey (1987, 223). On the other hand, Rasheed El-Enany notes the stark incongruity between al-Hakim as an artist and al-Hakim as a polemicist. While al-Hakim's fiction is anti-Western, his polemical writing shows great admiration of the West and denunciation of the East. Furthermore, El-Enany unearths an article by al-Hakim entitled *Tabi'atuna nahwa al-shabab* (Our responsibility towards youth)

illusionment in love, "perceived as an autobiographical narration of disappointments with women," along with his critical emphasis on the artistic shortcomings of the novel, has diverted attention from postcolonial elements located in the "discarded portions of the text" (2003, 191). According to him, the statue of Alfred de Musset, which Muhsin contemplates at the beginning of novel, together with the meeting with Anatole France, as well as the story about his father's refusal to be coerced by the British colonial administrator into making an unfair indictment of Egyptians, are all key moments of signification in the novel and shed light on al-Hakim's literary postcoloniality. The father's resistance of colonial intimidation confirms Muhsin's anticolonial commitment. At the same time, the affinities between him and Alfred De Musset and Anatole France seem to ameliorate the colonizer/colonized conflict. Notwithstanding, the Manichean paradigm continues to operate in other layers of the novel, exposing much ambivalence.

Al-Hakim's depiction of the East/West agon is heavily gendered. He reverses the colonial trope of the West as representing manhood and manliness and the East as representing femininity and womanhood. In this novel, Europe is "a blonde young woman" who is "pretty, graceful, and intelligent, but is also trivial and selfish, and totally unconcerned except with her own self and with the enslavement of others!" (1938, 130). She is the child of a marriage between Asia and Africa at one point in history. These two Eastern places understood the meaning of true science as the pursuit of absolute truth. They passed on their treasures to their child, Europe, who kept a small portion of it and then dissolved all the jewels and turned them into money to be kept in banks (137). The East, on the other hand, where Muhsin's roots are, represents true manhood, a manhood that is attained through a life of solitude, abstract ideas, and abstinence. It is the place of absolute values, a place that appreciates science and art and the world of the intellect. All of this is now lost, but lives as a memory in people's souls. When Ivan expresses his

---

published in *Akhbar al-Yawm* (28 May 1949) and later in the collection *Yaqazat al-Fikr* in 1986, in which he rescinds some of the views expressed in his fiction and tells young people: "Do not let the inferiority complex which dominated Muhsin dominate you, and make you over-protective towards your subjugated civilization" (quoted in El-Enany, 2006, 50).

desire to go to the East in pursuit of happiness and peace, Muhsin laments the fact, according to him, that the East is no longer what it used to be, that the sources of civilization and truth have been poisoned, in fact contaminated by the "young blonde woman." "Today there is no East! There is only a wilderness with monkeys in trees, wearing Western clothes, and showing no sign of order or discipline, or understanding or awareness" (145).

Commenting on this image of monkeys in trees, George Tarabishi maintains that it pithily summarizes al-Hakim's civilizational philosophy. He links it to the colonial trope about the effeminacy of the colonized elite, who, because of their mimicry of Western styles and habits, occupy a space that is in-between, neither Western nor Eastern, masculine or feminine: "Like monkeys whose movements trigger laughter because they are neither human nor bestial, but somewhere in-between, so does an effeminate man *al-khuntha* evoke loud laughter *qahqaha* because he is neither male or female but is in-between. The image of the East as a monkey [*sharq mutaqarid*] is this effeminate man. . . . It is doomed to be in-between, *mutashaghrib* or *mutaghashriq,* carrying all the caricature implications of these labels" ([1977] 1997, 44). Al-Hakim's representations of masculinity and femininity extend beyond defining relationships between men and women to become signifiers of cultural relationships. As exemplified in *'Usfur min al-sharq,* the East is masculine while the West is feminine. That explains how Western women, or European women, are often symbols or representatives of their culture in Arabic literature. The novel certainly belongs to a trend in the Arabic novel described as *al-riwaya al-'arabiyya al-hadariyya* (the civilizational Arabic novel). In these novels, the Eastern intellectual accepts the premise that "the relationship between nations and civilizations is similar to the relationship between men and women: a relationship of power, control and domination" (Tarabishi [1977] 1997, 16). Tarabishi's chapter on *'Usfur min al-sharq* is significantly subtitled: "*hija' algharb bi ta'nithuhu*" (satirizing the West by feminizing it) (18). However, this reversal of colonial violence does not empower the colonized male, as he does not possess real epistemic power over the colonizer, as knowledge of the European woman remains beyond his reach (Hassan 2003, 317). More important, it consolidates patriarchal oppression of women, forging an alliance between colonial and anticolonial masculine domination over women. This collusion is clearly exemplified in the last part of the trilogy, *al-Ribat al-muqaddas.*

Al-Ribat al-muqaddas ([1944] 1972; The sacred bond)[10] is about the encounter between the protagonist, Rahib al-fikr (a monk devoted to the worship of thought), clearly another persona of al-Hakim, and a young, modern, "liberated" Egyptian woman, whom he idolizes as a goddess at the beginning, but who flatly falls from grace as the story progresses and she becomes *ma'bud min tin* (an idol of clay) (154). The novel begins with a description of the protagonist as a recluse, a worshipper at the altar of thought, a monk whose goal is to abstain from worldly pleasures in order to attain moral and spiritual ascendance. He lives "an elevated life," like "a man on the seashore, throwing crumbs to the fish, watches the fish as they come together and then separate, aware that his writings had an impact and that his ideas had echoes" (9). His life embodies his thoughts and beliefs: he eats very little, and has no contact with women, like ancient Egyptian *kahana* (priests) who renounced worldly temptations. He is also an embodiment of *sufis'* ascetism in their spiritual voyage toward union with the divine. This modern-day monk receives a letter from a female admirer who wants his help to introduce her to the world of ideas and literature. After some hesitation, he agrees to meet her. His disdain for women, for their assumed triviality, superficial pursuits, lack of understanding of the matters of the soul, and inability to comprehend the higher values, is expressed clearly. He describes the young woman, who remains nameless throughout the novel, as *ta'isha* (reckless), *tafiha* (silly), *hamqa'* (idiotic). He struggles to figure out how to show her the way to *din al-fikr* (the religion of thought), as he realizes that he will need to "re-create her completely" (32). His eyes fall on a book in his library, *Thais* by Anatole France, the story of a prostitute who finds salvation with the help of Pavnos. He gives her the book and asks her to read it and to come and see him again. On her second visit, she invites him to watch her play tennis and argues that it is the duty of the savior, or prophet, to descend to the level of the people they are trying to save so as to be able to raise them

10. All quotations are taken from this edition. All translations are mine.

to higher levels. Rahib al-fikr is taken aback by the strength of her argument but stubbornly refuses to budge from his *sawma'a* (monk's cell). He is then paid a visit by the woman's husband and discovers that she lied to him. He confronts her with her lies on her next visit and asks her to leave. Imagining that she is bound to come back again, he is tortured by her absence and starts writing letters to her shadow (*rasa'il ila tayfiha*). He eventually learns from the husband that she had an affair with an actor, and he is asked to act as a go-between to finalize divorce arrangements. The couple are divorced, and his opinion of women is confirmed when he learns that "she married a man well-known for his triviality and modest intelligence and realized that she finally got the ideal husband for the modern woman" (271).

The novel is a conscious intervention in national debates about the ideal modern woman. As George Tarabishi has argued, al-Hakim does not condemn this particular woman in the novel, but his condemnation encompasses all women ([1977] 1997, 130). She is not just one wife, but all wives, or more accurately all contemporary Egyptian wives aspiring to be modern and liberated. Her negative portrayal is accentuated by comparisons to the wife of Karl Marx, who supported her husband and followed him everywhere; to the wife of Disraeli, Mary Anne, who concealed her terminal illness from her husband so as not to add to his worries and still managed to provide him with an ideal home; to the goddess Isis, whose loyalty and devotion to her husband Osiris is legendary; and finally, to Khadija, the first wife of the prophet Muhammad, who provided him with financial and moral support in the early years of the message. These positive role models however, only serve to emphasize the failure of the modern woman, rather than her potential. Like the *fallaha,* whom he blames for the ills and dire conditions of rural life, the modern liberated woman is blamed for all the trivialities and superficial mimicry of Western civilization.

The novel is replete with monologues and dialogues about ideal womanhood and manhood, about modern marriage, about the ideal relationship between a modern couple, so that the reader is left in no doubt as to al-Hakim's views on the subject. Both husband and wife are given a chance to present their views on marriage and the ideal relationship between the modern husband and wife. The husband comes from a well-to-do middle-class family who sent him to study in England, where he learned to appreciate the pleasure of reading and the mind. He always wanted to share his life with a wife with whom he could interact on an intellectual level. Despite the fact that his wife comes from a good middle-class family, like most women of her class her education was superficial and very trivial. He calls her *al-fatah al-ta'isha* and wants to reform her ways and "to transform her into the woman I want" (159). He introduces her to sports, and she later acquires the habit of reading. Unfortunately her pursuit of reading and literature leads to her downfall, as it enables her to write in her red copybook, where she confesses to her sins and her illicit love affair. The husband continues to voice his incredulity at her infidelity and her lack of respect for their relationship. He treats her like "a lady from the English aristocracy" (163), never interfering in her affairs, never interrogating her about her friends. He cannot comprehend why she says that she is bored, as he takes her everywhere and humors all her whims. In short, he is the ideal husband, who cares for his wife, is faithful to her, treats her with respect, and expects her to be his soul mate. All of the above representations are typical of the *nahda* male hero, as depicted by Qasim Amin, Haikal, Lutfi al-Sayyid, and others: an ideal modern man who searches in vain for an ideal modern woman.

The wife, on the other hand, voices what al-Hakim believes to be the ideas of the modern woman. She believes in sexual freedom, in the necessity of adventures to avoid boredom, that the meaning of a woman's honor has changed in the modern world, so that the honor of a beautiful woman is now compromised if it is said that she has no admirers, *'atila min al-mu'jabin* (210). She fails to achieve the "modern-yet-modest" dictum of national discourses. Listening to her, Rahib al-fikr is amazed as he concludes that her views are based on her beliefs and "nature." He then embarks on a moralistic condemnation of her views and actions: "Have moral principles been abrogated in this society? Have the words, virtue, chastity, and modesty been deleted from the accepted dictionaries without our knowledge?" He notes her casual dismissal of his outpour, as she carelessly powders her nose and applies lipstick, and he looks back with nostalgia to "the day when a woman's finery was concealed, happened behind closed doors . . . [when] cigarettes were only smoked by loose women, and alcohol only consumed by prostitutes" (211–12).

Al-Hakim's denigration of the modern woman does not just rest on moral grounds. It is deeply embedded in his civilizational philosophy, in which the

West, as woman, represents materiality and trivial pursuits of worldly pleasures. According to this paradigmatic construct, the East, which stands for spirituality, is masculine, a masculinity that is the radical opposite of the feminized West, and the national modern woman. Al-Hakim's writing constitutes one of the most powerful manifestations of a common theme in the *nahda* narrative, namely, the celebration of bachelorhood. Critics have noted the frequent recurrence of the theme of the unsuitability of marriage to artistic life in al-Hakim's oeuvre (Starkey 1987, 50–54). As discussed previously, al-Rafi'i harshly satirized what he perceived to be a renunciation of authentic Islamic masculinity, where marriage is an achievement in and of itself, in addition to being a national duty in colonial contexts. Al-Hakim's extolling the virtues of bachelorhood, and consequent hostility to women, can, however, be seen as a subconscious, defensive rejection of colonial representations of the masculinity of the colonized male. Here the anticolonial intellectual countervails colonial feminization by emphasizing a nonsexualized manhood that thrives on spiritual and intellectual pursuits. Steve Derne has demonstrated how Indian nationalists counteracted colonial representations by emphasizing celibacy and ascetic practices, in addition to bodybuilding, as well as sexual potency in relationships with good women. In India in particular, Gandhi's "celibacy and sexual self-control [was] an important part of Indian nationalism" (2000, 243). Celibacy as a theme certainly surfaced as a concern in the discourses of the middle-class male elite as they lamented their inability to find the right Egyptian woman. However, it was tempered by Islamic dictums about the importance of marriage for believers.

Al-Musawi has argued that Muhsin's position in *'Usfur min al-sharq* is not identical to Ivan's polarized view of East and West (2003, 194). Al-Hakim's persona does not reach conclusive decisions but sustains an inquisitive outlook that tries to make sense of an aggressive and complicated anticolonial as well as ontological struggle. Moreover, al-Hakim's admiration of Western civilization comes across in all his writings. He regarded his French interlude as formative, marking a break with his earlier years. In his two autobiographical accounts of his life before and after France, his French interlude is significantly entitled *Zahrat al-'umr* (1943; The flower of life), while its sequel, about his life before France, is also significantly called *Sijn al-'umr* (1964; The prison of life). France introduced him to the treasures of the West and the life of the mind. Ivan, on the other hand, is Muhsin's alter ego, who articulates feelings and views that are suppressed by the conscious mind. Al-Hakim consistently uses voices from the West to defend the East, as noted above with reference to the French archaeologist. This technique also reveals the levels of defensiveness experienced at the conscious level.

In his later writing, al-Hakim transfers the struggle to national grounds, where his civilizational other is embodied in women. An affirmation of a national masculinity becomes contingent on power and control over women, creating a strange alliance of colonial, national, and patriarchal domination over women's bodies. *Al-Ribat al-muqaddas* was seen as a contribution to the sociocultural debates on gendered roles in the new nation. In 1956, ten years after its publication, it was chosen by 'Ihsan 'Abd al-Quddus, popular writer and journalist, to be reprinted as part of the series *al-Kitab al-dhahaby* (The golden book) by Dar Ruz al-Yusuf. In the second edition, Al-Hakim tells us that the novel caused a stir and that 'Abd al-Quddus said that it paved the way for a new kind of writing.[11] This claim is certainly borne out by the popularity of the theme of the misguided modern woman who abuses her newly acquired freedom and requires the firm control and guidance of a man to put her on the right path. The theme thrived in the 1960s in popular literature as well as cinematic adaptations of novels, notably those written by Ihsan 'Abd al-Quddous.

Anne McClintock has argued that colonial desire was not the same for men and women. For men, it is "a politics of substitution," as the colonized man aspires to take the place of the master, whereas for women it is "an act of appropriation"(1995, 362). Al-Hakim's misogyny, widely acknowledged by his reputation as "the enemy of women," is the direct outcome of a beleaguered colonized consciousness, a defense mechanism against colonial aggression. His prolific literary and polemical output had a far-reaching influence on the national imaginary and can be detected in more subtle misogynist views and attitudes. As Ashis Nandy has rightly pointed out, "colonialism is first of all a matter of consciousness and needs to be defeated ultimately in the minds of men" (1983, 63).

11. Cited by Therese Fabi Kamal (1988).

PART TWO

4

Naguib Mahfouz's Trilogy

A National Allegory

Naguib Mahfouz's (1911–2006) Cairo Trilogy, *Bayn al-qasrayn* (1956; English translation, *Palace Walk,* 1990), *Qasr al-shawq* (1957; English translation, *Palace of Desire,* 1991) and *al-Sukkariyyah* (1957; English translation, *Sugar Street,* 1992,[1] is acknowledged as one of the masterpieces of the writer and a landmark in the history of the Arabic novel. His career is quite remarkable for its prolific output as well as its artistic development. His status and contribution to modern Arabic literature received international recognition in 1988 when he was awarded the Nobel Prize in Literature. The Trilogy, in particular, occupies a prominent position among his impressive oeuvre as regards its artistic as well as discursive imprint on the canon of Arabic literature. It has been described as a "saga of the birth of modern Egypt" (Leeuwen 1995, 93), a "national allegory" (Haydar and Beard 1993, 6), a form of "*roman fleuve*" (El-Enany 1993, 70), "a period novel" (al-Qutt 1982, 134), an example of "intellectual literature" ('adab al-qadaya al-fikriyya) (Shukri 1964, 7), and a novel that "radically changed the whole balance of Arabic literature" (Jayussi 1993, 13). The Trilogy is certainly an important document, a masterpiece of social history, as it chronicles the life of a prototypical Egyptian family in the first half of the twentieth century against the backdrop of the turbulent sociopolitical and cultural transformations that took place over the three decades before the July 1952 revolution by the Free Officers.

1. *Bayn al-qasrayn* ([1956] 1983); *Qasr al-shawq* ([1957] 1984a); *al-Sukkariyyah* ([1957] 1984b). All quotations are taken from these editions. All translations are mine.

The story follows the lives of members of Sayyid Ahmad 'Abd al-Jawwad's family from 1917 until 1944. The plot is punctuated with major political events, such as the 1919 demonstrations against British occupation, the exile of Sa'ad Zaghlul and his subsequent return to Egypt, two world wars, and the political arrests of communists and members of the Muslim Brotherhood. The protagonist is Kamal, son of 'Abd al-Jawwad, who is Mahfouz's persona according to critics and to Mahfouz himself, who stated: "I am Kamal 'Abd al-Jawwad in the *Trilogy*" (quoted in Shukri 1964, 7). There are many actual resemblances between Kamal and Mahfouz. Kamal's infatuation with 'Ayda is similar to Mahfouz's teenage love for a young woman who "was not traditional like other young women in 'Abbasiyya, but was more European in appearance and attitude, qualities which were not common at the time" (Mahfouz interview, Naqqash 1998, 105–6). Also, speaking about his parents, we discover that Kamal's relationship with his mother was similar to Mahfouz's. Like Amina, Kamal's mother, Mahfouz's mother was illiterate, but "a storehouse of popular culture" (14). She loved al-Husayn and paid daily visits to his shrine when they lived in Jamaliyya. And her father, too, was an Azharite sheikh. However, the two women are not identical. Mahfouz's father was not a tyrannical figure like Ahmad 'Abd al-Jawwad in the Trilogy, but still Mahfouz tells us that he was closer to his mother, as his father was not available most of the time. Kamal is also a representative of the generation of *nahda* intellectuals. His ontological and intellectual crisis encapsulated the crisis of an entire generation, as attested to by Mahfouz (cited in Shukri 1964, 7). His dilemma is similar to that of Hamid and Ibrahim al-Katib, that is, the dilemma of the *nahda* hero torn between two cultures and feeling alienated and unable to have a meaningful relationship with a woman. Mahfouz also reveals that like Kamal, he had decided at one point not to get married at all in order to devote himself entirely to literature, foregrounding a major *nahda* debate about which type of woman to marry (like Hamid and Ibrahim al-Katib) and also about the impact of marriage on intellectuals (like al-Hakim's personas) (cited in Shukri, 1964, 107).

The Trilogy has been described as a "national allegory" in the Jamesonian sense, that is, as reflective of sociopolitical concerns, marking the 1919 revolution as the central event in the narrative (Haydar and Beard 1993, 8).

Many have noted the direct correlation between the development and fate of members of Sayyid 'Abd al-Jawwad's family and the larger political and social upheavals that befall the nation. The death of Fahmy, 'Abd al-Jawwad's son, in the 1919 demonstrations, for example, signals a new era in Egypt and a series of disruptions and conflicts in the seemingly static social order of the family in *Bayn al-qasrayn*. Also, much has been said about the closeness to reality, or how the Trilogy is a truthful mirror to the real world. I argue that the Trilogy is a *canonical* national allegory in as much as it typifies the national, modernist discourse of the liberal *nahda* elite. That is not the same as saying that the personal lives of the characters are linked to historical or sociopolitical developments. Rather, the events, characterization, and plot all reflect and constitute the dominant national discourse about the road to modernization, about the inevitable linear development from a traditional society to a modern one, about the radical opposition between traditional and modern values, and about the imperative of relinquishing the old ways in favor of new ones. The Trilogy is an artistic enactment for the accession of the nation to modernity from the point of view of the *nahda* elite, as propagated by Qasim Amin and other *nahda* reformers. Shifting constructions of ideal femininity and masculinity in the three novels reflect a dominant national discourse that shaped the canon of Arabic literature and exemplify the imaginary of the national elite. A critical examination of the trials and fate of characters in the novels will demonstrate how Mahfouz projected his own vision of the present, past, and future of the nation, a vision that was congruent with the dominant liberal discourse espoused by the *nahda* literati.

Amina: The Iconic "Traditional" Woman

Amina is one of the most famous female characters in the history of the Arabic novel. She is the iconic traditional woman in the Arab national imaginary, as mention of her name immediately conjures images of traditional female virtues: obedience, devotion to family, and motherly affection. The opening scene of *Bayn al-qasrayn* introduces Amina to the reader and gives a brilliant snapshot of her relationship with her husband, Sayyid Ahmad 'Abd al-Jawwad, the ultimate patriarch, and of the rules that govern marital relationships from a "traditional" perspective.

> She woke up at midnight, as she always did at this hour of every night, without the help of an alarm clock or anything else. . . .
>
> Habit woke her up at this hour, an old habit she acquired when she was young, and continued with her into her old age. She learned it as part of the rules of married life: she was expected to wake up in the middle of the night, wait for her husband's return from his night out, and attend to his comfort until he went to bed. ([1956] 1983, 5)

Amina is portrayed as a traditional Egyptian woman who unquestioningly accepts her husband's authority and control over her life and surrenders to his every whim. We meet her first when she is in her forties and has had four children. She married at the age of fourteen and moved to her husband's family house. Since then, she literally has become a prisoner in her own home, as she is rarely allowed to go out, not even to visit her own mother. Her isolation is almost complete, as her house has become her entire world, allowing her to peep through the narrow openings of her *mashrabiyya* at the street outside. When her mother-in-law died, she took charge of the house with the help of one old woman. She is often scared when left alone in the house, is apprehensive about the presence of jinn and demons, and only feels safe when her husband is at home. Amina compensates for her incarceration for more than a quarter of a century by creating a world of her own on the roof of the house. There she keeps pigeons, chickens, and a little garden, which she tends and which provide her with a beautiful alternative to the world she misses. Every now and then, she still wishes that she were allowed to visit her mother more, or to visit the shrine of al-Husayn, which is within walking distance of where she lives. "She was not angry or complaining. Far from it. But when she peered through the gaps in the jasmine tree and the ivy plant, and saw the sky and the minarets and other roof tops, she smiled tenderly and dreamily" (36). Her husband took to staying out all night in the first year of their marriage. She tried once to object "very politely" to his daily absence, but his violent reaction silenced her forever. She learned her lesson: she had to obey unconditionally, "to the extent that she chided herself if she blamed him in silence. She became convinced that true manhood, tyranny and staying out late after midnight, were all characteristics of the same essence" (8). She breaks the rules once in her forties, when, encouraged by the absence of her husband for a night, and strongly urged by her children, she decides to visit the shrine of al-Husayn. The day ends in catastrophe: she is hit by a car, breaks a collar bone, and her secret adventure is found out. 'Abd al-Jawwad kicks her out of the house for a while as punishment. His harsh reaction is measured to ensure maximum fear and control over his household.

Amina is the iconic traditional woman, a modern social construct rife with contradictions and ambivalence in the national narrative. On one hand, she is a warm, affectionate, and kind mother who is loved by all her children and valued by society for her dedication to her family. On the other hand, she is the traditional, ignorant, and superstitious mother who was the target of reform projects proposed by the *nahda* elite. In the liberal national narrative, superstitious beliefs were signifiers of the backwardness of a tradition that the reformers rejected and sought to supersede. Amina asks her children never to mention the names of jinn or demons to avoid their wrath (63). We are told several times that she is incapable of disciplining her children, a quality of which Khadija, her daughter, is critical. We are also told that her lax approach does not lead to the dissolution of the family because of the awesome presence of Ahmad 'Abd al-Jawwad. She is the counterpart of the modern, educated mother who raises her children, following modern scientific methods of child rearing, to become modern citizens of the new nation. Her traditional style of mothering and taking care of the family might have been warm, but it was not efficient, nor sufficient for meeting the demand for citizens of the modern nation. Amina was uneducated but was oblivious to her limitations and felt content with her inherited popular culture about religion and religious stories because her father was a religious man who had memorized the Qur'an. Amina's total seclusion and lack of education is reflected, for example, in her almost complete inability to understand the political scene, the threat posed by the British occupation, and the role of Sa'ad Zaghlul. Her ignorance is kindly tolerated by her sons, who try to explain to her the complexities of political conflicts, but her limited world makes it impossible for her to understand concerns that are outside her immediate world (331). In Amina's household, when men talk politics, the women remain silent (336). Amina was also a staunch guardian of the traditions that shackled her. She was shocked by the behavior of her daughter-in-law, Zaynab, Yasin's wife, who broke the rules of propriety when she agreed to go out with her husband for a late night in town. Zaynab's actions transgressed the boundaries of what was allowed women. Amina "found fault with this behavior, seen through the eyes of a woman who spent her life a prisoner behind walls" (296).

Although Amina is the most developed female character in the Trilogy, as we get glimpses of her inner psyche on several occasions, she is not as complex or deep as Ahmad 'Abd al-Jawwad, or other male characters. It is only after the death of her husband, her master, *Sidi,* as she called him, in the final volume of the Trilogy that Mahfouz focuses on her response to the tragedy and gives her a voice to express herself at some length. Throughout the Trilogy, Amina's access to the world is controlled by her husband and proportionate to his entitlement and access. In *Bayn al-qasrayn* she is rarely allowed to set foot outside the house, and she is punished with banishment when she dares do so to visit a shrine without permission. In *Qasr al-shawq,* and after the death of her son Fahmy and the relative mellowing of her husband, she is allowed some mobility. It is only in *al-Sukkariyyah,* however, as 'Abd al-Jawwad grows old and less formidable, that she is able to go out every day either to visit holy shrines or her daughters. His death, though, releases her voice. It is an elegiac voice that mourns not only his death but also the passing of a way of life to which she has grown accustomed. Her words, "the house is now empty without my master, *Sidi*" ([1957] 1984b, 271) are symbolic of the emptiness she feels now that the raison d'être that sustained her throughout her life—to serve her husband—is gone. In her grief, and consistent with her submission to the social order imposed by her husband, she is nostalgic for the days of her sequestration: "How lovely were the days, when the *mashrabiyya* constituted the boundaries of my world, where I used to wait for my master's return in the middle of the night. With his strength, he almost shook the ground as he got off the carriage, and then he filled the room, tall, wide and strong" (275).

Amina's submission to patriarchal control is portrayed as a prerequisite for respectability in the traditional social order. Her respectable standing is juxtaposed to the disreputable fate of Yasin's mother, 'Abd al-Jawwad's first wife. This ultimate patriarch divorced his wife because she would not surrender totally and unconditionally to his commands. She had insisted on having the freedom to visit her father every now and then, a request that resulted in her being severely reprimanded, then harshly beaten by her husband. When she fled to her parents' house, he divorced her in order to discipline her and pretended to neglect her, confident that she would come back to him. Told that she would go back to him only on condition that he did not lock her up or beat her, he was enraged and swore never to take her back. Yasin was raised by his mother until he was seven and was then taken to his father's house. He grows up very much like his father and shares his views on women. Hence, any sign of freedom of will or movement on the part of his mother, who remarried, is perceived as sinful and dirty. "Every woman is damned and dirty. Women do not understand the meaning of virtue unless the routes to sin are denied. Even my father's kind wife [Amina]. Only God knows what she is capable of if it had not been for my father!" ([1956] 1983, 76). Yasin's invective against women, his conviction that they are all promiscuous, hence dangerous, if not controlled by a man, is borne out by Bahija, mother of Maryam, Yasin's fiancée. After her husband's death, she sexually approaches 'Abd al-Jawwad, hence shedding the robe of respectability provided to her by marriage. Her "respectable" status is further eroded, and her maternal credentials are brought into question when she flirts and has an affair with Yasin, her daughter's suitor. Mahfouz clearly wanted to complicate the traditional structure of mores by depicting a respectable married woman who loses her respectability once she is no longer under a man's control. Mahfouz's depiction of the "traditional" social order allows women only two choices: submissive respectability or liberal disrepute.

Critics have focused their attention on the position of prostitutes in Mahfouz's fiction. Referring to Hamida in *Zuqaq al-midaq* (1947; English translation, *Midaq Alley,* 1966), Miriam Cooke maintains that she makes a conscious decision not to marry and gain "social acceptability" through marriage (1994, 109). Cooke concludes that "Mahfouz's prostitutes are not fallen women, but rather modern women who have been exposed to new options and values and who have rebelled against traditional social expectations. They are forging a different future during a period of transition" (115–16). In the Trilogy, however, Mahfouz's prostitutes do not rebel against the social order, but rather are an integral part of it. In fact, their presence ensures the continuation and solidification of the patriarchal structures. They are the foils of Amina, the paragon of respectable and submissive womanhood, and at the same time a corollary for her "respectability." Their presence in the narrative serves to expose the intrinsic paradoxes in patriarchal structures, in which the woman-as-angel paradigm is contingent on the woman as whore. Jalila's sexualization in the narrative in her role as 'Abd al-Jawwad's mistress "is a necessary part of the economy of desire in which desire is redistributed away from 'respectable' women towards concubines and prostitutes" (Mondal 1999, 9). Although prostitutes ensure the sustainability of patriarchal structures, their location on the peripheries can potentially disrupt and threaten the seeming stability of social order. At his daughter's wedding, the wall 'Abd al-Jawwad has erected between his two lives, the bawdy life with prostitutes and his respectable life with his family, is shaken when Jalila crosses the boundaries and taunts him about their relationship in front of his friends and male members of his family. Her transgressive actions are not lost on Amina, who had always known about her husband's secret life but chose to disregard it. He, on the other hand, feels threatened and vulnerable as his hypocritical existence is exposed. The wedding incident acts as an early reminder of the fragility of a social order sustained by fear and hypocritical values. The fate of prostitutes, and their forays with various members of 'Abd al-Jawwad's family, highlight the fissures in the patriarchal order and forecast its demise. Kamal's despair and loss of faith lead him to the world of prostitutes. He also joins the circle of Jalila and finds comfort in her home. Jalila becomes her own boss and presides over a business. Zubayda ends up alone and destitute, roaming around in the streets like a madwoman. Zannuba, the younger musician in the band of 'Abd al-Jawwad's old mistress, Zubayda, whom he takes as mistress at one stage, leaves him for Yasin, his son. She becomes his wife and acquires the status of a respectable woman. She establishes herself in her husband's family and gains acceptance by perfecting the role of the devoted mother and obedient wife. When Khadija objects to her son's marriage to Zannuba's daughter, who is also her niece, no one pays any attention to her. Zannuba's story demonstrates the fluidity of the social order and its potential for change, despite its apparent fixity and inflexibility.

Sayyid Ahmad 'Abd al-Jawwad: The Icon of "Traditional" Manhood

Sayyid Ahmad 'Abd al-Jawwad is something of a Dr. Jekyll and Mr. Hyde type. He rules his family with an iron fist: harsh, uncompromising, deliberately stern to ensure their total submission and obedience. Outside the home, however, he is a different man: funny, pleasant, diplomatic, fun-loving, and promiscuous. He is the ultimate patriarch, whose masculinity is contingent upon his control of women and his authority over his household. His excessive control over his family, as a marker of his manhood, extends not only to the women, but also to his sons. His sons are denied the masculine privileges he reserves for himself; they are not allowed to exercise the same brand of manhood. As members of his household, he expects them to obey his rules, just like the women in the family. Fahmy is reprimanded for his participation in demonstrations, despite the fact that 'Abd al-Jawwad is also a nationalist who supports Sa'ad Zaghlul and his movement for change. His son defies him by not securing his approval for his actions, because according to 'Abd al-Jawwad's authoritarian logic, he is the only one who can decide the limits of freedom for his sons. In fact, 'Abd al-Jawwad's oppressive traditional masculinity practically feminizes his sons, as they live in mortal fear of him. In *Bayn al-qasrayn,* when Amina is banished from her home after paying a visit to the shrine of al-Husayn, her sons and daughters are utterly helpless in the face of their father's wrath. They are terrified of him and make only meek attempts to have him reconsider, but do nothing really assertive. During their visit to Amina in her mother's house, the grandmother challenges them: "If you were real men you would have managed to find a way to your father's heart to make him give up his stubbornness. Yasin and Fahmy exchange cynical glances about this alleged manhood, which melts away at the mention of their father" ([1956] 1983, 203). In the same vein, he is furious with Yasin for going to brothels—for leading a life similar to his. He also reprimands Yasin for escorting his wife, Zaynab, to a nightclub, a place unfit for married respectable women, according to 'Abd al-Jawwad. He expects all decent women to accept the fate of Amina, and blames Yasin for allowing this mistake to happen. From his point of view, Yasin's permissive manner with his wife makes him less of a man: "What kind of a man are you? . . . Women are spoiled by men, and not all men are worthy of ruling over women" (300). Throughout the narrative, the detrimental effect of 'Abd al-Jawwad's tyrannical brand of masculinity affects all members of his family, both men and women.

Yet despite his dissatisfaction with Yasin's laxness with his wife, he is still able to make excuses for him on the grounds of his manhood, "this manhood that legitimizes his independent actions" (367). Conversely, he is unable to find any excuse for Zaynab, who in his view is a shameless woman who caused a scandal for her husband and his family: "Yasin made a mistake but her mistake is much more grave" (368). Furthermore, when Muhammad 'Iffat, Zaynab's father, and 'Abd al-Jawwad's friend and drinking companion, insists on divorcing his daughter from Yasin after he learns of his neglect and his affairs with other women (especially the maid), 'Abd al-Jawwad is baffled by his friend's position. 'Iffat's desire to protect his daughter from the fate of her mother, that of having a husband who spends all his nights outside the house in nightclubs with prostitutes, was incomprehensible to 'Abd al-Jawwad. To allow a woman to ask for divorce was tantamount to a reversal of the order of things. The same view is shared by Yasin, who, when his father informs him that he had agreed with Zaynab's father on a divorce, is infuriated: "Who is the man and who is the woman [in this situation]? It is not strange if one throws away one's shoe, but for the shoe to reject its master!" (387). In a patriarchal world, becoming like a woman is the ultimate insult. When 'Abd al-Jawwad is faced with Fahmy's disobedience, insisting on his participation in the national struggle, he blows up and shouts: "I will not become a woman" (401). The idea that women are vassals of men becomes problematic within in the father-daughter relationship. 'Abd al-Jawwad hates the thought of his daughter's marriage because "A daughter is a real problem. Don't you see how we raise her, discipline her, protect and guard her? But then, don't you see how, after all this, we hand her over ourselves to a strange man to do with her as he pleases?" (252).

'Abd al-Jawwad's world is shaken to the core by colonial aggression. Going home one day after a late night out, he is stopped by an English soldier and forcibly taken to fill a trench that was dug by some of the resistance fighters. Like many other men of his age and standing, he finds himself powerless and humiliated. One of his main concerns is the potential destruction of his formidable, godlike image before his family if they see him in this degrading situation: "Could his family imagine the extent of his degradation, this family that only knew him as all-powerful, venerable and great" (422). He confides in Amina and shares with her the humiliating details of his detention, as she was the first one who saw him after the incident. In the morning, however, he regains control over himself and recounts the story with nonchalant humor, in an attempt to salvage his image and self-esteem before his family and friends. His world is invaded once more when a sheikh visits him and tells him the horror stories of two villages attacked by English troops, where they shot and killed men and raped women. The story brings home fears of colonial violation of women as a tool for the subordination of men.

In the *al-Sukkariyya,* we witness the waning of Ahmad 'Abd al-Jawwad's authority and the demise of his brand of traditional masculinity. This happens as he grows older, as his health declines, and as he suffers the pain of losing members of his family. We see him for the first time watching the road outside his house from the openings in the *mashrabiyya,* while Amina goes out daily ([1957] 1984b, 201–3). This scene highlights the ironic reversal of roles that takes place as he now occupies Amina's place behind the *mashrabiyya,* while she ventures onto the streets, armed by the sanctity of age and heightened religiosity. The order he had invested his life in enforcing on his household has been dissolved. Mellowed by age, and watching the world go by, he realizes that Amina is the only one he has left to take care of him (238). His deterioration, at one level, is part of the inevitable cycle of life, but it is also symbolic of the inevitable decline of his worldview and what has become an obsolete lifestyle. I disagree with the view that the "peaceful coexistence of opposites in the character of the father [Abd al-Jawwad] is a masterly rendition of a culture at peace with itself, a protected culture with neither external influence nor inner conflict" (El-Enany 1993, 82). There is nothing peaceful about 'Abd al-Jawwad's world, as it rages with multiple tensions and psychological problems. The decline of his "traditional" masculinity is a function of the advent of modernity and is congruent with an ideology that favored a radical break with the past and tradition.

Kamal: The Icon of *Nahda*/National Masculinity

Kamal is the central character of the Trilogy. We meet him in the first part, a child of ten, attached to his mother and her world. Like her, he is captivated by religious stories he heard at school and shares them with this mother, who then complements them with stories she had learned from her father, an Azharite sheikh. Kamal loves his father, in the sense that he holds him in high regard, influenced by the general atmosphere in the family. He is, however, terrified of him to the extent that he avoids walking in front of his shop on his way to school. Despite his fear, Kamal does not abide by his father's rules all the time, as he realizes early on that it would mean sitting around doing absolutely nothing.

Kamal comes into his own in the second part of the Trilogy, *Qasr al-shawq*. He has just finished high school and is preparing himself for university. His first major confrontation with his father occurs when he declares his desire to enroll in the School of Education, contrary to his father's wish that he join the School of Law. He is drawn to the world of the intellect and wants to study philosophy, art, and religion. His role model is Mustafa al-Manfaluti, a prominent intellectual and social reformer. His father's disapproval is pragmatic as well as in tune with social hierarchies of power: the School of Law means a good job with status, while the School of Education would destine Kamal to a career as a school teacher, a job that was socially less prestigious.

The appeal of the life of the intellect, a major *nahda* theme, is not exclusive to Kamal but is shared by Husayn Shaddad, Kamal's classmate and closest friend. Unlike Kamal however, Husayn agrees to join the School of Law, but only temporarily in order to convince his father to send him to Paris to study and thus partake of its vibrant cultural life, in art, music, theater, and philosophy, a life that he finds missing in Egypt. Husayn's dream extends beyond access to the world of culture and intellectual pursuits, as his ambitions include settling in Paris and marrying a French woman. His life and worldview are depicted as representative of a Westernized upper-class elite who are disconnected from national projects and aspirations, whose interests are more linked to the monarchy and the British presence, and whose eyes are riveted on everything European. Kamal loves his friend and admires his family and way of life, but he is troubled by their tenuous adherence to some national constants, such as the love of Sa'ad Zaghlul as a national hero and a symbol of resistance against the British and the corrupt monarchy. Husayn considers Kamal's nationalist fervor "a disease" ([1957] 1984a, 183) and disparages Sa'ad Zaghlul, accusing him of instigating hatred against the British.

Kamal falls in love with 'Ayda, Husayn's sister, an upper-class young woman whose lifestyle is modern and European. He is able to meet and talk to her because the strict rules of segregation that apply to the women of Kamal's family do not apply to the women of Husayn's family. In fact, her entire family does not follow the "traditional" social codes that are taken for granted by Kamal's family. Kamal admires the freedom and the easy-going atmosphere in the Shaddad household, but he is nevertheless often shocked by some of their customs, which are more European than Egyptian. Joining the Shaddads at a picnic, Kamal is surprised to find that 'Ayda has packed ham sandwiches and beer, contrary to Muslim practices. She laughs at Kamal's religious qualms and teases him about his conservative habits and mannerisms. Moreover, Kamal's appearance is perceived as a sign of his conservative stance: Husayn comments on his wearing a tarbush and on his short hair and jokingly concludes that "he is a good example of a conservative man" (187). As discussed in chapter 3, the tarbush was a marker of a traditional masculinity that was subject to negotiation and contestation in national narratives on identity. As he grows older, Kamal takes off the tarbush. On the other hand, Husayn tells Kamal that his parents abide by traditional customs and celebrations during the month of Ramadan. 'Ayda is impressed when she finds out that Kamal regularly reads the Qur'an and the Hadith, and she tries to remember some verses from the Qur'an. Husayn and 'Ayda's Westernized lifestyle and outlook is not depicted as a deliberate choice, or conscious iconoclastic standpoints, but rather as an inevitable outcome of their specific histories, their colonial education and social class. Husayn explains: "Our parents had no religious knowledge to speak of, our governess was Greek, and 'Ayda knows more about Christianity and its rituals than she knows about Islam. Compared to you [Kamal] we are virtually atheists" (200).

In fact, the whole family is portrayed as Europeanized. When 'Ayda refuses to eat because she is worried about her figure, Husayn explains that she considered herself "Parisian" (201). The Shaddads' standards of beauty for women are quite different from traditional standards, where a rounded figure is considered more attractive (201). They are secular, not religious, and lead what may be described as a Western lifestyle in Egypt. By making their acquaintance, Kamal, like other *nahda* elites, who actually traveled to Europe and had real encounters with European women, goes through a European experience in Egypt. And although their manners and mores are Westernized and very different, even contradictory to Kamal's familial mores, he admires them and refrains from judgment. He is captivated by their easygoing lifestyle, their enjoyment of life, and their openness to the world, qualities that are not present in the severe atmosphere of his house. It is noteworthy that his enchanted encounter with the Egyptian version of Europe had started a long time ago, through the numerous representations of the liberated European woman that flooded Egyptian media and public life. In *Qasr al-shawq,* Kamal stops on his way home from school in front of a billboard with the picture of a woman, blonde hair and blue eyes, reclining on a sofa, with cigarette smoke coming out of her crimson lips. He calls her *'abla* 'A'isha, as she reminds him of his pretty sister. He admires the woman in the picture tremendously, as "he imagined her enjoying life to the fullest, and imagined himself sharing her carefree life, in a tender room . . . with access to a country scene, with all its land, its palm trees, its water and its sky. [He imagined] swimming in the green valley, or crossing the river in a boat, that appeared in the background of the picture, like a shadow. . . . [He imagined himself] sitting in the arms of this beauty, gazing into her dreamy eyes" (48).

Kamal's love for 'Ayda is platonic, idealistic, and hopeless: he places her on a pedestal and calls her his idol. She is inaccessible by virtue of class differences, lifestyle, and worldview. On the other hand, her seeming "relative accessibility" increases his agony (Leeuwen 1995, 99). More important, Kamal thinks of her as an angel, an immortal being who does not belong to earth. At the picnic, he eagerly waits to find out if she is going to eat like other mortals. Watching her eat, "he was beset by two contradictory feelings. He was initially worried as he watched her perform a function human beings shared with animals. Then, he was relieved to know that this function brought her slightly closer to him" (199). Kamal's road to disillusionment begins when 'Ayda announced her engagement to marry Hasan Salim, a friend from her class with a promising future. He discovers that his secret adoration of her is common knowledge among their friends and is a source of humor. At the wedding, Kamal realizes that he really knows very little about 'Ayda's world. He is shocked to find out that the wedding proceeds without a singer and is told that the "Shaddads are half Parisian, and despise traditional wedding rituals" (319). Listening to his friend Isma'il's declaration that he will never marry, Kamal, reeling with disappointment, muses: "it is either heaven or nothing" (323). This thought basically becomes a correct prediction of the course of his life. In a discussion about marriage, Isma'il says that he will postpone it as long as possible. Husayn adds that if he has a chance to go to Europe, he will be able to find the right wife. Kamal is tempted to agree, but Isma'il responds by saying: "Do you know what marriage to a European woman means? One word, the conquest of a woman from the lowest class in society, a woman who accepts to sleep under a man she feels deep down is a slave" (324). The passage invokes the marriage debate discussed earlier, again to signal standpoints and attitudes vis à vis the relationship of the national self with the West and modernity.

'Ayda is the Westernized modern woman in national narratives, a construct wrapped in deep ambivalence: she is coveted and rejected at the same time. She promises happiness and the possibility of a relationship that is not feasible with "traditional" women like Kamal's mother. Like most *nahda* heroes, Kamal dreams of companionate love, a relationship that is diametrically opposed to that of his parents. His role models were Husayn's parents, whom he saw walking side by side, "not as master and slave, but as equal companions" (170). Kamal notes that Husayn's mother is not younger than his own mother, but she wore an elegant coat, her beautiful face was unveiled, and she spread fragrance and a captivating brilliance (170). These were the parents of his goddess. And this was the relationship he coveted but could not attain.

The ambivalence of the nationalist discourse toward its constructed traditional motherhood is exemplified in Kamal's relationship with his mother. He loves her, was totally integrated in her world as a child, but ultimately rejects her and her world. His gentle dismissal of some of her more blatant blunders, about politics or other worldly matters, is symbolic of the *nahda* hero's attitude to tradition, to Egypt, to mothers: he loves her but is embarrassed by her shortcomings and wants to change her. The representation of her warm, but "embarrassingly" antimodern, irrational existence is comparable to the representation of rural Egypt in Tawfiq al-Hakim's novels: like al-Hakim, who loves the countryside while being acutely conscious of its failings, Kamal loves his mother but is embarrassed by her perceived failings.

At the end of *Qasr al-shawq,* Kamal's disillusionment with his beloved goddess, 'Ayda, initiates a domino effect on the other constants in his life: his belief in God, his respect for his father's authority, and his attachment to his mother. Yasin reveals to him the other side of his father's life and personality, carefully hidden from his family. Kamal is filled with bitterness as he questions the reasons behind his father's sternness with his children and ascribes it to ignorance, as it has no justification in the rules of *tarbiyya.* Kamal uses modern ideas about child rearing that were widely spread in various media to analyze his father's failure as a parent and educator of his children. He concludes that his father's harshness deprived him of the friendship of his children, who only knew him as a tyrannical presence that ruled over their lives. Loss of faith in his father leads to loss of faith in God and religion. Kamal also blames his father for his blind adoration of his beloved 'Ayda and for his naïve acceptance of the wrongs she inflicted on him. He finally blames his mother for her role in making him who he is:

> My father represents rude ignorance, and you [my mother] represent tender ignorance. And, for as long as I live, I will remain the victim of these two opposites. Your ignorance is what filled my soul with legends. You are the link that ties me to the world of caves. I am suffering now to liberate myself from your influence, and I will suffer tomorrow to free myself from my father. . . . I therefore suggest that . . . we abolish the family . . . and abrogate fatherhood and motherhood. (385–86)

Kamal's rebellion against his parents and his rejection of their worldview and what they stand for is depicted as the quintessential conflict between science as the new god of the modern world and religion as the domain of superstition, myth, and irrationality. In a telling confrontation between Kamal and his father, after the father stumbles on an article by Kamal about Darwin's theory of evolution, the discussion foregrounds the huge schism between the two worldviews at war. It also brilliantly encapsulates the moral dilemma that faces Kamal, the new secular modern intellectual at this point in history. Kamal has rejected religion and is firm in his new belief, but he is unable publicly to declare his adherence to his new god, the god of science. 'Abd al-Jawwad, on the other hand, is equally firm in his rejection of Darwin's theory and insists that Kamal recants his views (343–50). Their clash is irrevocable and foretells the future. The persistence of the clash accentuates Kamal's agony, as, from his point of view, all the gods have failed, and he is left to fend for himself in a world without absolutes. His disillusionment in love is concretized in his decision to have sex with a prostitute, tormented by Yasin's statement that "an angelic woman does not exist in reality" (379).

In *al-Sukkariyya,* Kamal is a lost man with no soul. He is a regular contributor to a philosophy journal called *al-Fikr* (Thought), is still unmarried, and works as a schoolteacher. He enjoys the company of his nephews, the sons of Khadija, as they grow up to hold very different beliefs: Ahmad becomes a communist and 'Abd al-Mun'im joins the Muslim Brotherhood. He is unable to share their enthusiasm for politics, or anything else, as his intellectual standpoint, doubting everything and believing in nothing, has rendered him a skeptic, incapable of taking action. However, he sometimes makes an effort to overcome his intellectual cynicism and attends, on one occasion, a political meeting in which Mustafa al-Nahhas (1879–1965), leader of the Wafd party, speaks. It is during these rare moments that he temporarily shelves his cynicism and seeks refuge in "the heart of the community" ([1957] 1984b, 42). On the other hand, Kamal's philosophical explorations have not led him to espouse any particular point of view: he recognizes that he is a "tourist in a museum that does not belong to him, a mere chronicler, who does not know where he stands" (125). His position of doubt and lack of commitment to any school of philosophy encourages the editor of the journal of philosophy to which he contributes to say: "You are a bachelor in mind, as you are a bachelor in life" (126). Later, in a conversation with Khadija, who persistently reminds him of the necessity of marriage, Kamal recognizes that he avoids marriage to dedicate himself to intellectual pursuits. Yet he wonders, now that he has lost faith in the intellect and the intellectual, why he still avoids marriage (153). In a telling conversation with his friend Riyad Kaldas, another contributor to the philosophy journal, but who writes fiction, Riyad tells Kamal that if he ever writes a novel, he will be one of its main characters, exemplifying the typical Eastern man torn between East and West (227).

Bachelorhood as the inability to commit or decide on a clear path intellectually and practically resonates with *nahda* debates about the meaning and role of marriage in nation building and indicates that Kamal's marriage crisis is representative of the crisis of an entire generation of an intellectual elite. Critics have disagreed, though, about the nature and implications of the crisis of this generation. 'Ali al-Ra'i maintains that Kamal's tragedy is not as much about his unrealistic idealism as it is about his inability to act because of his paralyzed will, like Hamlet. Kamal, he continues, pays a heavy price for not rising to the historic challenge of the moment, by playing a dual role, "of an estranged and alienated *la-muntami* [individual] . . . and the role of a human being with a big heart whose noble sentiments place him above the actual battle" (1964, 269–70). Ghali Shukri, on the other hand, disagrees and argues that Kamal is not estranged but is someone with "a deep sense of belonging (*muntami*) who is facing a crisis" (1964, 14). Bearing in mind the consensus about Kamal as a representative of a generation of an intellectual modern elite, al-Ra'i's analysis constitutes a sharp criticism of their perceived inertia and ambivalence regarding the implementation of their reformist vision. Discussions of attitudes toward marriage and bachelorhood entail a visioning of new masculinities needed for the new nation.

The coming of age of a new generation of national citizens, represented by the grandchildren of 'Abd al-Jawwad and their friends and partners, perceptively foretells the future of the nation. Ahmad is drawn to communism and publishes articles in a magazine called *The New Human Being.* At the magazine, he meets Sawsan Hammad, a liberated young woman, who eventually becomes his wife. Ahmad rebels against traditional structures and values, both political and social. His marriage to Sawsan (a working woman and the daughter of a worker) defies the social values upheld by his family, as well as class hierarchies. 'Abd al-Mun'im, on the other hand, joins the Muslim Brotherhood and represents the rising forces of Islamism in the 1940s. His religiosity is different from his father's and grandfather's, as it becomes a driving force for political activism and engagement in society. The two brothers represent the rising political forces in society that are working to achieve independence and social justice. At the end of the novel, both are arrested by the police for holding meetings in their houses, perceived as threatening to the existing political system.

Sawsan Hammad represents the new modern woman in the Trilogy. She is intelligent, educated, and has a mind of her own. She is also the voice of the proletariat, which is critical of bourgeois intellectualism. Commenting on Kamal's articles on philosophy, she tells Ahmad: "[Your uncle] has no clear position on issues. . . . He is like the bourgeois intellectuals who enjoy reading and asking questions. He may doubt the Absolute, and may even be pained by his doubt. However, he will pass by unaware of the people who are in real pain. . . . His work is passive when compared to the real battle" (250). She recommends to Ahmad that he read the novels of Maxim Gorky. Ahmad's decision to marry her is met with the disapproval of his family, especially Khadija, his mother, but he holds firm. Sawsan moves to Ahmad's family house, but, despite her efforts to fit in the family by not reacting to attacks directed at her by her mother-in-law, she maintains a distance. Khadija, on the other hand, is constantly annoyed by what Sawsan represents, by her version of womanhood. She considers her participation in political discussions a sign of manliness (332) and remains convinced that "a working woman can never be a good wife" (350). Sawsan, however, the new woman and the counterpart of Amina, is a flat character, like 'Ayda Sabri; we get to know about her political views, but not about her inner self, the way we do about Kamal and 'Abd al-Jawwad and even Amina to some extent. Sawsan is educated, modern, and from a working-class background, but she still accommodates herself to family traditions and rules of bourgeois respectability. She embodies the enigmatic construct that occupied the *nahda* imaginary.

Conclusion

Critics have tried to answer the question about the extent to which Mahfouz's oeuvre is progressive on social issues, particularly regarding the status of women. In other words, was Mahfouz an advocate for women's freedom or did he reaffirm the status quo? In her foreword to Mahfouz's *Echoes of an Autobiography,* Nadine Gordimer wrote that after a lecture she delivered at Harvard on the Trilogy, feminist students were outraged by his "depiction of women characters." Gordimer defended Mahfouz in the following manner:

> It was a case of killing the messenger: Mahfouz was relaying the oppression of Amina and her daughters as it existed; he was not its advocate. His insight to the complex socio-sexual mores, the seraglio-prison that distorted the lives of women members of Abd al-Gawwad's family was a protest far more powerful than that of those who accused him of literary chauvinism. (1997, xiii)

This argument, that Mahfouz only portrayed the oppressive reality as a form of protest, or "to draw the attention of both the reading public and the authorities . . . to the necessity of reform" (el-Sheikh 1991, 98) supports the view that his work is socially progressive and ahead of its time within the conventions of the realistic novel. Rather, I have tried to show that the Trilogy is an artistic rendition of a national liberal discourse propagated by the dominant intellectual elite in the first half of the twentieth century. This discourse was modernist and was premised on a binary opposition between modernity and tradition, with tradition carrying negative connotations and obsolete values, and it was very ambivalent about gendered roles ascribed to both men and women. The characters of Amina and ʻAbd al-Jawwad are modernist parodies of a traditionalism that threatened to hamper the advent of modernity and hence had to be denigrated and destroyed. ʻAbd al-Jawwad's contradictions, double standards, and tyrannical rule are all designed to lead to a rejection of his value system and the acceptance of the new forces of change, an endorsement of the reform project of the generation of the *nahda* elite. Also, the relative paleness of women characters in the Trilogy, especially the modern types in *al-Sukariyya,* is congruent with the *nahda* ambivalence about what is meant by the "new woman." In this sense, the Trilogy is an emblematic "national allegory" that both reflected and constructed the dominant imaginary of a national elite at a particular moment in history.

5

Latifa al-Zayyat

Gender and Nationalist Politics

> Why is it that the advent of the politics of nationalism signals the subordination if not the demise of women's politics?
>
> —Radhakrishnan (1992, 78)

Latifa al-Zayyat (1923–1996) occupies a unique place in the Arabic cultural field. In the nationalist narrative, she is the exemplary committed Arab intellectual who participated in the national liberation movement against colonialism and continued her fight for freedom and justice throughout her career as a writer, academic, and political activist. Al-Zayyat's involvement in political protest started at an early age, in 1946, when, still a student, she was elected secretary general of the National Committee of Students and Workers. In 1979, she cofounded and was president of the Committee for the Defense of National Culture, which consisted of a group of writers and intellectuals who opposed Sadat's peace treaty with Israel and organized to raise awareness against the dangers of the normalization of relations with Israel in the cultural sphere. She was imprisoned twice: the first time was in 1949, when she was charged with conspiring to topple the regime; the second time was in 1981, when, among more than fifteen hundred prominent public and opposition figures arrested by Sadat, she was charged with conspiring with a foreign country. Sayyid al-Bahrawi pays tribute to her for being "a rare model among Arab women who engage in a struggle for liberation" and for possessing traits "that unite her with the general lot of the Arab nationalist intellectuals" (al-Bahrawi 1996a, 31). At the same time, she figures strongly in the Arab feminist narrative as a role model and inspiration to women writers in search of a tradition of women writing in Arab culture. Somaya Ramadan writes that her awareness of the complexities of her position as a woman in a man's world was shaped by al-Zayyat.[1] Hala al-Badri remembers how the film based on her novel, *al-Bab al-maftuh* (1960; English translation, *The Open Door,* 2000), left a lasting impression on her consciousness as a young girl, as it triggered discussions in her family about the daring ideas treated in the novel, for example, the dialogue between Layla and her cousin about a woman's body drying up as a consequence of a failed relationship (al-Badri 1996, 31).

Notwithstanding her prominence in both nationalist and feminist narratives, al-Zayyat's life and literary oeuvre embody the precarious and tenuous location of gender politics in Third World nationalist movements. After the appearance of her first novel *al-Bab al-maftuh* in 1960, al-Zayyat did not publish any literary work for a quarter of a century, that is, until the appearance in 1986 of a collection of short stories, *al-Shaykhukha* (Old age). More work followed at the end of the 1980s and into the 1990s: an autobiography, *Hamlat taftish: 'awraq shakhsiyya* (1992a; English translation, *The Search: Personal Papers,* 1997b); a play, *Bay' wa shira'* (1994a; Buying and selling); *Sahib al-bayt* (1994c; English translation, *The Owner of the House,* 1997a); a novella, *al-Rajul al-ladhi 'arafa tuhmatahu* (1995; The man who knew what he was charged for). Al-Zayyat's strikingly long literary silence has been the topic of some speculation and has been interpreted by some as a kind of literary laziness.[2] She defended herself against this charge, saying that her drawers were full of short stories and beginnings of novels, but that she was a perfectionist who was also concerned about the reception of her work by audiences, two factors that limited her literary production (al-Zayyat 1990, 143). She also revealed that after the defeat of Arab armies in 1967, she felt deceived and "hated words, and consequently literature" (146). This last point is extremely telling, especially in view of al-Zayyat's vision and overall

1. Somaya Ramadan counts al-Zayyat among the five most important women who made a mark on her consciousness; the others are Mary Wollstonecraft, Simone de Beauvoir, Nawal al-Sa'dawi, and Virginia Woolf (Ramadan 1995a, 12).

2. This interpretation was put forward by Radwa Ashur in an interview to allow her to explain why she stopped writing for such a long time (al-Zayyat 1990, 142).

message in *al-Bab al-maftuh.* The novel is a period piece par excellence, as al-Zayyat captures the idealism and euphoria of the dominant nationalist discourse of independence and freedom that was empowered by the Free Officers' revolution in 1952 and confirmed in 1956 with the failure of the Tripartite attack on Egypt following the nationalization of the Suez Canal. It was a historical moment that did not last very long though, as it was soon succeeded by frustration and disillusionment, first with the growing awareness of the many oppressive measures that were taken by the revolutionary officers against civil liberties and eventually by the shocking defeat in 1967, a defeat that was all the more harsh because it exposed the deceptive propaganda of the ruling regime. In fact, and because of the dominance of the radical shift in mood and direction of Arabic literature in the 1960s, *al-Bab al-maftuh* has been faulted for its positive take on events.[3] With this in mind, al-Zayyat's reaction to the deceptive power of words and, by extension, literature does shed some light on her literary silence.

In an interview four years later, after the appearance of her last novel, *Sahib al-bayt,* al-Zayyat is more open about the reasons for her literary silence. She addresses the limits of freedom available to writers in general but posits that women writers face more restrictions, which "multiply even more for a committed woman because we had been raised in a very disciplined and serious manner, and in order to face the aggressive campaigns directed against us, we had to purify ourselves, or behave like the purified" (al-Zayyat 1994b, 76). Referring to *Sahib al-bayt* in particular, she adds that it was delayed because she exercised political self-censorship, believing that it was the duty of writers to instill hope, and that the projection of a hopeful vision in bleak contexts could be a distortion and a form of deceit.

With these words in mind, and with reference to her later work, published toward the end of her life, it is clear that her silence was precipitated by more than a disillusionment with a nationalist discourse that failed her as a political activist; she was disillusioned with ideologies and ideologues that failed her as a woman in search of freedom and self-fulfillment. Al-Zayyat's

3. Hilary Kilpatrick has argued that the novel is dated "irremediably" because "the revolution and all its works are bathed in a positive light" (1992, 251).

novel *Sahib al-bayt,* published thirty-four years after *al-Bab al-maftuh,* is a powerful feminist critique of the ambivalence of nationalist and Third World leftist politics toward gender.[4]

Gender within nationalist politics has been widely researched in general and with reference to anticolonial nationalisms in particular. I have already discussed how the liberation of women was seen as a condition of modernization and a marker of national identity in the imagined independent nation-state. During the wars for liberation, women were constructed as icons of nation, and the bearers of identity and national values.[5] More to the point, the need to unite all national efforts in the battle against imperialism superseded everything else and was presented as a priority on the national agenda. Accordingly, women activists in many parts of the world were asked to postpone their demands for gender equality until the battle of independence was won. In effect, the idea was that the route to gender equality came via a national struggle. That was certainly the view of Frantz Fanon, whose insights about the centrality of the woman question in the dynamics of power relations between the colonizer and the colonized remain crucial to any discussion of colonial/national politics. However, as Ann McClintock aptly pointed out, Fanon stopped short of developing his insights into a theory of gender power. For him, women's agency is contingent on their joining the nationalist struggle, and only when invited to do so by men. It is an "agency by designation" that does not acknowledge their independent agency, their history, or their resistance prior to nationalism (McClintock 1995, 365–68). However, history has proven these assumptions wrong, as more and more women confronted their second-class status within nationalist politics and asserted their voice and independent agency.

Salwa Bakr talks about her disillusionment with her leftist partners when she realized that their practical lives belied their declared ideals: "Returning home from a demonstration in which both I and my husband, a leftist

4. This argument was made in an earlier version of this chapter published in 1995. Magda al-Nowaihi also noted that her silence resulted from al-Zayyat's "ambivalence about power and its structures" (2001, 478).

5. See Baron, *Egypt as a Woman* (2005).

intellectual, participated, he sat down to catch up on the latest news and I went to the kitchen to prepare dinner."[6] In 1987, more than two decades after Algeria gained its independence, Marie-Aimee Helie-Lucas, an Algerian sociologist, exposed the practices and ideologies that discriminated against women during the liberation struggle. Although Algerian women were equal partners during the struggle, they were never awarded the honors or the benefits that were later given to male resistance fighters. Referring to the Algerian archives for veterans, she observed that "if a man carried food to the armed fighters at great personal risk, he was called a 'fighter.' A woman doing the same was called a 'helper.'" More important, women accepted these discriminatory practices without questioning them, as they feared that they would be perceived to be undermining the national struggle, and also because they had, at one level, accepted the idea that they would gain their rights after independence. The subsequent disillusionment is painful: "What makes me angrier in retrospect is not women's confinement but the brainwashing that did not allow us young women even to think of questioning" (Helie-Lucas 1990, 106–7). This experience was shared by many women across the globe. In 1990, the ANC (African National Congress) stated: "The experience of other societies has shown that the emancipation of women is not a by-product of a struggle for democracy, national liberation or socialism" (quoted in McClintock 1995, 383).

The publication of *al-Bab al-maftuh*[7] in 1960 coincided with two other novels by women writers, *'I'tirafat 'imra'a mustarjila* (The confessions of a masculinized woman), by Su'ad Zuhayr, and *Mudhakkirat tabiba* (Memoirs of a woman doctor), by Nawal al-Sa'dawi. All three novels depict women's rebellion against forms of oppression that are specific to women in a society trying to recover from the setbacks of both traditional and colonial bondage. And all three novels project a vision of hope toward a better future. *Al-Bab al-maftuh* has received wider recognition in Arab literary history because of the link established between national liberation and the liberation of women,

6. This observation was made during a discussion with Salwa Bakr in 1993.

7. Latifa al-Zayyat ([1960] 1989). All quotations are taken from this edition. All translations are mine.

a cornerstone of nationalist discourse. The novel begins in 1946 with the mass demonstrations against British presence in Egypt that took place on 21 February in the 'Isma'iliyya square and ends in 1956 with the celebration of the resistance movement against the Tripartite Assault on Egypt by Israel, France, and Britain in Port Said. A chronicle of key events in a decisive period in the history of anticolonial resistance frames the coming-of-age of Layla, a young girl from a middle-class background, and defines her journey toward the attainment of a new consciousness that befits the model of the new national woman. There is a direct link between the public and the private: Layla's journey toward freedom parallels the nation's journey toward independence; her private struggle with her family, with tradition, with stereotypical roles imposed on women, corresponds to the national struggle against colonialism and exploitation. Al-Zayyat situates Layla at the center of events as she contributes and is a key player in three simultaneous and interlinked battles: a feminist battle for women's freedom; a Marxist battle against middle-class morality and the primacy of the family as a locus of tradition and power; and the larger anticolonial battle. The national struggle against colonialism acts as the impetus and the driving force that enables individual selves to overcome personal and class restrictions. In fact, every phase in the national struggle brings about a transformation in Layla's journey toward knowledge and self-awareness and enables her to break loose from the chains of her class and her family.

Layla's immediate battle is with her family, portrayed as a microcosm of the social order and political struggle: "For those people [who participated in the 1946 revolution], the battle was over, and the gains and losses were counted. But, the battle was not yet over, nor were the gains and losses counted, for the family of Muhammad Effendi Sulayman, the employee at the Ministry of Finance, who lived in house No. 3, Ya'qub Street in Sayyida Zaynab" ([1960] 1989, 2). Layla is characterized as a bright woman who questions at a very young age the hypocritical middle–class rules of propriety and decorum imposed on women in particular, and men in general. She receives contradictory and illogical messages from her parents about the proper conduct of young women, messages that do not make sense and only confuse her. The word *'usul,* meaning decorum or rules of propriety, is a recurrent idea that underlies the narrative and becomes a key target in Layla's fight against middle-class morality. Rules of propriety are the instruments of Layla's oppression and the target of her rebellion. They also concretize the discrimination against women in society, as there are different sets of rules for men and women. The mother persistently drills in Layla the rules and values of *al-'usul:* sitting up straight, speaking in a low voice, and so forth. These rules are satirized throughout the novel as hypocritical and illogical, but they are also presented as obstructive to the national good. Layla's participation in anti-British demonstrations with many school children, which, according to the rules of propriety, is deemed inappropriate behavior for young women, results in a beating by her father.

Men, too, are victimized by rules of propriety and decorum. Mahmud, Layla's brother, is also harassed by his father for joining the resistance movement and later for marrying against his will. However, for men, rules are more lax and more tolerant of individual preferences. Also, young men, in their relationships with young women, are trapped in the web of rules, as they are unable to overcome the *'usul* mandate, despite their avowed rebellion and belief in gender equality. Mahmud, for example, Layla's "hero" in many ways, is portrayed as a passionate nationalist determined to fight for his country. He supports his sister and is sympathetic to her rebellion against rules and restrictions, but he still oscillates between upholding conventional expectations of young women and his belief in their right to freedom. After her father beats her, she turns to him for help and support, but he stands against her, maintaining the traditions about what girls should and should not do. She confronts him with his contradictory views, saying that his actions belie his declared support for women's rights ("You know very well that I respect women, and I believe that they are equal to me in every way" [50]), and she exposes the double standards he applies when it all boils down to words on paper or declarations without practical applications in the real world. Layla wins the argument with her brother, who keeps silent and realizes that "the problem is not hers alone, but that it is his problem too, the problem of an entire generation" (51). In another incident, during the battle against the Tripartite Assault in 1956, Mahmud assumes the role of patriarch and insists on sending his wife, Sana', and Layla back to Cairo, to save them, despite their wish to stay and participate in the fight. It is only when Layla finds her inner strength and defies his authority that he accepts her as an equal.

Al-Zayyat explores the impact of a traditional society with obsolete values on a range of characters. All of them, with the exception of Dr. Ramzi, are portrayed sympathetically as victims of old traditions that are destined to becoming extinct in a modern national world. 'Isam, Layla's first sweetheart, who struggles with his sexual attraction to Layla and has an affair with the maid, eventually overcomes his cowardice (opting at first not to join the resistance movement with Mahmud and surrendering to rules of propriety during the marriage of his sister), joins the resistance at the end of the novel, and dies a hero. Jamila, Layla's cousin, is trapped in a loveless marriage of convenience and copes by having an affair. In many ways, she is Layla's foil, a harsh reminder of the possible fate of young women who simply accept illogical rules. Dr. Ramzi, however, is an obnoxious character throughout. He is the hypocritical intellectual who wants to marry a bright but obedient young woman on whom he can exercise intellectual and sexual control.

Layla goes through a series of revelations as she confronts acts of infidelity on a personal level, manifested in 'Isam and Jamila's affairs. These private moments of failure and betrayal coincide with a larger national act of treason, the Cairo fire in January 1952, which demolished large parts of the city center and triggered rumors and speculation about conspiracies against the interest of the nation. Layla is also betrayed by Dr. Ramzi, her university teacher and a representative of decadent intellectualism. She finally finds a way out of the various forms of oppression to which she has been subjected when she joins the popular resistance movement in Port Said that battled against the Tripartite Assault in 1956. She becomes an equal partner in the battle only after she gains confidence in herself and is able to impose her will and determination on her male comrades: "She left the family circle, and moved from the circle of the self to the circle of the collective" (332). Only then, when the individual self unites with the larger community, is Layla able to achieve her freedom. For the first time, Mahmud stops patronizing her as his young sister and shakes her hand as an equal. In a symbolic gesture, Layla witnesses the destruction of the statue of Ferdinand de Lesseps, who symbolized colonial exploitation of the Suez Canal. First the head came tumbling down, leaving the statue still in place "as if its roots extended into the earth" (350). The roots of the statue symbolized for Layla all the rules of propriety, the *'usul,* that curtailed her freedom. She cried out "al-'usul, daruri al-'usul" (the rules, the rules must go), when she meant to say that the foundations of the statue must also be demolished. This Freudian slip serves to foreground the collusion between colonial exploitation and obsolete traditional values against personal and national liberation.

The novel ends in an upbeat tone: the resistance movement is victorious and the invading armies withdraw; at the same time Layla gains confidence in herself as a woman and in her ability to have an equal relationship with Husayn, a friend of her brother's and her comrade in the resistance movement. The novel epitomizes an idealism that imbued the late 1950s and early 1960s in Egypt, based on dreams of prosperity and independence. It represents an optimistic worldview on the national as well as on the personal level. "*al-Bab al-maftuh* was the door for people, the door for the nation" (al-Zayyat 1990, 139).

Al-Zayyat's vision developed throughout the years, paralleling the social and political developments in society. A comparison of the artistic vision in her early novel, *al-Bab* (1960) and her later collection of short stories, *al-Shaykhukha* (1986) indicates a change in the relationship between the individual and society, as perceived by the main character or narrator. In *al-Bab,* to use al-Zayyat's words, "the individual is relatively at peace with his society. His/her freedom corresponds to the freedom of his nation: there is no contradiction" (1994d, 120). The novel progressed in a realistic style with a beginning, middle, and end. In *al-Shaykhukha,* however, it was no longer possible to portray "this organic body that makes its way, easily and inevitably, from beginning to middle to end" again to use al-Zayyat's words (1994d, 124).

"Al-Shaykhukha," a long short story or novella in the collection, crosses the boundaries between genres and reminds us of Paul de Man's statement that all writing is at one level autobiographical. It tackles a new theme in Arabic narrative in general, where the writer attempts to portray an objective correlative of the crisis of a writer regarding her self-image vis à vis her own self, as well as others. In the beginning, she tells us that what we are about to read are her diary entries that were written in the mid–1970s, that is, ten years before their publication date in the mid-1980s. These texts were written from the perspective of a woman in her fifties, but she is reading them and interacting with them from the perspective of a woman in her sixties. Moments of time intersect and overlap in the writer's consciousness as she attempts to dissect the overwhelming state of mind that dominated her relationship with herself and with others. This state of mind is identified by the writer as old age, or, "the feeling that one's existence is superfluous to other human beings" (1986, 55). It is a condition that drives the individual into a vicious circle of pathological attachment and distance from surrounding people. The diaries shed light on the relationship between the self/the protagonist on the one hand, and her daughter and her son-in-law on the other. The story brilliantly depicts hidden and declared conflicts at the center of strong relationships, rethinking ideas about love, protection, and control. Having reached the age of sixty, the protagonist seeks to rearrange her relationship with the world and with people. She recalls the state of mind of old age, as recorded in her diaries, written in her fifties, which overshadowed her relation with her daughter after her marriage and her separation from the mother. We come face to face with a double consciousness: the consciousness of a woman in her fifties, totally immersed in the minute details of her problem, and the consciousness of a woman in her sixties, confronting herself. She goes through her neglected papers and takes another look at her diaries, which were lost amid piles of forgotten papers (23). This very rich text begs the question: were these papers not just lost, but possibly hidden, or silenced? Al-Zayyat squarely confronts the silence imposed on her, not just in her relation with the world but, in a more important way, as it affects her relation with her own self. Another question is raised: to what extent is old age a state of mind of an individual? And did al-Zayyat mean to create a metaphor for a more general condition, a national condition characterized by inertia and a general feeling of inadequacy? Was this story her first step in breaking the silence she imposed on herself as a creative writer deeply involved in the affairs and travails of the nation?

It is noteworthy that the collection of short stories, *al-Shaykhukha* (1986), was the first creative work to appear by al-Zayyat since the publication of *al-Bab al-maftuh* in 1960. This means that al-Zayyat stopped writing, or more accurately, did not publish any literary work for over twenty-five years. In 1992, she published her autobiography, *Hamlat taftish: 'awraq shakhsiyya,* in which she revisits difficult moments in her life and reassesses their significance from the perspective of a woman approaching her seventies. According to Faysal Darraj, *Hamlat taftish* is "an iconic text about the tragedy of the noble intellectual who united with the group to liberate it, but ends up alone, after discovering that he/she was not free while leading the group towards freedom" (1996, 183). The autobiography is completely steeped in the present: in fact the writer is obsessed with searching for reasons behind transformations. This search is reflected in the structure of the autobiography, which is not linear but is divided into sections that respond to questions posed by the present (Barrada 1996, 175).

In 1995, al-Zayyat published a novella, *al-Rajul al-ladhi 'arafa tuhmatahu,* about 'Abdallah, a defeated Arab antihero, a man who has lost his manhood: his ability to act, to be proactive, to engage in a healthy manner with the world. Unlike Kafka's Joseph K. in *The Trial,* whose crisis is existential and related to the emptiness of the modern way of life, 'Abdallah's crisis is particularly Arab, or specifically political: he is the logical heir to failed social and economic policies and long years of political oppression and a parody of defeated Arab masculinities. The opening lines of the novella set the tone: "'Abdallah could not snatch a few moments of sleep as he usually did, while standing in the co-op queue, waiting for a bottle of oil which became sparse in the house. He was thinking—something he does not usually do—since, last night, he found in his house something that required thinking and quick action" (1995, 33). 'Abdallah belongs to a political family. His father is an old political activist who was imprisoned several times but never gave up. The father is now an old man, and 'Abdallah refers to him as a "senile man" who wasted his life trying to change conditions for the better, to no avail. "Does he know that the price of a kilo of meat is seven pounds, that a morsel of fried aubergine costs his son hours of standing in the co-op queue waiting for a bottle of cooking oil?" (37), wondered 'Abadallah. 'Abdallah's son and daughter show a deep awareness of political matters and express their views openly and clearly. He, on the other hand, is extremely apolitical, in fact antipolitical: he does not think, does not have opinions, refuses to watch the news, and only watches unrealistic soap operas on TV. He forbids his household from engaging in anything political, but fails even to do that.

While 'Abdallah is standing in the queue, police officers show up at his house with an arrest warrant. This takes place on 6 September 1981, the year when President Sadat ordered the arrest of more than fifteen hundred political opponents. In 'Abdallah's case, the whole matter seems ridiculous and is described as such: "They came to find him at nine o'clock in the evening of

6 September 1981. He was absent, in the co-op queue. They asked for him by name though they did not know his age, what he looked like and they had no picture of him" (40). The scene that follows is absurd: his father keeps shouting slogans; he swallows the piece of paper with his son's name on it, leaving the police officer at a loss to verify the name of the wanted man. The absurdity of the whole matter is multiplied by the arrival of 'Abdallah, who cannot comprehend the reason for his arrest. The officer comes back for him, and he is led to prison. There he comes in contact with political prisoners, but he shuts himself out and insists that his arrest was a mistake and that he will be released soon. Following the advice of his fellow prisoners, he decides to deny everything during the interrogation. He does so in an absurd manner, responding with "no" to every single question. The interrogating officer is infuriated; he shouts, "Don't you do anything at all?" (83) and charges him with disrupting national unity. Unable to comprehend the actual meaning of the charge brought against him, 'Abdallah reaches the conclusion that he is being charged with doing nothing.

'Abdallah's prison interlude does not lead to any transformation in his worldview or apolitical position. Unlike prison experiences in Arabic literature,[8] which usually lead to radical changes, 'Abdallah is in such a deep state of apathy that he is incapable of change. He is a caricature of a generation of men who relinquished their ability to act and to insist on their rights. By doing so, they lost their manhood and the respect of their children. 'Abdallah's son declares that his generation has no fathers (46). Al-Zayyat tells us that she wrote the novella as a parable to satirize unbearable conditions that seem to persist with no hope for change (1992b, 239).[9]

In 1994, al-Zayyat published her masterpiece, *Sahib al-bayt.* She began writing the novel in 1962, immediately after she finished writing *al-Bab*

8. Prison experiences in Arabic literature abound. They either lead to emasculation (see Sonallah Ibrahim) or to a revival of national commitment (see Sahar Khalifeh). Prison is said to be for "strong men," or is seen as as a school, with reference to the formative influence on prisoners.

9. Ferial Ghazoul, on the other hand, finds that this novella is part of a tradition of resistance literature that presents a caricature of the hegemonic other, which is belittled through satire that evokes the reader's laughter (1996, 197).

al-maftuh. But the novel was actually completed and published more than thirty years later. In *Hamlat taftish,* al-Zayyat tells us that *Sahib al-bayt* was originally called "The Apricot Tree" and that she had wanted to write in it about the period when the police chased her and her husband into hiding. She had wanted to portray the "victory of fallible human beings over all kinds of societal oppression," and decided to use juxtaposition as a structural element. The chase was going to end with prison, "that is failure at the material level, whereas failure was in fact a spiritual victory, whereby human beings flourish despite very harsh circumstances, and the soft and fragile apricot flowers bloom out of rough wooden stems" (1992a, 141). As the writing of the novel developed, she moved away from her original plan, and the novel was retitled *al-Rihla* (The journey), "a metaphor for the journey of man from birth to death" (1992a, 141). She found herself unable to complete the novel and could not find its essential flaw, which became clear to her only later, after she had gotten a divorce. Her analysis of the flaw in the novel is worth quoting in full:

> The vision in this novel was a tortured vision. It was my vision during a period in my marriage, but it was strange and alien to the overall development of my life. In this novel, man is an asocial individual: his freedom constitutes a burden that only he can carry. He is an ahistorical individual who finds himself thrown into an ahistorical position. His ahistoricity is concretized by his eternal isolation and eternal loneliness. For this individual, the other represents hell. In the novel, the individual acts, but his actions . . . lack justification and reconstruct neither reality nor the self. Action in this novel is incidental not cumulative. It is not the action of a well-developed character with a history, neither does it build a well-balanced character that undertakes actions that extend from the past to the present and into the future. (1992a, 142)

Sahib al-bayt is about the journey of Samya, wife of a member of a political opposition group in Egypt, toward self-knowledge. The plot revolves around Samya's going into hiding with her husband, who has just escaped prison and is being chased by the police. They are accompanied by a friend, a fellow rebel who has organized the escape and plays a major role in planning their course of action. Although Samya took a conscious risk when she married her husband and defied her family, she is nevertheless not allowed by the two men to share, or even to know about the important decisions that have to be taken during their escapade. Her exclusion from the confidence of her partners in the escape evokes recollections of other moments in her life, which accumulate in her consciousness and gradually lead to a moment of revelation. The linear events of the plot are laden with layers of experience and emotional struggles as the novelist uses stream of consciousness to give each event historical and psychological depth. The result of this technique is crucial to the vision of the novel: it establishes an unmistakable correlation between the oppressive attitudes of Samya's comrades on the one hand, and the social and familial oppression she suffered all her life on the other. The narrative technique also makes it quite clear that the main reason for Samya's oppressive exclusion is her gender. The novel guides the reader to recognize different kinds of gender discrimination practiced against women, by society, by the family, and also by partners in a struggle for liberation.

The title *Sahib al-bayt* refers to the owner of the house where Samya and her husband hide from the police. Reading al-Zayyat's autobiographical novel, we realize the significance of houses in her life. She describes her journey to freedom and maturity as a journey away from the old family house to a new house: "The old house was my destiny and my heritage; the house in Sidi Bishr was my creation and my choice" (1992a, 29). We also discover that the house in Sidi Bishr had an apricot tree blooming outside its window. As mentioned earlier, al-Zayyat had intended to call her novel "The Apricot Tree." Also, Amina Rashid tells us that al-Zayyat's second house, the one in Sidi Bishr, was the house to which she escaped with her husband to hide from the police (1995, 8). Hence, the house where Samya and her husband hide gains added significance as it has been described as "my creation and choice," and as it was supposed to have an apricot tree blooming in front of it. This same house is described in very different terms in *Sahib al-bayt,* projecting a radical change of feelings and perception.

Samya arrives at the house at night, having been jerked out of bed only a while before. The atmosphere is one of danger and suspense. The door opens before they knock. The place looks strange and frustrates her expectations: "The garden is not a garden; there are no flowers, just land cultivated with lettuce" (1994c, 23). On top of the building, there was a tower with round openings. "Was it a pigeon house or a control tower?" she wondered (24). The building was small, as small as a "doll's house." She goes up the stairs, and the landlord produces "a large ring of keys" to open the door to the flat. Samya feels trapped. She finds herself in "one lonely room, long like a passage, which you would expect could lead somewhere, but leads nowhere." An iron bed with rails is placed in the center of the room. On the right, there is a sofa with its "metal entrails" (25) hanging from it, and to its left stands a closet with a broken mirror. The house is portrayed as a prison into which she is forcefully dragged. She enters obediently, led by Rafiq, her husband's comrade, and the landlord. Gradually, as she begins to show signs of resistance, "she is dragged against her will to the kitchen by the owner of the house" (27). As he leaves, Samya screams for the key, but he refuses to give it to her.

Samya's perception of and relation to the new house goes through a major transformation. It is no longer the house with the apricot tree blooming outside, nor is it the house of her choice, as she is dragged into it against her will. It reminds her of a doll's house, Ibsen's *Doll's House,* where Nora, the protagonist, was trapped, just like Samya. At the end of the novel, and after Samya gains self-knowledge, the house is transformed into a pigeon tower from which flocks of pigeons fly, signaling hope and a new beginning.

Samya's trials help her understand her constant feeling of inadequacy and insecurity in her relationship with the comrades. Because she is a woman, she has been forbidden access to knowledge. Her mother covered her up in darkness and trimmed her nails (32), impeding her ability to explore and discover new territories. She was raised to become a helpless human being, totally dependent on others. She is never informed and never trusted by her partners to act on her own initiative. After another blunder she commits because she was never told of the emergency plan should the owner of the house become suspicious, she has a moment of illumination:

> Everything here, all the planning happens without her: she is totally excluded, totally dispensable. What then makes her stay in this place? Why do they deliberately withhold knowledge? Is it pity, or condescension, or is it a conviction that if she is informed she is bound to spoil everything? . . . Her ignorance of the course of events doubled her fear and drove her to commit a series of mad actions that only increased the danger rather than

> decreased it. Did it all happen because she did not know or because she cannot stand on her feet? (84)

Samya sets out on her journey to freedom and self-discovery. She repeatedly asks the question: who am I? All her life, she had been denied the privilege of exploring her own desires and of acting on her own initiative. As a first step toward knowledge, she identifies Rafiq as the "other," the stranger. "Rafiq is my opposite in everything" (52). The opposition between the two characters in the novel is an opposition between stereotypical notions about masculinity and femininity: Rafiq is aggressive, violent, uncaring, arrogant, conceited, self-assured, domineering, and very authoritarian; Samya is submissive, hesitant, and quiet. She cannot keep up with the two men as they take quick and strong steps. Samya perceives of herself as absence, as nothing, as the weak side of the binary opposition between male and female. She decides to leave her husband, and although she comes closer to attaining her freedom, she initially sees her departure as failure in her womanly duties.

Samya's tense encounter with the landlord brings back memories of other domineering figures in her life: "the one-and-only ruler? . . . her father? . . . the preacher in the mosque threatening people with fire and a dire destiny? . . . the teacher telling her to extend her hand to receive punishment?" (27) She is drawn into a game, and the landlord is the game master. Samya soon realized that "those who go through the door [of the house] have to play the master's game" (26). She also realized that she has always played the game and has always abided by the role assigned to her. Her encounter with the landlord recalls other encounters and relationships. He represents all the oppressive inherited values that had always hindered her quest for freedom. He is a patriarch and a representative of dominant patriarchal values and power structures. He also reminds her of her mother, disciplining her and trying to fit her into a submissive feminine mold. The landlord in the novel is the sum total of cultural and societal values and structures that perpetrate the oppression of women.

Halfway through her journey of self-discovery, Samya acknowledges her deep hatred of him: "There is an old vendetta between her and this man. What kind of vendetta? . . . She does not know but she is certain that there is an old vendetta between them and that matters will not be resolved until it is settled" (75). At the end of the novel, when she finally rids herself of her bondage to the comrades and starts to act on her own initiative without fear of rejection, she goes back to face the owner of the house. She battles with him and overcomes him, hence overcoming her oppression and oppressor. The final scene, her victory over the owner of the house, symbolizes her victory over the oppression of her gender.

The owner of the house also owns the world she inhabits and sets the rules to be followed. Samya's world is portrayed as a game with players who perform artificial and limiting roles. Al-Zayyat employs the metaphor of a game to comment on the gender roles of men and women. The oppressive nature of the game is criticized by rendering it absurd, even childish. The metaphor of the game runs throughout the novel and develops into a recurrent motif, almost a refrain:

> Whoever enters into this house must play a role, the role prescribed by the owner of the house. . . . (24)

> It occurred to her that she has always played the game of the owner of the house. . . . (26)

> He plays, therefore he is a player. This is the best definition of the required behavior. . . . Our world allows us no choice. Play, her mother said, and she persistently repeated her words while she [Samya] could not desire the calculated game. (32)

Deciding to leave the house to save her husband from spending the night outside in the cold, she is intercepted by the owner of the house, who insists childishly on going out with her. The scene portrays an absurd situation in which a grown man acts petulantly, stamping his feet when his wishes are denied. The absurdity shocks Samya and results in her scrutinizing the reasons she agreed to participate:

> Play, Samya, play. All your life, you have been forced to play. Why hold back now? Play, in spite of your worn out body and your strangled voice, play. Your mother's orders that break stones in half and your husband freezing in the car: you must play. You have no choice. Gather the terms of the game with your inherited and acquired baggage and play. (35)

Although Samya is a partner in the escape from the police and has consciously agreed to join Rafiq and her husband in their hideout, she is never treated as an equal partner. She is only told to follow their instructions, without question, and without being properly informed about the whole plan. Requests by her partners for her help are based on their preconceived ideas about her gender, like when asked by Rafiq to resort to her "feminine wiles" to charm the policeman with a smile and pretend to be his beloved.

Samya's prescribed gender role in the novel is perceived by her, and presented by the writer, as a continuation and reaffirmation of her other roles throughout her life. The representation of her life as a continuum, as variations on the same theme, is portrayed through the use of the stream-of-consciousness technique and the recurrent use of words and sentence structures creating a musical refrain. After the seduction scene, Samya wonders:

> Has she turned into the monstrous being prescribed for her? A monster with no roots, no motives? Lifelong training has borne fruit: the exclusion from eyes and hearts; the isolation and the deprivation; the beatings and the threats; the promises and the warnings; the blame and the punishment; the whispers in corners. Woe betide those who differ! The road with the comrades is prescribed, like the road to the old house is prescribed. Woe betide he who goes his way! . . . Oh my father, my mother, my grandmother. Oh minaret overlooking our old house. Oh comrades, everybody, make room for me among you. I am about to belong. I have come to you, the way you wanted me, a monster with no roots and no motives. (15–16)
>
> Oh mother, hide me, mother hide me. I have ceased my quest. Cover me with darkness. (62)

Sentences and words are repeated with variation throughout the novel, creating a dominant motif and establishing a continuum of Samya's experiences as a woman. Repetition serves to strengthen the similarities between the various forms of gender oppression to which she has been subjected. The narrative is both linear and cumulative, emphasizing that her alienation from the comrades is one more instance of her alienation as a woman living in a patriarchal society. She gradually comes to the realization that she cannot win as long as she abides by the rules of the game.

The novel concludes with hope. Upon seeing Rafiq's and Muhammad's pictures in the daily paper, Samya is given a chance to help her comrades and warn them that their hideout is no longer safe. She returns to the house to confront the landlord with whom she has been in conflict from the beginning of the novel. She realizes that her struggle is not with Rafiq or with her husband, two victims of the same oppressive social order, but with the owner of the house, the symbol of social, religious, and political oppression. She enters the house, no longer hesitantly and shyly, but forcefully and with determination. She realizes that "she either kills him or she dies" (113). They fight as he tries to intercept her advance: "She dug her claws in his throat. It was as if they had never succeeded in trimming her nails, never broke the sword of the warrior inside her, as if they did not transform her in a lifetime into a fragile doll" (113). Samya discovers who she is when she rids herself of her prescribed role and stereotypes of her abilities and qualities and acts on her own initiative. By exposing the oppressive and stifling acts practiced against women by proponents of liberation ideologies, al-Zayyat creates a space for women to get in touch with their subjectivity on their own terms and makes them better able to attain self-knowledge. At the end of her quest Samya cries out: "Oh father, mother, and grandmother. Oh minaret overlooking our old house. Listen everybody. Yes, I am alive. In spite of you, I am alive" (114). Magda al-Nowaihi has suggested that "it is not unreasonable to see shades of president Gamal Abdel Nasser in the figure of the owner of the house" (2000, 293), an allusion to political oppression practiced by the revolutionary elite. Also, in the 1990s, and after more than thirty years, al-Zayyat testified to the political pressure exerted on women writers by national ideologies, the belief that their freedom is not a priority issue, and that it will automatically be achieved after the success of the larger national struggle. This is a familiar story to activist women involved in national struggles, who have agreed to overlook exclusionary or discriminatory practices against them so as not to distract attention from the larger struggle. Many women lived to regret their decision.

Al-Zayyat's literary silence exposes the ambivalence of national liberation discourses toward women. *Al-Shaykhukha,* published in the mid-1980s, brings her closer to self-knowledge and allows her to face her demons, so to speak. Gradually, she reaches a point in her life, armed with a long history of struggle and a highly valued career, where she is able to voice the unsaid and the silenced. *Sahib al-bayt* is al-Zayyat's final work and her masterpiece. It is also an important landmark in the history of Arab women's writing. After confronting the social and cultural restrictions that forced her to suppress her identity as a woman, she also faced the political taboos that prevented her from criticizing the gender hierarchies within national liberation movements.

Conclusion

In a testimonial delivered in 1990 at a Forum for Women's Creative Writing in Fez and published in 1994 in *'Adab wa naqd,* al-Zayyat directly addresses the stigma associated with the title "feminist" or "women's literature":

> I am a woman, and this in my view is an important element in the definition of the self. . . .
>
> Our creative writing is consequently different from writing by male writers who belong to the same society. It might be on the same level artistically, or it might be better or worse, but in all cases it will be different. Why was it so hard for us to admit this difference? Why did I, and why do we, stubbornly deny any attempt to classify my creative work as women's or feminist literature? . . .
>
> I entrenched myself, like all women writers, in the trenches of literature. I persistently refused to have my creative writing classified as women's literature. It is either literature or no literature, art or no art. There is no such thing as male literature and female literature. I said this over and over again to anyone who posed the question, just like all Arab women writers do. These statements were said in self-defense, against persistent efforts in our Arab world to classify the literature written by women in a lesser artistic and literary status compared to literature written by men; against the use of the category "women's literature" in a derogatory manner to undermine its importance. (1996, 17–18)

Al-Zayyat's place in the Arabic canon has certainly been adversely affected by her long literary silence, compared to her male contemporaries in particular, but also by her acute awareness of the precarious position occupied by women in the national imaginary, as they are simultaneously required to affirm and to deny their female identity. Referring to al-Zayyat's position in the 1960s, Richard Jacquemond remarks that "the woman writer needed to minimize her 'difference' and deal with the large social themes in order to be recognized" (2008, 187). This she managed to achieve throughout most of her career, and she therefore has been lauded for not confining herself within the "narrow interests" of women writers.[10]

Toward the end of her life, al-Zayyat was able to lift the lid that repressed her creative writing. *Al-Bab al-maftuh,* her only novel for a long period, was very well received as belonging to a "period of maturity" in the development of the Arabic novel (Allen 1995). Its status was also enshrined in the canon because it situated women's freedom within the larger context of national freedom and Marxist class struggle, and not as a battle between men and women. This last point, the assumption that women's critique of patriarchal oppression is a battle against men, remains a dominant perception in cultural circles, and a weapon used to undermine Arab feminists, who are constantly put on the defensive and deny these allegations. Al-Zayyat steered a careful course but never undercut her feminist standpoint. She always emphasized, as she did in the novel, that both men and women are victims of cultural and social structures, but she always acknowledged the double oppression of women enforced by "public opinion, men as fathers, brothers and husbands" as well as by women who assimilated the dominant class ideologies and fell prey to false consciousness (1989, 39).

However, the importance of the novel as a worthy addition to the national literary canon was initially contested: it was nominated to the State Encouragement Prize in Literature, but despite a unanimous vote by the committee in favor of her nomination, the award was withheld because 'Abbas al-'Aqqad, a permanent member of the Higher Council for Literature and the Arts, threatened to resign in protest. His reason for objecting to

10. Despite her rejection of these cultural constraints on women writers, particularly in her late career, al-Zayyat continued to be praised for distinguishing herself from other women writers. Ibrahim 'Abd al-Majid praised al-Zayyat for not limiting her writing to the oppression of women by men they loved, a kind of "masochistic writing about a sadistic phenomenon" (1996, 25), again revealing male prejudice and derogatory assumptions about literature written by women.

the award was her "exaggerated use of the colloquial" (quoted in al-Zayyat 1993, 57). This claim is particularly interesting, as critics have subsequently identified al-Zayyat's innovative manipulation of different levels of language to accommodate and reflect the "educational background of characters and the nature of the subject discussed" (Zeidan 1995, 169). In the 1990s, *al-Bab al-maftuh* was rediscovered by feminist critics. In an article about the novel, Hiba Sharif explored the distinguishing characteristics of a feminist literature. Using the novel as an exemplary feminist text, she concluded that feminist literature is "a committed literature" that acknowledges the challenges facing women and tries to effect change; that it demonstrates "an ability to transcend the limits of a woman's personal experience and link it to larger human concerns"; and that feminist literature is directly linked to the writer's experience and often contains some biographical undertones. She also makes the point that texts that reduce the issue to the relationship between men and women cannot be counted as feminist literature (1993, 137). In the introduction to the English translation of the novel published in 2000, Marilyn Booth emphasizes the extensive use of the colloquial in *al-Bab al-maftuh* in both dialogue and internal monologue and finds this use of language a "feminist act . . . her colloquial is lively, precise, *female:* characters emerge in their choice of expression" (al-Zayyat 2000, xxvi). Certainly, the appearance of more creative writing by al-Zayyat coincided with the changing cultural scene in the 1990s, particularly the ascendance of women writers and feminist researchers. She was awarded the prestigious State Prize a few months before her death in 1996.

6

Defeated Masculinities in Sonallah Ibrahim

The second half of the 1960s ushered in a new era in the national history of Egypt, and new imaginings of nationhood and belonging. The national dream of modernization and independence from colonialism, which had climaxed in 1952 with the revolution by the Free Officers led by Gamal Abd al-Nasser, started to falter and gradually to dissipate. While Nasser continued to inspire the national dream of freedom and dignity, standing up to colonial exploitation, nationalizing the Suez Canal, implementing laws for land reform, and initiating large national projects such as the building of the Aswan Dam, signs of the dictatorial direction of his regime were soon felt. In 1954, the Muslim Brotherhood party was disbanded, in 1959 members of the Communist Party were arrested, and these events were followed in 1960 by the arrest of the Muslim brothers, initiating what has come to be known as the era of fear. Many writers and intellectuals who had welcomed the 1952 revolution with joy and much hope hesitated publicly to denounce the many signs that all was not well. This unwillingness, or cautious hesitation, to criticize the icon of the national dream is behind the tragic fate of one of his first critics, Duriyya Shafik (1908–1975). An activist in the women's movement who founded a woman's magazine in 1945 and a political party in 1953, she went on a hunger strike in 1957 to object to Nasser's dissolution of independent nongovernmental organizations and also asked for the withdrawal of Israel from Palestine. She was put under house arrest, banished from public life, accused of collaborating with imperial powers, and denounced by her friends and colleagues. She eventually committed suicide.

The above sheds some light on the reasons that Sonallah Ibrahim's *Tilka al-ra'iha* (1966; English translation, *The Smell of It,* 1971) is a seminal text in the history of Arabic literature. It has been described as a "ground-breaking novel" (Mehrez 2008, 76), and as a novel of identity that signaled a paradigmatic shift toward literary modernism in Arabic literature (Stehli-Werbeck 2006). Critics have drawn attention to the shift in mood in the literature of the 1960s, as writers grappled with feelings of alienation and disillusionment (Starkey 1998) and started searching for new beginnings and a new identity (Hafez 1976, 78). However, the novel occupies a unique place within this generation because it foregrounds the theme of the emasculation/desexualization of the national hero as a consequence of political oppression, and ushered in a breed of disempowered, impotent, and disenfranchised protagonists, or anti–national heroes.[1] It was published and immediately banned in 1966, yet it earned instant recognition and a place in the literary scene. It has also been credited with crossing the boundaries of the permissible in the political as well as artistic spheres. It is certainly a transgressive novel, as is attested by the history of its publication: it was banned in 1966, published in an expurgated edition in 1968, translated into English by Denys Johnson-Davies in 1971, and finally published in its complete form in Morocco in 1986.[2] The title of the novel is a brilliant and pithy commentary on the political contradictions under Nasser: there is a bad smell beneath the surface of a dazzling project of social and economic transformation. The novel had just hit the market when it was quickly picked up by the censor as a dangerous example of political criticism of the regime. After the 1967 defeat, it became iconic of an era when opposition was smothered in public spaces and could only be expressed obliquely in literature.

Tilka al-ra'iha constitutes a significant break with earlier texts, particularly as regards representations of masculinity. The protagonist has been described as an antihero, but more accurately as an anti–national hero, when compared to the prototypical *nahda* hero as exemplified by Hamid and later

1. Sabry Hafez fits *Tilka al-ra'iha* in his typology of the 1960s where the protagonists have "a violent desire for a new beginning . . . [and] a craving for a new identity" and describes the protagonist in *Tilka al-ra'iha* as a "nameless hero . . . [who emerges] from the womb of the prison . . . [and] welcomes life in search of a new identity" (1976, 78). This analysis does not give credit to Ibrahim's radical introduction of the disempowered and defeated antihero.

2. Paul Starkey finds the story of *Tilka al-ra'iha* proof that publishing in the Arab world is "a considerably more hazardous activity than in most western countries" (2006, 141).

by Kamal in the Trilogy. The novel ushers into Arabic literature a long array of impotent, defeated Arab men, who have been emasculated by oppressive political regimes and are rendered icons of the general political weakness and powerlessness of Arab nation-states. Unlike the previous generation of writers, Ibrahim had firsthand experience of incarceration as a political prisoner: he was arrested for his affiliation with the Communist Party; tried before a military tribunal; and sentenced to seven years in prison, of which he spent only five, between 1959 and 1964. Ibrahim's experience of oppression was inscribed on his body as he endured mistreatment and violation of his dignity. The novel belongs to the genre of prison literature, or *'adab al-sujun,* a genre that is particularly important in Arabic literature (Hafez 2002); many writers were political prisoners at some point because of their oppositional stances toward dictatorial Arab regimes, rendering the "emasculation of men under autocratic regimes" (Aghacy 2009, 96) a dominant theme.

Since making his mark on the literary scene in the late 1960s, Ibrahim (born in 1937) has occupied an ambivalent space between the margin and the center in the literary field. He continued to have a career on the edge, often finding himself in the midst of controversy.[3] His work has been subjected at the same time to vitriolic attack and resounding praise and has consistently occupied an ambivalent position in the literary field. Again the story of his first novel is a good metaphor for his later career. On the one hand, *Tilka al-ra'iha* triggered a scathing critique by a formidable writer, Yahya Haqqi, who found it disgusting and devoid of taste.[4] On the other hand, this same novel was first published with the support of, or under the patronage of, Yusuf Idris, "a master writer" who was given the manuscript by Ibrahim, suggested some changes to the text and the title, and then wrote a preface to the first edition.[5]

3. For a detailed account of Sonallah Ibrahim's cultural battles and position in the literary field, see Samia Mehrez (2008), chaps. 1 and 4.

4. See Mehrez's discussion of the reception of the novel (2008, 29).

5. Jacquemond recounts this story and interprets it as proof that "relationships between generations are not necessarily ones of conflict" (2008, 172). Mehrez's analysis, on the other hand, emphasizes the conflict between Ibrahim and representatives of the literary establishment.

In many respects Ibrahim is a typical Arab writer struggling to preserve his independence and integrity against overwhelming odds. He certainly belongs to the generation of writers who embraced the value of committed writing, interpreted largely as commitment to a national project that elevates the values of independence and freedom. He is recognized as a prominent writer, and his work has received many awards.[6] On the other hand, he has been portrayed, by some critics and writers, as the ultimate committed intellectual in the purest sense, who stands apart from his peers, insists on his freedom, hence occupying a marginal place vis à vis mainstream literary establishments. Samia Mehrez in particular makes a case for Ibrahim as the "autonomous anomaly within the Egyptian cultural field that is predominantly dominated by the state" (2008, 76). She traces the publishing history of his work and highlights key moments in his career, such as his famous rejection of a distinguished literary award by the Egyptian Higher Council for Culture in 2003, to argue that he consciously and consistently stayed away from literary centers of power in the Arab world in order to preserve his freedom and integrity as an intellectual who speaks truth to power. She also refers to an incident in 1992, when Ibrahim's novel *Dhat,* which is highly critical of the state and its apparatuses, was not nominated for the award for the best book of the year for the twenty-fifth Cairo International Book Fair, contrary to all expectations. She concludes that Ibrahim's marginalization in official cultural circles manifests Bourdieu's characterization of an autonomous field of cultural production, where the basic principle "he who loses wins" applies (Mehrez 1994, 120). Richard Jacquemond maintains that "Ibrahim's refusal [of the award] was not only a vivid expression of the freedom of the intellectual and of his mission as 'the conscience of the nation.' It was also a political stand and the exact equivalent of a parliamentary vote of censure" (2008, 229).

Accounts of Ibrahim's acceptance or rejection of literary prizes, however, are not just about a writer trying to protect his autonomy from the state: his stances shed light on the power struggles taking place between various

6. For a detailed account of Ibrahim's career and achievements as a writer, see Samia Mehrez (2008, 25–40 and 72–88).

cultural centers and elites over the shape and character of the national canon. Mehrez also tells us that Ibrahim turned down the Naguib Mahfouz award in 1996, which is granted by the American University Press in Cairo, but unlike the rejection of the award in 2003, he did not do it publicly but privately, when the committee called him to say that he was being considered. Also, in 1998, he did not show up to a ceremony to celebrate the selection of his novel *Sharaf* as the novel of the year at the Cairo International Book Fair (Mehrez 2008, 86). Ibrahim's refusal of the second award supports Mehrez's argument that he diligently tried to safeguard his autonomy from state institutions. His refusal of the AUC Press Naguib Mahfouz award, however, indicates his reluctance to legitimize another cultural center of power, also contested, because of perceptions of its affiliation with neocolonial American influence in Egypt. At the same time, Ibrahim accepted the al-'Uways Award in 1993, a fact mentioned by the minister of culture, Farouk Hosni, in 2003 to discredit Ibrahim's defiant gesture against the Egyptian state. In a footnote, Mehrez defends Ibrahim by saying that the award "was established by a wealthy, independent arts patron from the Emirates," then recounts all the prominent figures who accepted it along with Ibrahim, and concludes by saying that "Ibrahim has argued throughout that he accepted it because it was an independent award" (2008, 287). The issue is more complex than it is made out to be because state awards have also been granted to very prominent figures who accepted them, including writers who have opposed state policies. Also, cultural awards sponsored by rich Gulf Arabs or rich Egyptian businessmen have attracted much controversy and speculation about the role of money in the creation of new elites and new cultural centers that shape the canon of Arabic literature and, ultimately, new cultural and national identities. Mehrez's very insightful portrayal of Ibrahim falls in the trap of establishing rigid oppositions between writers and the state in a context that is extremely complex.

Ibrahim's work is particularly important in understanding the relationship between representations of gendered roles and the nation. The hierarchies of power governing the relationship between East and West, the nation-state and the global world order, or the new modern citizen and the national elite are invariably depicted in sexual terms, a gendered power struggle over domination and control. *Tilka al-ra'iha* portrays the devastating effect of oppressive autocratic rule on male identity. Ibrahim's worldview is tainted by the darkness of the prison cell: he does not romanticize the prison experience as a test of steadfastness and manhood, nor does he wear it as a badge of honor, as is the case in many prison novels. *Tilka al-ra'iha* inaugurates the character of the ineffectual, impotent male who has lost interest in everything and everyone. The protagonist is released from prison but is bound to report to a police officer every night. The events are told in a style that is "de-emotionalized" (Starkey 2006, 148), dispassionate, and aloof. He has lost his ability to interact with people and the world and receives the news of his mother's death without showing any feelings. He is sexually frustrated, as he is unable to have a sexual encounter with a girlfriend and also fails with a prostitute. In fact, his withdrawal from the world is almost complete, as he is unable to resume old relationships or start new ones. He is also powerless and destitute; he envies a taxi driver who smokes hashish because he has managed to find something to help him get through life. The text is interspersed with dreams and memories of times past that are a reminder of his earlier existence, prior to the prison experience. The time of the novel is almost static, as the protagonist visits friends and family, but nothing much happens. The novel also contains a letter written by a prison inmate to his wife and is delivered by the protagonist. The insertion of extraneous texts in novels becomes a stylistic characteristic of Ibrahim in his later novels.

After his "groundbreaking" novel, which registered a radical shift in the national imaginary, Ibrahim decided to devote himself to writing. In an interview, he revealed that his ambition as a young man was to become a political activist as the only way for changing the world, that he never intended to be a writer because he believed that "literature was a waste of time, an affectation." However, his prison interlude changed his life, as he "began to feel the need to tell . . . that certain things must be communicated and expressed" (Ibrahim 2003). This urge to tell, to record and document, and, in effect, to produce a counternarrative to traditional mainstream history as told in official archives and media, became Ibrahim's project and artistic trademark. Ibrahim's novels are characteristically packed with extraneous excerpts from newspapers and historical records, as is the case in *Dhat,* for example; summaries of articles and scholarly presentations, as in *al-Qanun al-faransi;* lengthy analyses of historical events delivered from the point of view of an "informed" protagonist, as in in *al-Lajna* and *Amrikanli;* and other literary conventions, such as having a play within the novel, as in *Sharaf.* These techniques, it can be argued, cross generic boundaries between fiction and historical narrative and secure a place for Ibrahim's fiction in the historical archive.[7]

Al-Lajna (1981; English translation, *The Committee,* 2001) is about a nameless man who appears before an unidentified and sinister committee. The committee, we are told, consists of three military personnel, a spinster, an old man with thick glasses who can hardly read—a large group of people wearing dark eye glasses and speaking a language that is not Arabic. The man is thanked for electing to go to the committee, an ominous undertaking, as we find out that it took him a whole year to prepare for the event. The man is expected to lay bare his life and soul to the scrutiny of members of the committee to gain approval. He is also subjected to humiliating requests and acts: he is asked to dance, and he complies with enthusiasm as he imitates the moves of professional belly dancers. He is also asked to take off his trousers and underwear and has a finger inserted in his anus. The committee member who carries out this procedure interprets the protagonist's compliance with his request as indication of his sexual orientation and turns triumphantly to the head of the committee saying: "Haven't I told you so?" ([1981] 1991, 18).[8] In response to a question about the most significant event of the twentieth century, the protagonist decides that it is the introduction of Coca-Cola to the world market, and proceeds to give a lengthy presentation that links this product to modern consumerism, wars, and globalization, as well as definitions of masculinity ("the image of the American man opening a can of Coca-Cola with his teeth became a symbol of heroism and manhood" [21]), among many other things. We discover that his quite elaborate litany is delivered while he is naked, with his pants still down. He is then asked to say something about the Great Pyramid. He tells the story of its construction and concludes

7. With reference to *al-Lajna* in particular, Noha Radwan has argued that it constitutes a "counterdiscourse to the hegemonic narrative of Egypt's socio-economic and political development" on the Egyptian American relationships (2008, 80–81).

8. All quotations are taken from this edition.

that because it required highly skilled knowledge and creativity, it is more than likely that the Egyptians sought the help of the Israelis. This story, which adopts the point of view of an Israeli narrative that is distinctly opposed to the Egyptian narrative, dissipates the tension in the room and persuades the members of the committee that he can be won over to their "global" narrative. He finally pulls up his trousers and leaves. The committee then sends him a telegraph asking him to choose and conduct a study of an Arab luminary. After dismissing all politicians and public figures, he decides to research the life of a man, the Doctor, who rose from a life of poverty and destitution to become one of the wealthiest men in Egypt. Information about the Doctor's life is not easy to find, in fact was deliberately erased, as he finds out, from public records and media. However, the protagonist manages to find alternative sources in the archives and succeeds in constructing the life of this enigmatic man. As he gets close to exposing the clandestine dealings of his subject, he is asked by the committee to stop. The committee members are convinced that he could not have arrived at this information about the Doctor on his own, so they ask the protagonist to reveal the names of his accomplices in the plot. As he is unable to comply with their request, they then decide to inflict upon him the utmost punishment and sentence him to eat himself, or self-destruct. He goes on with his life, experiencing a few moments of defiance or attempts at resisting exploitation or aggression (he threatens a medical doctor who overcharges patients for his services with a lawsuit [117]). He quickly loses steam when, after standing up to defend a woman who is harassed in a public bus, he becomes the aggressor, is attacked, and is asked to get off the bus. Still trying to express some bravado in the face of oppression, he wishes he had another chance to tell off the committee, to say that "he had made a mistake, . . . that his duty should have been to stand against them not before them" (119). Nevertheless, the novel concludes with the protagonist raising his wounded arm to his mouth as he proceeds to eat himself.

Ibrahim's antihero is defeated not by local dictators, nor by colonial aggressors as such, but by their united front in the global world order. Globalization has ushered in neocolonialism, where former colonizers have combined forces with a corrupt ruling elite to ensure their control and hegemony on the lives of all citizens of the world, especially populations in the south with a history of colonialism. The tragedy of the protagonist in *al-Lajna,* however, is not precipitated by the onslaught of globalization on the nation-state, as suggested by al-Musawi, who argues that the protagonist "stands in the position of the post-colonial nation-state: both are powerless, exposed and turned into mere recipients of the leftover" (2007, 314). Al-Musawi's analysis is in accordance with much of the literature on globalization, which is premised on an oppositional relationship in the global/local nexus, an opposition that is extended to the global and the national. Ibrahim's vision goes beyond the global/national divide, as boundaries between the global and the local are transgressed and as local actors are major players in the global hegemony and vice versa. It is useful here to refer to the concept of glocalization, introduced by Roland Robertson to "transcend the tendency to cast the idea of globalization as inevitably in tension with the idea of localization" (1995, 40). Ibrahim's project is to expose the glocal hegemony of the new world order, especially its impact on the lives of individuals. The conflict is no longer between the colonized nation-state and the colonial, but between the individual against the combined aggression of both. The protagonist's predicament, while overtly political, is also existential, as there is no hope in sight, absolutely no glimmer of light at the end of the dark tunnel. His defeat is inevitable; his impotence in the face of aggression is complete. His fate has been predetermined from the very first encounter, when he accepted the committee's invasive assault on his body. For Ibrahim, as we shall see in later novels, this penetrating assault on his manhood symbolizes ultimate surrender and humiliation.

Described as Kafkaesque,[9] the novel deliberately disturbs readers' expectations, as horrific events are told in a matter-of-fact way, heightening the tension. Elements of the grotesque permeate the text, as we witness the big-brother control of the members of the committee on the fate of the protagonist and the bizarre actions required of him, culminating in his final act of eating himself. Ibrahim's text is highly subversive. His narrative strategies

9. See Samia Mehrez (1994, 46). Roger Allen also makes a comparison with Kafka: "Sun'allah Ibrahim can be regarded as a true pioneer of Franz Kafka in his ability to make use of a disarmingly undramatic level of discourse to convey a reality that is genuinely disturbing in its routine callousness" ("Afterword" to *The Committee,* Ibrahim 2001a, 160).

and choices satirize the new world order, exposing its superficiality and perniciousness at the same time. His choice of Coca-Cola as the ultimate global consumer commodity is particularly ironic. Not only is it a symbol of American global influence, it is also marketed as an indicator of modern American/global manhood. Ibrahim satirizes the commodification of ideals of modern manhood, "hegemonic masculinity" to use Connell's phrase, while his protagonist struggles to hold onto his sense of worth and identity. And although the novel ends tragically with the defeat of the protagonist, the story remains about his ontological struggle against overwhelming odds and his persistence in challenging the glocal deluge.

In *Dhat* (1992; English translation, *Zaat*, 2001), another highly acclaimed novel by Ibrahim, political setbacks are also experienced as ontological challenges. Dhat is the name of the main female character and means "self" in Arabic.[10] It is the story of Everywoman's struggle for survival against overwhelming odds and, equipped with a miraculous ability to absorb shocks, emerge better able to deal with more hardship. It is also the specific story of every Egyptian middle-class woman whose life was transformed by the open-door economic policies introduced in the 1970s by Sadat, which resulted in a radical move away from the socialist era of Gamal Abd al-Nasser, a rise in consumerism, and the demise of the middle classes. Dhat's quest for identity and autonomous selfhood encounters obstacles, or shocks, from the moment of birth. She experiences her first shock when she enters the world and is "raised in the air, turned upside down, and smacked on her bottom" ([1992] 2003, 9),[11] the second when she is circumcised, and the third on her wedding night. Dhat's personal setbacks run parallel to the larger, macro setbacks that befall society as a whole, as a consequence of global and national transformations. The story of Dhat is punctuated with a large amount of information presented in the form of newspaper clippings, arranged in chapters that alternate with the chapters about Dhat. The information chapters shed light on

10. Quoting Ibrahim Fathi, Mehrez says that Dhat can also be "an inversion of the mythical character of Princess Dhat al-Himma who 'fought against the Romans and defended the forts during the early Abbassid period'" (1994, 130).

11. All quotations are taken from this edition.

the workings of the glocal world order, exposing callous statements about the poor by rich businessmen, the absurdity of popular religious discourse and religious figures, the contradictory statements made by politicians, corruption scandals, multinational takeovers of national businesses, and so forth. The insertion of factual extraneous sections in the novel is a form of contextualization and not documentation in order "to surround the text with a relevant discourse," according to Ibrahim (2003).

Dhat marries ʻAbd al-Majid, a minor bank employee with no university degree and limited prospects. At the start of their married life, Dhat willingly accepts his wish that she stay at home and devote herself to domestic duties. However, the Nasser ideal of a middle-class home soon dissipates with the rise in prices and consumer mentality. She takes a job in a newspaper in the monitoring department entrusted with revising printing, linguistic, political, and professional errors. The futility of her job, as no one in her department performs the assigned duties, sheds light on the absence of ethical and professional standards in newspapers, as well as the unreliability and corruption of media in general, an important theme in Ibrahim's critique of the new world order. She is then transferred to the archive department, where she struggles to be accepted by her coworkers, or the "transmission machines," who compete with other transmission machines in her building or among her family in a contest over marks of distinction, defined as wealth, in a culture dominated by vicious and unethical consumerism. On one level, Dhat's journey is depicted as a race to keep up with the Joneses. She fails repeatedly, especially with her encounters with the "transmission machines," not only because of her limited means, but also because she is basically "kind and tolerant." However, Dhat is relentless in her desire to fit in and to keep up. With every setback, she escapes to the toilet and weeps, only to pick herself up and prepare for the next round: "Does she ever despair? Never. As soon as she sheds the appropriate amount of tears, she tries again" (27). On the other hand, Dhat's "tears" are caused not only by "the marathon of transmission" (51) but also certainly by the physical changes that have befallen her immediate environment. The street that was once quiet and peaceful is now crowded with shops and covered in sewage, "the neighboring empty land, which was intended to become a garden, is a garbage dump" (51). Characteristically, Dhat takes the initiative to clean the building, but her efforts go awry. Finally, Dhat's journey is also in search of self-worth and justice, but she is consistently thwarted. A decision to report an incident of commercial fraud when she discovers that the expiration date on a pack of olives was tampered with takes Dhat, and her reporter friend, Himmat, on a futile quixotic trip that brings her face to face with the pervasive inefficiency of a corrupt bureaucracy. The unimaginable complexities of going through the system, only to arrive nowhere, are so absurd that they constitute a comic snapshot of the lack of purpose of the postmodern human condition as experienced by Dhat. At the end of the novel, she is driven by the sense of the futility of all action to her weeping place, the lavatory. Despite this final note of defeat, the fact that Dhat has been knocked down too many times already but has consistently managed to pick herself up remains a ray of hope that she will eventually summon her courage and continue to face life's trials and setbacks.

It is noteworthy that Ibrahim's tragic but unbeatable protagonist is a woman, not a man. From the moment of birth, she has been subjected to one act of aggression after another, culminating in her wedding night ordeals, which are dictated by patriarchal cultural values that seek to rob women of their sexuality. Her dissatisfaction with her life and limited means is fueled by the new consumerism that accompanied the open-door policy in the 1970s and into the 1980s. Dhat's resilience and resourcefulness are juxtaposed to her husband's. 'Abd al-Majid is also the victim of social transformations beyond his control, but whereas she resorts to practical solutions to survive, his survival mechanisms lead him first to watching porn, then to wandering in the more affluent quarters and fantasizing about young women eating ice cream, and to imagining heroic feats. At one point, Dhat decides that her son would be better off in a private school and works "quietly, drawing on all her talents in careful management of resources, saving and borrowing," while 'Abd al-Majid spends his days "rolling back and forth between the suburbs and the center, enjoying himself as he watched the ice cream, and striking numerous futile comparisons" (208).

Sharaf (1997),[12] the title of Ibrahim's novel, and the name of the protagonist, means honor. Sharaf is originally called Ashraf, meaning the most

12. All quotations are taken from this edition, and all translations are mine.

honorable. The title is extremely symbolic not only of the main conflict in the novel, as Sharaf struggles to protect his honor, but also of Ibrahim's perception of himself, as well as his perception by others, as an honorable writer in pursuit of the truth in a world governed by lies and deception.[13] We first meet Sharaf as he is walking aimlessly in downtown Cairo, staring at shop windows stacked with imported merchandise that is way beyond his means, or the means of the majority of young men his age. He reviews his options (using the English word *'ubshanz*) for passing time based on his very limited finances and is then approached by a foreign blond man who offers him a ticket to a movie. Sharaf first refuses the offer but "like all blond foreigners in Egypt, our friend was not used to being denied his request" (12). Sharaf accepts and finds out that the man, John, is an Australian who is actually English, though Sharaf thought he was American. Sharaf is invited back to John's apartment for drinks. John makes sexual advances to Sharaf, who rejects them with horror. John becomes violent. Sharaf defends himself and kills John.

In prison, Sharaf goes through many ordeals in order to survive. One of the prisoners, Batsha, tries to rape him, but he is saved by another prisoner, whom he thanks for saving "his life and his honor" (104). We soon discover that Sharaf is basically incapable of standing up for himself and generally does as he is told. At the end of the novel, Sharaf submits to what he considers to be the worst fate, when he begins to shave the hair on his body in preparation for having a sexual relationship with his cell mate. Sharaf is defeated and willingly participates in his humiliation.

The prison is depicted as a microcosm of society with all its ills and contradictions, with prisoners convicted for all sorts of crimes and coming from various walks of life. The prison is divided into two main wards, the *'anbar miri* (military ward) for the poor and the *'anbar malaki* (civilian ward) for the "rich." After a tough period in the first ward, Sharaf is transferred to the second ward, thanks to his mother's contribution to provisions on a regular

13. Mehrez discusses at length this point and analyzes an editorial by Gamal al-Ghitany entitled "Sharaf Sonallah" (Suna'allah's Honor), which pays tribute to Ibrahim's career as a writer on the occasion of the publication of *Sharaf,* making direct links between Ibrahim's honorable reputation in the literary field and the plight of his protagonist, Sharaf (2008, 25–39).

basis. In this other ward, he meets Dr. Ramzi, whose life and overall worldview are pitted against those of Sharaf. Unlike Sharaf, who is in his twenties and belongs to the "peace generation," or the "October generation" as they are sometimes dubbed, Dr. Ramzi is from an older generation who espoused the dreams of the 1950s and 1960s. He represents the ideal modern national man: middle class, well-educated, widely traveled, sophisticated, and with a social conscience. He worked for a pharmaceutical company and worked in Europe and Latin America before returning to Egypt to run the company's office in the Middle East. His twenty years experience in an international pharmaceutical company makes him a staunch critic of capitalism and the detrimental effects of globalization on Third World countries. In Egypt, he tries to resist corruption in his own company and in government offices, is implicated in a bribery charge, and ends up in prison.

The novel is divided into three parts. The first and last are narrated by an omniscient narrator, who traces the fate of Sharaf. The second part consists of three chapters that are told from the point of view of Dr. Ramzi. The first of these chapters comprises newspaper clippings, which document major cases of corruption on the national and international level. Dr. Ramzi is almost obsessive about these clippings, which he hides carefully, hence arousing the curiosity of the prison warden, who eventually manages to get hold of them with the help of Sharaf. The second chapter consists of a well-documented and well argued defense of Dr. Ramzi's case, in which he tells the story of his life, answering the question of what made him who he is, and why, though innocent, he is destined to end his life in prison. The third chapter in this part dedicated to Dr. Ramzi is a play, written and directed by him and performed as a celebration of the 6 October victory in the 1973 war against Israel. He had submitted many requests to be allowed to organize this activity with his fellow prisoners, which was finally granted by prison authorities who did not check what it was about. The performance gets out of hand, and Dr. Ramzi is put in solitary confinement, where he continues to shout out his views, trying to educate other prisoners and to encourage them to take a stand. Life in prison, however, proceeds as usual, as nobody heeds his words and he ends up "crazy" and alone.

The play, which is structured as a trial-like debate between members of the audience, representing the voice of the people or the ordinary citizen, and various figures who represent American global policies, Israeli conspiracies against Arab countries, corporate interests, and local businessmen who collaborate with international companies, just to give a few examples, is a typical critical account of exploitative global politics delivered by a character who voices the author's take on the affairs of the world. These political-historical analyses have become a trademark of Ibrahim's writing. Ibrahim's readers would typically expect a large dose of documentary information, presented as newspaper clippings, or as lectures delivered by an intellectual. In *Sharaf*, the historical analysis is presented through a play, which allows for a multiplicity of voices, but only to confirm one narrative: that we are all inevitably and irrevocably "screwed."[14]

At the end of the play, and after a repartee between audience and characters about the exploitation of the human and material resources of Third World countries in the new global order, a member of the audience tells the story of two Egyptians who went to the jungles of Africa in search of work. They were captured by a "savage" tribe and given the choice of two fates: Honga or death. From the gestures of the chief, they immediately understood the sexual implications of Honga. One of them, who valued his honor over life, chose death, while the other chose Honga. The chief then ordered both to be "Honga'd till death" (377). This becomes the final message of the play that is picked up by the prisoners as they walk away from the performance and the rioting that broke out after it, laughingly shouting: "Honga'd till death."

In his analysis of *Sharaf*, Joseph Massad has pointed out that "the Honga versus death joke is an old racist one, known in a number of colonial contexts to show how sexually depraved and mendacious Africans are" (2007, 378). He finds Ibrahim's employment of the "sexual dichotomy of civilization and barbarism [which] is part of an imperialist episteme" in relation to Africa problematic.[15] On the other hand, one can argue that Ibrahim is

14. The word repeatedly used by Ibrahim in the novel is *sakhmattuhum,* which, like screwed, has offensive sexual connotations, but also, to be cheated, made use of, exploited.

15. Massad takes issue with Ibrahim's representation of same-sex relations: "the very traps which Ibrahim sees his characters fall into are traps which he cannot avoid himself. The metaphor of rape and male honor, which structures the entire novel, beginning with its title

reversing the moral of the joke, turning it on its head so to speak, by reasserting the aggressive nature of imperialism reincarnated as globalization, and the victimized status of the peoples of the world. The irony implied in the humorous repetition of the sentence by the prisoners, in recognition of their condition, is definitely tragic and symptomatic of the tragic worldview presented by Ibrahim. According to Ibrahim, *Sharaf* is the Everyman of the global world order. He is the modern national antihero, impotent, effeminate, and violated.

Ibrahim's interest in exploring postcolonial identities under globalization, or glocalization, directs him to immerse himself in the centers of power in an attempt to better understand their psyche and sociopolitical mechanisms. His two novels *'Amrikanli* (2003), and *al-Qanun al-faransi* (2008; The French law) depict the intellectual and sexual encounters of Professor Shukri, a history scholar, with Western and Arab academics and students in the United States and France. Both novels shed light on competing historical narratives about Arab history, the role of Islam, liberation, the impact of colonialism, and the responsibility of the national elite. Shukri is portrayed as an objective and impartial historian who searches for truth and knowledge. He is radically different from an earlier generation of Arab travelers to the West whose search for identity was premised on an insurmountable opposition between the East and West. In *'Amrikanli,* he teaches a course to students at the University of California Berkeley in the late 1990s about his personal history as a contemporary Arab historian. The course highlights the connectedness between the personal and the public, the micro and the macro. At the intellectual level, Ibrahim's historical narrative is variously received by his audience of students, each according to his/her social, cultural, and political identities. For example, Fadya, who is of Egyptian origin, shows signs of dissatisfaction when Shukri flouts conservative rules of decorum in his

---

and ending with the final scene of feminization of men, is not interrogated at all, but rather confirmed throughout. Ibrahim's objection is to the literalization of buggery in the mind of his characters and their inability to see its metaphorical forms, which have more detrimental material consequences for their lives. Where Ibrahim seemingly agrees with his characters is that the crisis precipitated by globalization is a crisis of Arab masculinity" (2007, 380).

description of his feelings for a university lecturer. Muna, an Israeli student, consistently points out aspects of Arab and Islamic failure.

Shukri's personal contact with students and other ordinary American citizens, across diverse racial and social strata, sheds light on the internal conflicts within American society and the predicament of the American underdog facing challenges similar to those faced in Third World countries. The novel's title is particularly relevant to this point. *'Amrikanli* is a pun that suggests different layers of meaning.[16] It can be divided into three words, *'amri kan li,* as is the case in the subtitle, meaning "once upon a time, my fate was in my hands," or "I was the master of my fate," referring to the idea that the protagonist's life is controlled by forces beyond his reach. It also implies that some of the characters in the novel are following the American way of life, or have become "Americanized," an inversion of the colonial going native (Naaman 2006, 80). Or it can be a comment on the deceptive glitter of things American, as used by Shukri in one of his lectures, where he tells students that *'amrikanli* was used in this sense in Egypt after the Second World War, when the markets were flooded with less durable American goods to fill the gap created by the scarcity of durable goods from England and Germany (2004, 180). This last connotation is the most relevant to the main theme of the novel, which explores the internal ills, or the less glamorous side, of a rich superpower and portrays the United States as a decadent empire that is rotting from the inside and is on the brink of decline.[17] Mrs. Chadwick, the department secretary who is befriended by Shukri, shares with him her worries about her future and her helplessness in the face of her daughter's drug addiction. At the same time, we meet several Arabs who have escaped from grim futures at home, only to find themselves caught in other webs of corruption and disillusionment. Mahir, an Egyptian academic who left for the United States on a scholarship, decides to stay and is at pains to justify his satisfaction with his life choices by consistently pointing out the advantages

16. For an excellent discussion of the title see Naaman (2006, 79–80).

17. Mona al-Ghobashy has argued that *'Amrikanli* echoes *Osmanli,* "the disparaging Egyptian slang for the externally powerful, internally rotting Ottoman Empire that ruled the Middle East for centuries" (quoted in Naaman 2006, 79–80).

of life in the United States. He is forced to modify his research agenda to accommodate the Gulf Arab funder of his research center, and he disregards his wife's unhappiness in the land of plenty. Compared to other depictions of America in Arabic literature, Ibrahim's America is complex and multifaceted, seen through the "competing lenses . . . [of] the male gaze of the narrator, the critical gaze of the Third World Marxist critic, and the sympathetic gaze of the humanist writer" (Naaman 2006, 75).[18] Like that of the protagonist in *al-Lajna,* Shukri's narrative is not premised on a geocultural binarism between the oppressor and the oppressed, or a colonial West and a colonized East. His ability to empathize with the marginalized in imperial loci of power destabilizes the East vs. West dichotomy and allows him to go beyond the civilizational opposition.

We meet Shukri again a few years later, in *al-Qanun al-faransi,* on a trip to France to attend first a conference on Napoleon in Egypt, and then another one to protest the passing of a law that validates colonialism by paying tribute to the role of French colonials in spreading the light of civilization to the dark continent, among other things. The novel consists of detailed expositions of papers and arguments presented during the conferences, representing conflicting narratives about the impact of colonialism on the Arab region. Shukri puts forward a critical counternarrative to the dominant modernist one that marks the first sparks of the Arab renaissance with the encounter with Western civilization through Napoleon's "expedition," and he cites Western and Arab sources to prove his point. His critical stance is not necessarily shared by all Arab participants, nor is it rejected by all French scholars: Ibrahim is careful to show that positions are not demarcated by nationality or geographical location. The novel is primarily about the impact of colonial violence on both the colonized and the colonizers. The theme is explored through the intellectual characterization of

18. Naaman takes issue with Ibrahim's "painfully long lessons on US and Egyptian history" (79), his depiction of "America-as-hyper-sexualized space" (82), and his "caricatures of [American] women" (82) but concludes that he nevertheless succeeds in presenting a much more nuanced picture of the other. It is noteworthy that Ibrahim's "sexualized gaze" is not reserved for American women but is actually a feature of his work in general.

a diverse group of Arab and Western academics in their response to their colonial burden. To give just one example, the participation of an Israeli diplomat in the conference triggers conflicting responses that are indicative of their political stances in relation to neocolonial projects. Also, the narrator includes a presentation by a conference participant, Rafiq Sulayman, entitled *Lathat al-musta'mir* (The pleasure of the colonizer) (2008, 103–13), where he analyzes the political and cultural implications of the circumstances surrounding the commemoration of the French colonial interlude in Egypt, a highly contested moment in Arab history. He sheds light on the controversy that overshadowed the event and concludes that the insistence of state officials in Egypt on celebrating colonialism indicates a psychological aberration, in which the colonized finds pleasure in the colonial violence inflicted on his/her identity.

On the other hand, the two conferences take place in an imperial center and against the background of the riots that erupted in Paris in October and November 2005 in the poor suburbs where a majority of immigrants, mainly from France's North African ex-colonies, live. The riots expose the underlying racial tensions in French society and the long-lasting effects of the colonial past on the French metropolis. The intellectual confrontations about the meaning and implications of colonial invasions carried out inside the conference halls are paralleled, albeit violently, on the streets of Paris. In the second half of the novel, Shukri attempts to delve into the psyche of the colonizer through his encounter with a French woman, Celine, who manages an educational association that supports the integration of the children of immigrants into French society. The two are attracted to each other, have similar interests, and read the same books. Celine's attraction to Shukri, however, is offset against her repulsion of him as an Arab. Her prejudice is subtly hinted at in sarcastic comments that challenge Shukri's analysis of neocolonial exploitation of the Third World. In the final scene, Shukri is totally oblivious to her visceral rejection of his narrative and himself, which she finds threatening to her worldview. The contrast between his expectations of a night of intimacy and her final drunken outburst against his advances and expectations reveals the distance between his intellectual aspirations and reality. In the morning, he finds a note from her on his doorstep that leaves him in no doubt of her position: "My answer is that you are actually a naïve and backward person" (2008, 228). In this incident, Celine concretizes the scarring effect of colonial violence on Western civilization. Ibrahim's French interlude is very different from previous depictions, where civilizational differences are gendered and constitute reversals of colonial violence against the self. Here, Ibrahim quickly establishes the many similarities between Celine and Shukri. These however, are destroyed as Celine, like France with the immigrant rioters, is unable to accept the "other" and perceives him as a threat.

Tilka al-ra'iha ushered in the defeated and impotent antihero who has been deceived by revolutionary fervor and empty dreams. Much has been written about the predicament of this antihero in the novels of Jamal al-Ghitany (henceforth Gamal al-Ghitany), Yusuf al-Qa'id, and others. In conclusion, I would like to bring to light a forgotten but important text that appeared ten years after the publication of *Tilka al-ra'iha,* 'Asma Halim's *Hikayat 'Abdu 'Abd al-Rahman* (1977; The story of Abdu Abd al-Rahman),[19] about another impotent antihero. Unlike Ibrahim's hero, who is a political activist, the novel is about the life of a poor, working-class man who is victimized and oppressed before and after the Nasser era. The novel is written from the point of view of a first-person narrator, 'Abdu, and traces his journey from childhood to adulthood, as he moves from one impossible situation to another. It is a very powerful testimony to feelings of oppression and impotence in the face of dire poverty and systematic exploitation by various institutions. 'Abdu's father dies when he is very young, and he moves with his sister and mother to live with his maternal uncle. Although he is allowed to go to school, his sister is kept at home, and his mother becomes a servant who is mistreated by his uncle's wife. Upon his graduation, he is offered a job at his uncle's farm in return for food and accommodation. His uncle visits him once a week with his food provisions, which means that he goes hungry if the uncle fails to show up. After an unpleasant incident with one of the tenants at the farm, 'Abdu decides to leave and takes a low-paid job in a factory. His salary barely covers his basic needs. 'Abdu's predicament as a poor worker is

19. All quotations are taken from this edition. All translations are mine.

poignantly expressed in very simple terms: "I was paid seven piastres for a very long time. A very long time that extended to years. Holidays were not paid, and were always followed by a bitter struggle to survive" (32).

While still working at the factory, the July 1952 revolution takes place. 'Abdu was taken by surprise: "I woke up one day and found a revolution in the country . . . when workers at the factory told me that they had dethroned the King, I did not believe it" (72). He continues to wonder at the bravery of the officers who did that in the face of a powerful monarch supported by British troops. He goes out to celebrate with other workers, but he loses his voice and runs away feeling stifled. He finally manages to muster some hope for a better future and better working conditions, only to be disillusioned very quickly:

> A day passed and then a week and another week, and the feeling that fluttered in my heart subsided. What I expected did not happen, did not arrive: I am not sure what I expected. A revolution happened in the country, but it did not reach me. I should have expected this, as a wave does not reach all the sand pebbles on the beach unless it is overwhelming. My pains returned, the rheumatic pains in my joints, and the pain in my soul, and the ennui. (77)

In effect, the revolution has no impact on his life and does not satisfy his dreams for a better future. He eventually leaves the factory and takes a desk job in a company. His situation remains the same: he is exploited by his colleagues, as he does their work for them. His relationship with his colleagues deteriorates while he continues to make more concessions to them. He gets into a bloody fight with them and is arrested by the police.

For the first time in his life, 'Abdu stands up for himself when threatened with rape and humiliation by a gangster in his prison cell, who asks him to take off his trousers. He decides to fight for his honor: "I told myself: hold on to your trousers and die for them. He does not want your trousers, but he wants to expose your private parts [*'awratak*]. He wants to violate you, if not physically, then morally. Die wearing your trousers, 'Abdu, so that you die a human being. Resist. If you do not resist now, when will you resist?" (155). 'Abdu is acquitted and leaves prison a changed man. He has finally confronted his oppressor and gained the respect of his fellow inmates.

Unfortunately however, it does not last long, as once more he falls prey to exploitation and oppression, this time by his sister and her husband. The novel ends with 'Abdu's attempt to makes sense of his life:

> Am I a defeated human being, as I hear them say about me? Life has defeated me more than once, but the Nile made amends and comforted me.
>
> But, where is it now? . . .
>
> The Nile that tended to my wounds and cleansed my soul, where is it now? I do not know why my feet are heavy and have lost their way. (169–70)

'Abdu's impotence and lack of will and determination in the face of oppressive institutions and conditions is also played out on a sexual level. He succumbs to the unwanted and unsolicited attention of two women in the novel. The first one, an old woman in his uncle's farm, 'Umm Ibrahim, offers him food in return for his acceptance of her sexual advances. He is repulsed by her but acquiesces. Unable to bear this relationship, he decides to escape and leave the farm altogether, to get far away from this "depressing" woman. The second is a maid in his relative's house, where he spends two years. Again, she forces herself on him and he agrees unwillingly. Her flirtations gradually turn into aggressive attacks, and then into material exploitation as she extracts from him a monthly allowance for an alleged pregnancy. As with his encounter with Umm Ibrahim, 'Abdu is ashamed of himself but does not refuse her advances. And again he escapes by moving out.

Although he accepts these humiliating sexual encounters with women, in which he is overpowered, almost emasculated, when faced with rape later on in prison by one of the inmates, he decides to resist. His final act of resistance gains him some respect and a boost to his self-esteem. But it does not last long, as he returns to his old ways of uninterrupted surrender, powerlessness, and impotence.

Writing in the 1970s, after the 1967 defeat, 'Asma Halim concretizes the overriding feeling of national impotence and defeat in her depiction of a poor spineless victim of exploitation and oppression. 'Abdu is a far cry from the ideal national modern man envisaged as the logical outcome of the success of the national struggle for independence. His lot basically remains unchanged, and his life is almost untouched by the grand developments on the national front. His very existence begs the question of what went wrong with the projects of national independence. The novel is certainly a harsh indictment of the failed promises of freedom and prosperity meted out to the working classes by a revolutionary elite. 'Abdu's impotence in the face of adversary is a consequence of a life of oppressive poverty and exploitation. His personal defeat is symbolic or symptomatic of national defeat.

PART THREE

7

The Personal Is Political

Debating the New Writing in the 1990s

"The literature of the 1990s" has become a phrase widely used to refer to new directions in writing in Egypt, spearheaded by a new generation of young men and women who consciously distinguished their literary production from that of previous generations. The controversial "new writing" triggered many debates about the relationship between the writer and society, and also about the definition and contours of the national canon of Arabic literature. Two literary debates erupted in Egypt in the 1990s about the literary production of this new generation of writers. The first revolved around the value of their writing from a nationalist perspective, as critics and cultural commentators negatively judged them for not being "interested in *al-qadaya al-kubra*" (the big issues; Badawi 1999), for having relinquished the larger sociopolitical concerns that characterized the work of previous generations of writers, and for focusing too much on the narrow confines of the self and on the minute details of daily life. Prominent writers expressed their concern for what they saw as the "new generation's complete indifference to politics."[1] The debate about *al-qadaya al-kubra* is linked to another debate about the artistic contribution of women writers. References to the literary production of a new generation of young women writers as *kitabat al-banat* (girls' writing) and qualifying some of their work under the headline *kitabat al-jasad* (writing the body) were hotly debated

1. Baha' Tahir, in an interview with Elisabeth Kendall (2003, 55). Also, for a detailed discussion of the beginnings of the new writing see Kendall (2006).

as indicative of a hegemonic and patriarchal literary establishment. Again, their writing was deemed to be apolitical and too focused on the self. Young writers, both men and women, contested these critical judgments, arguing that they were based on false dichotomies that they consciously sought to supersede. Two texts, *Qamis wardi farigh* (An empty pink shirt) by Nura Amin, and *Dunyazad,* by May Telmissani, were at the center of the controversy about women writing their bodies and the apolitical characteristic of the new writing. I argue that both texts are emblematic of the feminist motto "the personal is political" foregrounding the act of writing as praxis, and consequently subverting essentialist oppositions between the public and private spheres.

Critics have tried to pin down the distinguishing characteristics of the new generation of writers. Many have noted that the novels are markedly short, typically 100 to 150 pages long (Mehrez 2001–2, 34). In addition, young writers have certainly benefited from a phenomenon that is probably peculiar to the Egyptian scene, namely the relative ease of publishing a novel or a collection of short stories or poems. This ease is partly behind the sheer quantity and volume of the Egyptian literary production at present, bearing in mind that Egypt is the most populous Arab country. Credit is always given for the establishment of new publishing houses, which are not state owned, but run by entrepreneurial publishers, particularly Dar sharqiyyat, and Dar merit (established in 1998). Critics have referred to the new generation of writers as the Sharqiyyat generation. Muhammad Hashim, owner of Dar merit, is acknowledged as a supporter, or mentor, of the new writing.[2] His office, according to many accounts, became the meeting hotspot for writers to get together and interact. And even though writers are often expected to contribute to the cost of publishing and are aware that it is highly unlikely that they will be compensated for their work, the fact that these small publishing

2. Muhammad Hashim, the owner of Dar merit, was awarded the 2006 Jeri Laber International Freedom to Publish Award by the Association of American Publishers International Freedom to Publish (IFTP) Committee. He certainly played a role in supporting young publishers by facilitating the process of publishing and distribution. See Mehrez (2001–2) and Jacquemond (2004).

houses are not state owned and not regulated by mainstream literary elite has resulted in encouraging new writing and new tastes.

The contemporary literary scene is also characterized by the advent of writers belonging to previously marginalized communities. Sabry Hafez has emphasized the significant literary presence of writers who are the product of the new informal housing settlements, *'ashwa'iyyat,* that have characterized urban spaces in the last two decades. In an influential study that attempts to construct a topology for the literary production in the 1990s in Egypt, Hafez refers to accusations leveled against the new generation of writers, namely that they are nihilistic and disengaged from reality. He argues that the transformations in the new literary text cannot be understood in isolation from "the transformations in the cultural reality from which they emerged": Sadat's ominous (*mash'um*) economic *infitah* (open-door policy); the consequences of the feeling of defeat; the spread of corruption even in universities; the eruption of political violence; the privatization policies that resulted in "selling (read pillage) of the property of the people without their consent, a fact which renders the process illegitimate" (Hafez 2001, 186–88). After painting a very bleak picture of the historical moment that gave birth to the new writing, he examines the defining role of place, the physical environment of the new generation of writers. He focuses on the rise of the *'ashwa'iyyat* in urban spaces, on marginal dwellings, on cemetery dwellings, on new forms of living that have mushroomed on the margins of the city of Cairo as well as in its center, resulting in the formation of new forms of expression (2001, 188–93). The state is almost nonexistent in the "third city," as he calls these new areas, and authority is concentrated in the mosque or in the hands of the neighborhood bully (*futuwwa*) (2001, 192). Hafez foregrounds the importance of place, or the landscape inhabited by the individual, as a significant indicator of influence and argues that the 1990s novel is the child of the "third city," that many of the writers of the 1990s are sons of this third city, and "even those who are not her biological sons are still sons of its imaginary, its time and its rhythm" (2001, 195).

In an article that posits the family as "the central national icon" in the tradition of the novel, Samia Mehrez notes a thematic variable in selected texts published in the 1990s that herald "the death of the family" (2001–2, 31, 34). This death is heir to the post-*infitah* generation of the 1980s and leads to unexpected results. Drawing on the modernist dichotomy between family (as community, collective belonging) and the individual, she argues that the death of the family, in this case, "rather than announce the birth of the individual . . . announce[s] his/her death" as well (2001–2, 33–34). At the end of her essay, she poses a question raised by Richard Jacquemond about whether the writers of the 1990s will return to the family/national icon after they are recognized and established.[3] She concludes that the journey undertaken by these writers is "one of no return, for there is, perhaps, nothing left to return to" (2001–2, 48).

Richard Jacquemond prefaces his discussion of the 1990s by noting the "unprecedented" freedom of expression available since the early 1980s (2004). This has been augmented with a "revolutionary push" by the new generation of writers, "ostensibly turning their backs to the 'great causes' (*al-qadaya al-kubra*) . . . [and] they give publicity to self discourses and self images which the dominant moral either condemns or tolerates on the condition that they remain within the sphere of orality and privacy" (2004, 42). Jacquemond proceeds to unpack the predicament of the new generation within a literary environment that is inimical to understanding their creative endeavor. He discusses three cases in which literary works were subjected to informal censorship and examines the arguments used by literary critics who came to the defense of the writers under attack, arguing that the problem arises from within the field of literary criticism itself. Citing Ferial Ghazoul's defense of Muhammad Shukri's novel *al-Khubz al-hafi* (English translation, *For Bread Alone,* a novel that was at the center of a notorious case of censorship at the American University in Cairo),[4] Jacquemond maintains that her main argument "is in conformity with the realistic-reformist theme: the immorality of the literary work is explained and justified by reference not to art's autonomy, but to a social reality itself immoral—the debasement imposed by colonial domination" (2004, 48). He concludes that "the dominant ideology in the

3. Richard Jacquemond, "Le Champ Litterraire," PhD diss., Université Aix-Marseille, 1999. Quoted in Mehrez (2001–2, 48).

4. For a detailed account of the controversy surrounding the novel, see Samia Mehrez (2008, 229–50).

field itself . . . the realistic reformist paradigm, has proven its ineptitude to establish an autonomous conception of art and literature." Jacquemond's analysis of the Shukri affair foregrounds the dominance of a reformist agenda as an essential function of literature, generally defined as sociopolitical relevance to the larger concerns of the national community, coupled with a realist paradigm, narrowly defined as verisimilitude, faithful depiction of the "real" world. In other words, much of the resistance to the new writing and its perceived inconsequentiality to *al-qadaya al-kubra,* a sort of nonnational allegiance, is first and foremost a function of the dominant ideology among an Arab literati that continues to privilege a national narrative narrowly defined to represent their particular worldview.

Finally, the new writing has been described as highly experimental in the use of both language and themes. These new experiments are constantly evolving, interacting with the changing conditions in the new global order, and inscribing new idioms and imaginaries. Moreover, some young writers have certainly taken the Egyptian cultural scene by storm. Their use of language has shocked the literary establishment and constitutes a significant diversion from conventional literary norms and structures. To quote Gamal al-Ghitany, the new generation of writers uses a language that no one in his own generation [that of the 1960s] "dared think about, a language that equips writers with better tools to depict reality" (quoted in al-Hadari 2007.

Many writers from the generation of the 1990s have directly or indirectly engaged with critical debates about their work, particularly the claim about its sociopolitical irrelevance, arguing that the problem lies with a literary establishment that is not up to speed with new developments and has fixed tastes that originated in previous decades. Yasir 'Abd al-Hafiz qualifies the ongoing debate about the 1990s as symptomatic of a generational war ignited by the hegemonic presence of critics whose literary tastes and criteria are biased toward the literary production of the generation of the 1960s.[5] Mansura 'Iz al-Din (henceforth Mansoura Ez Eldin) agrees, adding that one of the main problems lies in the critical scene: most critics are still caught up

5. Yasir 'Abd al-Hafiz, interview with author, 27 December 2006.

in the styles and the moods of the 1960s and have failed to decipher the specificity of the new generation.[6] Ibrahim Farghali agrees that the literary scene is still controlled by critics who "belong to old and obsolete schools of criticism" and who have failed to provide the necessary critical appraisal that would have guided the new generation, so much so that the new "texts are literally emerging on their own two feet."[7] He is optimistic about the future of "non-traditional literary writings" (2006a, 89). Another view put forward is that "there are no *qadaya kubra.* Had there been any, we would have written about them. . . . In the sixties there were real issues. . . . Songs were real; Salah Jahin[8] genuinely believed in what he wrote [with reference to the national dream]."[9] Mustafa Zikri concurs and foregrounds the national vacuum experienced by the new generation:

> Contemporary Egyptian writers have abandoned the big issues that occupied the older generation. There is no longer a nation, nor are there the dramatic breakdowns and defeats, only a narrative embodying all styles. . . . This is a genre of writing we might call existential, naked. . . . It is of a form that belongs to the individual, that turns away from the collective, and that views with suspicion issues of politics, history and society. (Zikri 2006, 82)

Other writers adopted a confrontational approach and resorted to a strategy of reversal, validating the claim that their generation is isolated and alienated from larger social concerns. Safa' al-Najjar describes the new writing as a "literature of the ghetto," entirely unaffected by political movements and circulating "within the circle of the literati" (2006, 100). On the other hand, many writers dismiss the debate as contrived and based on erroneous assumptions.[10] Hamdi al-Jazzar contests the critical tendency to categorize

6. Mansoura Ez Eldin, interview with author, 27 December 2006.

7. Ibrahim Farghali, interview with author, 24 December 2006.

8. Salah Jahin (1930–1986) was a prominent poet, cartoonist, and playwright.

9. Yasir 'Abd al-Hafiz, interview with author, 27 December 2006.

10. Yasir 'Abd al-Latif, interview with author, 28 December 2006. He concedes that perhaps this issue is relevant to poetry because "there was a tradition of political poetry with prominent voices such as 'Amal Dunqul, Fu'ad Haddad, and Salah Jahin . . . but now poetry is more individualistic . . . closer to lyrical poetry."

and to create typologies based on generations or characteristic features. About the absence of *al-qadaya al-kubra* in the writing of the 1990s, he cites young authors who do tackle sociopolitical issues in their work. He then adds that even if one accepts that there is an absence of the sociopolitical, then that is in itself a form of objection.[11] Finally, Mansoura Ez Eldin faults the new generation of writers for fueling a false controversy. She argues that "a lack of genuine critical scrutiny," a problem compounded with the "ease with which they [novels in the 1990s] can be published," has resulted in the entry into the literary scene of "writers who lack both talent and adequate knowledge of techniques and strategies" (2006, 52). She dismisses as banal and superficial the literary manifestos that were published in the early 1990s by writers who celebrated writing about the self in contrast to writing about societal concerns. According to her, such work only reveals their ignorance of what writing the self really means.[12]

The 1990s saw a marked rise in the number of women writers in the cultural scene leading to "gender equality in literary production," to use the words of Samia Mehrez (2001–2, 126). There were as many if not more women writers producing work worthy of critical attention, as manifested in numerous conferences, seminars, special issues in prominent literary magazines, and reviews that were devoted to women writers and their work. In addition, many of the writings by women, first novels by young writers, were selected for translation, hence gaining international recognition and status. There emerged a perception that there was an artificial prominence given to women writers, disadvantaging male writers and corrupting the cultural scene. What is new here is an unprecedented volume of literary production by women, coinciding with an increased market interest in women's issues in local and global contexts. The high profile of creative women's presence and visibility in the literary scene triggered an aggressive backlash, driven and orchestrated by gatekeepers troubled by the rapidly changing key players in the cultural field. The severity of the campaign launched indiscriminately against women

11. Hamdi al-Jazzar, interview with author, 25 December 2006.

12. Mansoura Ez Eldin interview, ibid.

writers is not dissimilar to the concerted effort to undercut the contribution of young writers of the 1990s: in this case, however, there is the added gender dimension thrown into the equation. A long-standing controversy around the value of using the terms "women's literature," or "feminist literature" was transformed into a deliberate effort, be it conscious or unconscious, to undermine the work of young women writers, by referring to their writing as *kitabat al-banat* (girls' writing).

The idea of women's literature, or feminist literature, has usually been met with skepticism and overt or covert hostility in Arab literary circles. "Feminist" in Arabic, is heavily laden with negative, even pejorative, connotations, ranging from man-hating, masculinized women to cultural traitors and agents of the West. This perception explains why the majority of Arab women writers refuse to use this label to describe themselves. The phrase "women's literature," on the other hand, is also suspect, as it has been used to suggest a lesser form of literature that cannot hold its own against mainstream literature, which is ascribed to universal standards of artistic excellence. Some writers and critics try carefully to position themselves in this debate. Yumna al-'Id, a prominent critic, rejects the term "women's literature" or feminist literature. She points out, however, that male critics have often disregarded important literary works by women, such as Labiba Hashim's *Qalb al-rajul* (The heart of man), published in 1904, ten years before the canonical first Arabic novel, *Zaynab* by Haikal (al-'Id 2002a, 8). The implication is that the category of women's literature can be misleading; it is potentially useful only insofar as it foregrounds women's contribution to the literature and exposes critical prejudice against women writers, hence eventually carving a space for them in the tradition.

It is important to note here that women writers in the modern period have carved a space for themselves through their many established contributions to the Arab literary tradition, beginning in the second half of the nineteenth century and throughout the twentieth. In other words, women's participation in the literary field is neither a novelty nor an unusual phenomenon that merits exceptional perusal. It is equally important to note that prejudice against literary women, manifested in critical endeavors to undermine their contribution, goes as far back as the reception of women's writing in the late nineteenth and early twentieth century. What is new is the scale and intensity of the antagonism, at a historical moment when many Arab women writers have succeeded in gaining prominence and status in national as well as international contexts.

The debate about women's writing in the 1990s escalated as growing numbers of young women writers entering the literary field were grouped together as *al-banat* (girls), after phrases such as *kitabat al-banat* (girls' writing), *mawsim kitabat al-banat* (season of girls' writing), and *al-banat yaktubna ajsadahunna* (girls write their bodies) were used by prominent critics and circulated widely in the media and in literary magazines. Many young writers, both men and women, challenged the labels and their implications, while some felt targeted and disadvantaged because of the exaggerated attention given to women's creative writing. In an article that mainly explores the reactions of young men writers to the phenomenon of "girls' writing," one writer recounted that the only time he felt bitter was when a German translator said that she could not translate his first novel because that only happened with women writers, and that publishers would only translate a second novel by a male writer.[13] Another expressed his bafflement at why the media is intent on celebrating women's writing, saying that much of the fuss was over mediocre writers who were only recognized because they were women.[14] Others pointed out that this attempt to approach literary phenomena as "isolated islands" cut off from their context was in line with the social isolation experienced in society.[15] Somaya Ramadan, a writer who started publishing in the 1990s, remarked that the use of the word *banat* to refer to young women writers, although seemingly an intimate manner of address, testified to "a patriarchal sense of superiority" toward younger women. She further argues that the labeling of new writing by women as a "phenomenon" is a clear indication of the hierarchical structures that attempt to diminish its dominance (1996, 36). Samia Mehrez objected to the term "girls' writing,"

13. Ahmad Gharib, quoted in al-Hafiz (1996, 8).
14. Mustafa Zikri, quoted in al-Hafiz, (1996, 8).
15. Muntasir al-Qaffash, quoted in al-Hafiz, (1996, 8).

describing it as crass, but also misleading, as it suggested that this is a new phenomenon.[16] Mehrez endorsed public and literary efforts to foreground women's literature and argued for the legitimacy of this critical trend as it sheds light on alternative voices that have been traditionally marginalized.

Kitabat al-jasad, writing the body, is another phrase that became associated with the new generation of women writers in the 1990s and was deliberately manipulated by some critics to suggest that women writers were at the forefront of the fight against conservatism and religious fundamentalism by openly challenging cultural taboos and writing explicitly about their bodies and their sexual relationships. This seemingly liberal attitude, however, was double-edged: while outwardly championing the "cause" of women by foregrounding the specificity of their voice and their experience, it became, to use the words of one writer and critic, synonymous with pornographic writing (al-Hafiz 1997b, 9). Thus it effectively undermined the literary value of the writers in question. Somaya Ramadan openly challenged Ahmed ʿAbd al-Muʿti Hijazi, prominent poet and critic, and editor of the state-owned literary journal *'Ibdaʿ,* who devoted a special issue of the magazine to short stories by young women writers under the title: *al-Banat yaktubna 'ajsadahunna fi khams ʿashr qissa* (The girls write their bodies in fifteen stories). Ramadan does not mince words; she draws attention to Hijazi's prejudices and patriarchal attitude to young writers, as well as his manipulation of the prevailing ambivalence of the concept of "writing the body" in Arab cultural circles in such a way as to consolidate misconceptions about its meaning.[17]

There is widespread consensus that the 1990s ushered in a new writing. Definitions of this newness, the characteristic markers that distinguish this generation from previous ones, have been the subject of debate and much critical reflection. Focusing on women's autobiographical writing in

16. Samia Mehrez, quoted in al-Hafiz (1996, 9).

17. Ramadan's, "Hawla malaff al-banat yaktubna 'ajsadahunna: lisan wa shafatan" (1996) was published as a direct response to a special issue published by *'Ibdaʿ* under the title "al Banat yaktubna ajsadahunna fi khams ʿashar qissa," which was prefaced with an introduction by the editor, Ahmad ʿAbd al-Muʿti Hijazi, a prominent poet and critic. Hijazi publishes Ramadan's rebuttal but precedes it with his response and says that she misunderstood the point (*'Ibdaʿ* 1996, 34).

particular, Khayri Duma, professor of Arabic and literary critic, rejects a view held by many critics and writers, such as Sabry Hafez, that all criticism of women's autobiographical tendencies harbors deep-seated prejudice against women and their contributions by claiming that they are narrowly focused on the personal and are radically removed from public concerns, social, cultural, or political. Autobiographies written by earlier generations of Arab writers, Duma argues, such as Taha Husayn and Latifa al-Zayyat, have always incorporated national concerns in their life stories. Even the generation of the 1960s who pioneered "experimental autobiographical writing to counter realism" integrated social and political concerns in their writing. He posits that the 1990s generation of men and women writers are completely wrapped up in their own private worlds (Duma n.d., 14–15) but are not necessarily uninterested in addressing issues of a larger magnitude. He concludes, however, that the emphasis on the personal is not an innovation they can claim, and that it is an extension of a direction that began with the generation of the 1960s. The difference lies in the increased participation of women writers in the literary scene in the 1990s. The other major difference is that the 1960s writers had "their own vision of life and the role of art," whereas for the young writers in the 1990s "everything around them is mired, confusing, with unclear horizons," a condition that makes it impossible to have any sense of purpose or vision for their own lives and their society (28). This is a variation on the idea that the younger generation are not interested in *al-qadaya al-kubra,* justifying their assumed lack of concern with the sociopolitical to a material reality defined by confusion and lack of clarity.

Nura Amin's *Qamis wardi farigh* (1996; An empty pink shirt) is an artistic enactment of *l'écriture féminine* championed by Hélène Cixous, the renowned French feminist theorist, an experimental praxis of writing the body. Amin (born in 1970) herself is a talented and avant-garde feminist writer, performer, and theater director. In addition to her literary publications, two novels and four collections of short stories, she has also written and performed many experimental plays and participated in numerous theater workshops. Amin trained with masters of the theater, particularly Augusto Boal (Brazilian dramatist, director, and founder of the Theatre of the Oppressed), an experience that "reunited [her] with the old notion of art as a tool for political and social change" (Amin 2004). Amin's career as a writer of fiction and dramatic performances is consistent with her quest to transgress established norms and to defy the status quo in order to attain self-awareness.

Amin uses the concept "writing the body" to describe her literary production. She argues that one of the crises her generation is facing is a crisis with their bodies, a crisis caused by the cultural values that are imprinted particularly on the female body (al-Hafiz 1997b), locking it in cultural taboos and stereotypes. Her literary project can be understood as a persistent struggle against hierarchical structures of thought, as well as cultural, literary, and linguistic conventions that restrict the horizons of expression available to women writers who are struggling to find a voice of their own. Amin is clearly influenced by Hélène Cixous's call to women to "write through their bodies" (1976, 866) because only in writing lies "the possibility of change, the space that can serve as a springboard for subversive thought, the precursory movement of a transformation of social and cultural structures" (879). *Qamis wardi farigh* is a transgressive text that consciously experiments with various strategies to disrupt readers' conventional cultural expectations about love relationships, as well as the conventions of writing themselves.

Qamis is a very short novel, approximately eighty pages long. It is about a love relationship between a man and a woman, but it is primarily about the writing of the story, the awareness of the author that she is constantly observing herself and recording her emotions and thoughts. The novel is semiautobiographical: Nura, the protagonist, is a writer, translates from French into Arabic, and has a daughter called Jamila, all corresponding to the biographical details of the author. The novel is dedicated to Marguerite Duras, the French novelist, and a major influence on Amin and her career. At some level, the act of writing takes over and controls the relationship. The protagonist admits to her obsession with writing all the details of the relationship and worries that her lover will eventually feel like a guinea pig rather than her muse. She wonders: "when will I be free from the bondage of recording your features in writing? When will I cease investing the details you give me as a literary opportunity?" (1996, 24).[18]

18. All quotations are taken from this edition. All translations are mine.

In *Qamis,* Nura, the writer/narrator, is besotted by "the writing of her hoped for ecstasy" (23). She sacrifices having a real-life relationship in return for "eloquent papers and a documented imagination" (23). Writing is "the only intimate friend" (36); all her "moments of ecstasy/pleasure are inscribed 'written moments'" (32); she recalls her lover through writing (35); she writes to pick herself up and regain control over her life (67); all is finite except writing (85). Writing is personified: it keeps her company as she sits waiting for her lover (43). Writing becomes a measure of time, "fifty pages ago" (86). In effect, her life is textual, as her writing takes precedence over life.[19]

The narrator/author is also aware of her artistic strategies and shares them with the reader. Despite the nonlinear narrative, as the novel develops according to a stream of consciousness, with flashbacks and numerous pauses to comment and reflect on the narrative, the narrative is tightly structured. It is divided into four parts, with titles that are variations on the main title of the novel. *Qamis* (shirt) has multiple connotations in the novel: it is the novel that contains the story; the experience of writing; the intimate bond that ties human beings in a relationship; the cover that shields and protects; or the weight that burdens and suffocates.[20] *Wardi* (pink) implies a rosy attitude to life, often a fantasy world where girls travel to escape reality. *Farigh* means empty, but also silly and inconsequential. From the very beginning, the prospect of creating another world with a different set of rules is cynically undermined as a futile endeavor. The second part of the novel is entitled *Qamis wardi la yurid an yakun farighan* (A pink shirt that does not want to be empty), and the last part is entitled *Qamis aswad tawil* (A long black shirt). The titles foreground the real and imagined struggle of the author to write a transgressive text while constantly feeling the weight of reality pulling her back to familiar territories. Her long black shirt is her real life, her awareness of the image to which she is supposed to conform, "the mother she should be and the writer she must revere" (67). It is her social prison as a divorced woman in a conservative environment.

19. Also see Ahmad al-Sharif (1998, 97–104) and Fatima Fawzi (2000, 118–25).

20. Khayri Duma also suggests that *qamis* has sexual connotations, as *qamis* is linked to sexual intercourse (*nizwa*).

Through writing, Amin aspires to create a world and a pattern of relationships that do not conform to conventional standards and expectations. In her text, her lover is "free from the world that imposes on [him] its masculinity" (11). Through writing, she becomes aware that she has mastered the art of fleeing from men who impose their love on her, and she embraces only those whom she actively attracts. Conscious of the dominant gender roles expected of men and women, she seeks to subvert these roles, to rid herself of the accusation of abiding by the image of the woman as object, a woman "who receives masculinized love while lying on her face, smothered, blindfolded, and bristling with rage" (15). She realizes that her flight from the conventional and the normal has led her at times to reverse the equation, "to perform the role of the man she is running away from" (15). In this textual praxis, she hopes to create an imaginary world that escapes the "ghost of the father" (16), the phallogocentrism that relegates women to the position of other and denies her presence in the symbolic order. This transgressive leap would also free her lover from bondage to a prescribed hegemonic masculinity and would allow him to practice his own subjective masculinity, a masculinity that does not compete with "the father." In an attempt to articulate the defining contours of her lover's manhood, the narrator describes him as follows:

> I admire your Egyptianness and your cheerful manhood. There is something about you that emits pure qualities: dark-skinned with no distinguishing features; an average body/physique. You wear what you will of clothes from any place you have visited in the world, but you wear them and do not allow them to wear you. . . . You remind me of the boys in the Pyramids surrounding the camels and the probably inauthentic papyrus papers. Fresh and friendly. Cheerful and available. An Egyptian devoid of the deceitful psychological epidemics that had penetrated him and had turned him either into a stone in agony, or a monstrosity that inflicts pain in love . . . a man, pure as you are, will make me search inside for a woman who resembles him, who was not corrupted by society, whose feminine sensitivity was not codified, nor was she alienated from it, a woman with a feminine history, an Egyptian who belongs to the good old days, like you, what a coincidence. (17–18)

Amin's articulation of a different relationship that does not conform to normative patterns slips into some essentialist patterns of thought, as it looks back to the idealized world of "her grandmother's stories" (17). This slippage only confirms the difficulties faced by women in transcending the heavily laden meanings of masculine language in their quest to write their bodies. Her lover, who is also an image maker, a successful film director, emerges as someone still inhabiting familiar territory. At the end, the narrator gives him voice to articulate her image in the eyes of others. His verdict is judgmental and stereotypical as he tells her that her existential reflections are an indication of bourgeois writing that has failed to find a cause (82–83). He goes further and disillusions her of her expectations of him that he be her savior, "her life-line in a tumultuous sea" (84), which, according to him, is another bourgeois image she holds about men. She accepts the limitations of both their abilities to transgress.

The novel is rich with intertextual affinities with the short stories of Nura Amin, as well as a novel by Marguerite Duras, *The Lover,* and a Meryl Streep film. Duras's novel presides over the narrative from the first page, as the novel is dedicated to her and "our lover." Duras is recalled more than once as a guiding presence. Her death in 1996 also coincides with the writing of the novel and is referred to directly. At the end, the narrator wonders whether the lovers' relationship was destined to end, or whether it was suggested to her by Duras's death (88). The other text is a Clint Eastwood film that starred Meryl Streep, *The Bridges of Madison County,* another love story that gives the protagonist a glimpse of happiness, but that ends with the lovers parting. These two stories epitomize love stories that defy traditions and expected norms: they are of course fictional stories, preserved in writing and through writing.

May Telmissany's *Dunyazad* (1997; English translation, *Dunyazad* 2000) is an autobiographical novel about the agonizing experience of a mother giving birth to a stillborn child. The novel was awarded the Ulysses Prize for best first novel in 2002 in France, and the State Encouragement Prize for best autobiographical novel in Egypt in the same year. In addition to her career as a creative writer, Telmissany (born 1965) is also a translator, a university lecturer, and a columnist in the Egyptian newspaper *Ruzalyusuf.* The title, *Dunyazad,* the name of the stillborn child in the novel, recalls the sister of Shahrazad, the legendary storyteller in *One Thousand and One Nights* who hid under the bed and listened to her sister telling one story after another to King Shahrayar, thereby putting off her execution. Dunyazad, the stillborn daughter, has no voice in the narrative, like her namesake in *One Thousand and One Nights*. Her presence is felt through the words of the narrator/author, the twentieth-century Shahrazad. Storytelling as a survival strategy adopted by women to fight against the looming specter of imminent death is similarly employed by Telmissany, as she inscribes the story of her unique experience to help overcome the shadow of death hovering over her life after the loss of a child.

The narrative is dominated by the consciousness of the mother, the narrator and author. She is obsessed by the paradox of her womb as a locus of birth and death. The image of her womb as a grave haunts her and prompts her to reflect on the relationship between life and death, how memory can beget forgetfulness, how a place for life can also harbor death. The tragedy has a transformative effect on her life: she quits her job and reconsiders relationships with friends. Everything and everybody reminds her of her lost child. She sees a man's picture in the obituary page in the newspaper and imagines his life and his wife's mourning. The sale of her husband's family house, where she spent memorable happy days, becomes a metaphor for the passing away of a way of life and the embodiment of the truth about mortality. Her decision to have another child is overshadowed by her awareness that she is compensating for her loss. The act of writing to overcome death, writing about waiting, about a failed memory, about conquering fear by identifying other fears, writing about anything but death, all lead to a realization that she is still obsessed with the death of her child. ([1997] 2002, 54–55).[21] At the end, she becomes aware that she has reached a turning point in her life, as she recognizes her ability to be bored, angry, and many other things. She is finally able to mourn her child as she writes *Dunyazad* and finds solace in words that help her forget (*asta'inu 'ala hurufiha bil-nisyan*).

The novel is also a metafictional narrative about the act of writing itself as a simultaneous inscription of remembrance and forgetfulness, memory and amnesia, life and death. Binary opposites are united and absolute dichotomies are superseded as the moment of birth is conflated with death, and

21. All quotations are taken from the 2002 edition. All translations are mine.

writing as an act of remembrance becomes the tool that aids forgetfulness. In writing, opposites unite and voices intermingle. This union is achieved with the use of a polyphony of voices that interact and converge through the use of association of ideas. The narrative is nonlinear: the novel starts in medias res, with the news of the death of the child, then unfolds gradually as it sheds light on the happy expectations that preceded the tragedy, the actual moment of death, the tribulations of the father as to how to break the news, and then the journey of both parents toward healing and reconciliation. The voices of the father and a friend are merged in the narrative of loss, giving the reader a multiplicity of points of view that complements the view of the narrator. Standing next to the bed of his wife, the husband is thinking that he will not be able to embrace his wife soon. The word "embrace" is echoed by the wife, who remembers when she embraced him while bearing their child, and how she laughed as the child kicked her husband away. She is describing her hospital room full of flowers, and he remembers the flower basket that carries his child to her grave.

This development of the narrative through association of ideas between two people, in this case the father and mother, renders the multiplicity of points of view complementary rather than oppositional. From the very beginning, the reader is informed about the loss of the child from the point of view of the mother and the father. Their feelings of loss and pain are similar and different at the same time. The point of view of the father is poignantly expressed, as he is the first to be informed of the death of the child and watches his wife's "death-like complexion" (12) as she comes out of the operating room. Following the advice of doctors, he decides to inform her gradually about her daughter's death. He has to direct his attention to the practical details of how to break the news to his wife, how to manage members of the family, the burial of the child, so he was unable to grieve properly. He experiences a sense of double loss, the loss of his child as well as that of his wife, as she emerges pale and aloof after the tragedy. Their pictures are "planted in his heart, like cactus, constantly defiant" (22). His emotions are juxtaposed to his wife's, especially how to deal with their pain.

Telmissany's depiction of the father of her child and her husband through the presence of his voice in her very personal narrative gives us a rare glimpse of conventionally hidden male weaknesses and emotions. Watching his wife cry in the arms of friends, he "had a childish need for friends and family . . . a genuine need for someone to pat him on the shoulder and wipe off his forehead images of approaching death, possible death, and imminent death" (23). He is aware of his wife's judgmental disapproval of his seeming lack of emotional distress, as she asks him incredulously, "why are you not crying?" and then "maybe I do not really know you" (23). His voice tells us that he has trained himself for years to hold back, to contain his grief (23), and not to show his sense of "fear and defeat" (22), as part of his inculcation into manhood. In another incident when he is discussing with members of his family the selling of his grandfather's house, he is deeply aware of his wife's presence in the adjacent room as she quietly awaits the family's decision. He observes his potential actions through her eyes: "if I agree to the sale, she will say that he succumbed to his uncle's will; if I object to the suggested price, she will say let us get this matter over and done with; and if I remain silent, she will say that he is always hesitant" (41). The tragic experience of the loss of a child accentuates his self-awareness and soul-searching in a manner similar to that of his wife's, even if his way of dealing with the loss is different.

Asked about what distinguishes women's writing from men's writing, Yumna al-'Id cites *Dunyazad* as an example of how women writers use a double voice, in the sense that it is not possible to separate the voice of the man and the woman in the novel (2002a, 8). In *Dunyazad,* there is a merging of the feminine and the masculine, which subverts stereotypical representations of men and women. The father's suffering and grief for his lost child is as deep as the mother's, albeit expressed and experienced differently. His traditional "male" strengths, controlling his tears or avoiding public expression of weakness, are identified and reconsidered as potential causes of miscommunication between the sexes. Telmissany's depiction of the male voice probes beyond stereotypical assumptions about masculine strength and emotional control. His acute awareness of and sensitivity toward his wife's feelings, coupled with his confrontation of his own weaknesses and fears, presents the reader with a new fictional representation of manhood.

Conclusion

Both novels by May Telmissany and Nura Amin are metafictional narratives that consciously reflect on the art of writing "in order to pose questions about the relationship between fiction and reality" (Waugh 1984, 2). Their concern with the craft of writing fiction reflects their desire to explore new areas of consciousness and new horizons of expression to give voice to their individual visions. According to Muntasir al-Qaffash, "previous generations of writers wrote about their lives, and were oblivious to the art of criticism. Our generation is different: we follow approaches to criticism, which are reflected in our writing. We are interested in the actual process of writing" (quoted in Duma n.d.). Amin identifies herself as a feminist writer and embraces *l'écriture féminine* as feminist praxis. Telmissany is more hesitant about affiliating herself with a theoretical direction linked to a social movement, yet her subject matter, her use of a double voice, and her preoccupation with writing as survival render her text a powerful expression of a woman's writing with a difference.

Khayri Duma has argued that the new generation of women writers are too wrapped up in themselves, hence echoing a widespread assumption about the absence of sociopolitical concerns in the new writing. May Telmissany describes her project, and that of her generation, as "writing on the margin of history," a writing that does not address sociopolitical issues, such as the woman question, or wars, or the effect of the open-door policies on individuals (1996, 97–98). She further adds, in an interview:

> the idea behind what we are trying to say from the very beginning is that the issue is not about the collapse of ideologies, or the decline of the national project and the rise of individualism. This might be true on the political and social levels, and it might have some repercussions on the creative process. However, and probably because of these reasons and many other reasons, such as the palpable falsification of everything due to the dominance of the image, everything around us has withdrawn inside because there is no longer any hope in the validity of the external image captured by the camera because the camera has been contaminated. The remaining hope is in the inside, as the image produced then may be new, or at least real. (al-Hafiz 1997a, 15)

The thrust of Telmissany's view is that a focus on the personal, the subjective, on life at a micro level, is potentially more powerful and more genuine for the search for truth in a larger sense. I have argued that the new generation of writers, notably the two writers discussed in this chapter, transgress the opposition between the personal and the political. Telmissany's loss of her child is paralleled by the loss of the family house of her husband, giving us a brief but accurate glimpse of the changes in the life of the middle classes in Egypt in the second half of the twentieth century. Nura Amin's empty pink shirt, while inward looking and verging on an egotistical obsession with the self, is also a commentary on dominant social norms and values, particularly as they pertain to relationships between men and women. Both writers interrogate dominant, national representations of femininity and masculinity. Telmissany's depiction of her feelings of loss as well as those of her husband problematizes stereotypical representations of masculinity as synonymous with strength and control of emotions in the face of crisis, and it highlights the destructive dimension of these constructs. Similarly, Amin's text dissects and subverts stereotypical gendered roles as she defies the gendered order of the status quo.

I will end with a quote by Baha' Tahir, who, in 2009, recalls with sorrow that he told May Telmissany that he did not like her first collection of short stories: "I made the same mistake made [by critics,] who attacked the writing of my generation when we first started. I only wanted to read what I was accustomed to. I needed some time to be able to appreciate the aesthetics of this new writing." Tahir's candid retraction of an earlier judgment is testimony to his openness and willingness to revise his definition of the political. It is also an indication that the new writing is gaining ground and recognition in mainstream literary circles.

8

The Postcolonial Nomadic Novel

> The conundrum is as follows: the world is divided between, on the one hand, those who divide the world, and on the other hand, those who don't. Nationalists and nomads.
>
> —Christopher Miller 1998, 6

Nations as imagined communities are nevertheless constructed geographically and historically, leading to the creation of borders and the demarcation of frontiers. Similarly, the discursive construction of nations and gendered national identities is predicated on the erection of boundaries premised on the difference between the self and the other. Said has pointed out that the definition of the national self is most of the time contingent on opposition with the foreign other, leading to his insight about Orientalism as "a style of thought based upon an ontological and epistemological distinction made between 'the Orient' and (most of the time) 'the Occident'" (1978, 2). Throughout the twentieth century, Arab writers have grappled with the encounter with the West, using a paradigm of sameness and difference and striving to determine the implications of both ends of the continuum on the definition of Arab identities. In the 1930s, when Egypt was still a British Protectorate, Tawfiq al-Hakim adopted a Manichean aesthetic and attempted to reverse colonial violence in an effort to bolster the national self. In his later work in the 1990s, Sonallah Ibrahim sought to go beyond colonial and nationalist binary thought and explore the ramifications of colonial violence on the psyches of both colonizer and colonized.

A noted feature in much of the literature of the 1990s is a determination not to be confined to fixed formulas of identity and belonging that have been prescribed by previous generations, by the state, by social mores, or by idealized representations of gendered roles. This resolve is certainly reflected in the way writers position themselves vis à vis the group, the collective identity, or the nation. The encounter with the West in the global age, and its implications for national belonging and representations of gendered identities, continued to preoccupy writers as we approached the end of the twentieth century and the beginnings of the new millennium. The works of Husam Fakhr and Somaya Ramadan are narratives of estrangement and exile written in the twenty-first century that revisit national gendered identities against the backdrop of a global neo-imperialism. Ramadan's novel *'Awraq al-narjis* (2000; English translation, *Leaves of Narcissus,* 2002) depicts the struggle of her protagonist, Kimi, for individual selfhood while traversing a space in between Dublin and Cairo and in between national and neocolonial representations of gendered subjectivities. Fakhr's work was written in exile and explores the migrant's experience of belonging to two places, Cairo and New York. Both these texts consciously attempt to subvert the colonial and national narratives that foreground difference from and opposition to the "other" as the basis for the depiction of gendered identities. Both writers complicate the meaning of home and exile and seek to step outside the paradigm of sameness and difference, alienation and belonging. Their novels exemplify a postcolonial nomadism that seeks to transcend fixed binaries and create a third space for the enunciation of nonessentialist gendered identities. While the figure of the nomad, as a metaphor for the postcolonial subject, can potentially illuminate new conceptualizations of identity, it remains highly ambivalent and fraught with tensions and contradictions.

Nomadism as a conceptual tool for understanding subjectivities in colonial and neo-imperial contexts has been used by postcolonial as well as feminist critics to shed light on discursive critiques to stereotypical representations of the colonized self (Orlando 1999; Lionnet 1995). According to Deleuze and Guattari, "the life of the nomad is the intermezzo" (2004, 419) because the nomad is deterritorialized and, unlike the migrant, "there is no reterritorialization afterward" (421). This status, moving between points but never fixed to any particular one, empowers critical thought, hence rendering the figure of the nomad in postcolonial literature a metaphor for critical thinking in general. However, the use of nomadism as a signifier of critical thought has spurred a large amount of skepticism, largely owing to the conflation of nomadism as a subversive standpoint, on the one hand, and the material reality of real people, on the other. Caren Kaplan has warned against the use of the deterritorialization of the nomad to denote empowerment, noting that there is a huge difference between those who choose deterritorialization and those who do not: "My caution is against a form of theoretical tourism on the part of the first world critic, where the margin becomes a linguistic or critical vacation, a new poetics of the exotic" (1990, 361). She also faults Deleuze and Guattari for disregarding the fact "that oppositional consciousness (with its benefits and costs) stems from the daily, lived experience of oppression" (361). Many feminists have further questioned the empowering value of a nomadic subjectivity, particularly for women, who have been historically marginalized and whose agency has not yet been established in particular contexts (Grewal and Kaplan 1994). Rosi Braidotti, however, has argued that Deleuze's anti-Oedipal conceptualization of woman as a "constant process of becoming," rendering her "the prototype of the nomadic vision of subjectivity," creates important usages for the figure of the nomad in feminist projects (1996, 307–8).[1] John Noyes also argues that Deleuze and Guattari's exposition of the theory of the nomadic is closely associated with empire, and nomad thought is "an arrangement of thought that escapes empire, conquers empire, and ceaselessly invents administrative apparatuses for empire" (2004, 162). Quoting Said on the centrality of the migrant and the intellectual in exile for the conceptualization of liberatory thought, Noyes concludes that the "the textual politics of nomadology must address the conditions of nomadic existence" (167).

Somaya Ramadan (born in 1951) published her first novel, *'Awraq al-narjis,* in 2000. Her previous publications consisted of two collections of short stories, *Khashab wa nuhas* (1995; Wood and brass) and *Manazil al-qamar* (1999; Moon dwellings). Asked why she waited so long before publishing her work, she responded: "For a long time I was unable to find a language to express

1. Braidotti also acknowledges the ambivalence of the question of Woman in Deleuze: he "remains caught in a structural ambivalence on the question of Woman . . . [manifest in his] inability to conceptualize his own speaking stance or situated position" (1996, 311).

myself. I first wrote in English, but I knew I did not want it. Had I had a chance, I would have written in Egyptian colloquial Arabic. I wasted a lot of time looking for a language that belonged to me in particular. I was looking for a female voice for me" (2001, 10). Finding a voice of her own that is independent of oppressive cultural representations delayed Ramadan's literary expression. Much has been written about how women writers tend to develop a dual consciousness as a consequence of their inability to see themselves in the dominant cultural representations (Rowbotham 1973; Du Bois [1903] 1968), resulting "in a peculiar sensation . . . of always looking at one's self through the eyes of others, of measuring one's soul by the tape of a world that looks on in amused contempt and pity" (Friedman 1998, 76). This double consciousness, though a consequence of a disadvantaged position within hegemonic structures that results in tension and alienation, is potentially a powerful vantage point. The possession of a dual consciousness is also the condition of men and women who live on the edge of languages and cultures in a postcolonial global context. Ramadan's search for a peculiarly female voice is conducted on more than one level: as a quest for a distinct female identity within a patriarchal culture, on the one hand, and a quest for an identity between languages and cultures as a postcolonial subject, on the other. She first writes in English, then realizes that it does not adequately express her identity and her thoughts because "it is my language, and it is not my language" (2000,[2] 49). She would have preferred to write in colloquial Arabic, but again decided that it was not possible. Her dilemma is not caused by an inability to write in Arabic, and standard literary Arabic for that matter; rather, her dilemma is the consequence of her knowledge of two languages and two cultures. Situated between two poles, she belongs everywhere but nowhere. Ramadan's search for a language of expression is a metaphor for her search for an identity that is not exclusively defined by either side, but that is a combination of both, an attempt to create a different space for home and belonging. Ramadan resolves her dilemma by writing in Arabic. The English dimension of her identity surfaces in the recurrent use of

2. All quotations are taken are taken from this edition. All translations are mine.

English expressions and words, some of them written in Arabic letters, as well as in the numerous intertextual references to English literature.

'Awraq al-narjis is about Kimi, a young Egyptian woman who struggles with cultural representations of her gendered, cultural identity at home and abroad. As a child growing up in a middle-class family, she is acutely aware of oppressive rules of conduct imposed on her by her mother as well as by her English teacher. She rebels and escapes to a world of the imagination fed by the folk stories told by her nanny, 'Amna, a mother figure who fills the void left by a middle-class mother unable to meet the emotional needs of her children. Estranged from her parents, Kimi identifies with 'Amna and the characters in her folktales, as she weaves imaginary stories of adventure and fulfillment. She goes to Ireland to obtain a doctoral degree. There, she becomes acutely conscious of colonial representations of her identity as an Egyptian, Arab, and Muslim woman. She is, however someone who studies and identifies with the traditions of James Joyce, Yeats, and Shakespeare. In fact, she carries with her multiple passports/identities, but only her Egyptian, Arab, and Muslim ones are recognized when she walks down the streets of Dublin. Pressure on her mounts as she is unable to accommodate herself to the constraints imposed on her by her material reality of oppressive national and colonial identities. She has a nervous breakdown and is admitted to Saint Patrick Hospital, where she smells "the odor of madness" (50). After this hospital interlude, which comes right in the middle of the novel, she returns to her father's house and is pursued by the odor of madness. No one asks her what happened or why, and an official tale about her journey to the West to obtain a higher degree is told.

The title of the novel, *'Awraq al-narjis,* signals an autobiographical dimension of the text. *'Awraq* means the leaves of the narcissus flowers, but also the pages in a diary. Referring to an unpublished testimony/manuscript by Ramadan entitled *Min bayn al-sutur* (Between the lines), Mohamed Birayri argues that the novel is clearly autobiographical, and that it is "a continuation of the testimony and vice versa" (2002, 98). Ramadan's assertion of her autobiographical self defies the successive assaults she/the narrator/ the female self experienced as a child and as a young woman against herself and her individuality. The use of the metaphor of the narcissus flower is particularly interesting and indicative of her subversive endeavor. In common usage, the flower is associated with extreme egotism and self-aggrandizement. In the novel, however, narcissism becomes an affirmation, an act of resistance against erasure of herself, by social expectations, her community of friends, and her family. It is a narcissism tempered by uncertainty and a desire to explore and discover. The title of the first chapter in the novel, "Perhaps," establishes uncertainty and indeterminacy as the guiding principle of the narrator's quest for self-knowledge. In the first scene, she depicts her struggle with her friends and family as they try to convince her to take a pill that will help her sleep. For her, the pill, which will calm her down and help her become the person she is expected to be, is like death and nothingness. Rather than conform to her prescribed role, she withdraws into the narcissus phase, focusing on herself and distancing herself from the community.

Kimi's predicament lies in her inability to conform to dictates of an essential prescribed identity. She belongs to two places that she cannot call her own. She is under pressure to choose her identity, her home, her belonging, but she is unable to choose. In a section entitled "Parable of a Nation" (35) she contemplates the walls of her room in Dublin, where as a foreign student she would be expected to hang trinkets and pictures that remind her of her homeland and her status as an exile. Her map of exile, however, is different from most other maps that recall a nation. Kimi's wall has a picture of James Joyce "deep in thought, eyes blurred behind round glasses . . . seemingly haughty, the way people with weak eye-sight unintentionally are" (35). It also has Gauguin's dark young women "smiling at suitors who never arrive" (35) and a cheap reproduction of a painting of a Chinese woman with a "confused head" gazing at a postcard full of very complicated directions and names of villages. Her map of exile is typically nonnational, nonethnic, nonreligious, and characterized by affinities with temperaments, fears, and desires. Her map changes as it reflects a nostalgia for "an imagined nation" that does not look like any other and cannot be verified by anyone (36). Upon her return to her father's house, she realizes that there, too, she is without a clear-cut map that determines her identity: "The walls have no maps here nor there. And I am no longer here, nor there. I am in purgatory with no hope of leaving, not even in the imagination. In limbo, a more appropriate word to describe the space created when two worlds intersect" (61–62).

In Dublin, Kimi's imagined nation, or her map of home in exile, collides with a material reality of colonial narratives and national narratives of what home is about. Her own individual experience is evidence of the multiple identities she possesses. Listening to a lecture on Egyptian history by a professor of the history of the Middle East, she does not recognize the diverse sides of the Egypt she knows and how multiple identities blend and fuse inside her:

> In her inner being and her head rages a civil war between all the [histories] of Egypt, and she is all Egypts: if she wears kohl and becomes Nefertiti; if she plants lentil and fenugreek before Easter and if she reads Arabic poetry; if she longs for her father's house in Alexandria; and if she remembers her mother's stories about the trousseau of her Turkish mother-in-law; . . . and in the midst of all this and from between its folds, she hears the voice of her mother telling the story of Little Red Riding Hood one sunny morning in the Fish garden. (37–38)

Ramadan is beset by the difficulties of transcending boundaries of colonial and national identities. She questions her own impulse to embrace more than one identity in an undivided whole. No matter how she might seem to fit in the Western city, she is acutely conscious of herself seen through the eyes of the Western other as she carries her history with her: "I carry on my back my ethnicity and my religion and all the Egyptian, Arab, and Muslim passports, marked by what I imagine others have learned to imagine about my country in jokes and caricatures" (48). This perpetual self-consciousness about her multiple identities is an effect of her being a postcolonial subject, conscious of the other's oppressive narrative and gaze. Ramadan uses a poignant metaphor to re-create for the reader this heightened self-consciousness of the other's critical gaze: "I go out to buy bread or milk from the grocer's and feel like I am wearing an evening dress, studded shoes, and my finest jewelry for a bicycle ride in the countryside" (48).

Back in Cairo, she is overwhelmed by the same self-conscious awareness of her identity as seen through the lens of discriminatory cultural representations. After a ten-year absence, everything is different—more conservative and more oppressive. She is confronted with old and new rules: "Cover your face woman. . . . Lower your voice. *Ya 'awra.* Lower your eyes. Off what? What do I lower my eyes from? . . . From everything" (76). She goes out of her way to flout social expectations and rules of propriety and demands that her loved ones accept her, whichever way she presents herself, or whichever aspect of her identity she decides to foreground, in defiance of expectations and social norms. She deliberately goes to a grand party in rags and in very poor shape, and, conversely, dresses up and wears an expensive and beautiful outfit to attend a casual outing. For her, these subversive games are sacrificial offerings that aim at disrupting the social mold to which she is confined, in the hope that society will be less judgmental, and that she will eventually be left in peace to be who she wants to be. Alienated because of the pressures to conform to a specific identity, she rebels against any attempt to confine her to a particular definition of home/identity. When her lover asks her to come home with him, she responds angrily: "Where is my home? What is it that you call my home? Why do you say my home?" and then quotes from Henry V: "My nation! What ish my nation? Ish a villain, and a bastard, and a knave, and a rascal? What ish my nation? Who talks of my nation?"[3] (45). As a nomad, Kimi moves back and forth between two poles, two identities, not wanting to choose between them.

On the other hand, she tries to train herself to fit into society by practicing the expected social and gender roles and by accepting the rules and constraints of a fixed identity, but she fails. In a conversation with a professor she reaches the conclusion that her quest to transcend boundaries and not to be restricted to a particular identity is not possible in the real world, and madness is her only recourse:

> —I wanted to be . . . to live as my own self, to experience my self. . . . I was training myself. This is what delayed me for so long.
>
> —Training does not lift boundaries. You have confused matters. Training is to achieve excellence within boundaries. Everyone knows that there are boundaries that cannot be crossed, no matter how hard they tried, except for . . .

3. The quote is from Henry V by William Shakespeare. "What ish my nation?" is also the title of a chapter by David Cairns and Shaun Richards in *Writing Ireland: Colonialism, Nationalism and Culture* (Manchester: Univ. of Manchester Press, 1988).

—Except for the mad?

—Except for the mad.

As well as magicians, novelists and short-story writers. (105)

Kimi's desire to erase boundaries becomes an impossible feat, given the realities of the outside world, and she ends up in a mental hospital. She escapes into the confines of her inner self, or the narcissus phase. The novel ends with the voice of the sirens luring Kimi with their enchanted songs. The figure of James Joyce hovers over the narrative; an intricate mesh of intertextuality with *Ulysses* renders Kimi another sailor at sea, attracted by the sirens and "the threat of forgetfulness" (Nestrovski 1988, 19). Kimi's head reverberates with a cacophony of voices, which, if we extend the analogy with the fugue of the sirens in *Ulysses,* "allows for a simultaneous reconciliation of various strands of self in the moment" (Zimmerman 2002, 110). Kimi's sirens transpose her to a dark, unfamiliar world that is both a threat and a promise. Hala Kamal described Kimi's madness as "a state of consciousness, rebellion, and an act of resistance" (2001, 132). It is certainly an alternative space for transcending imposed boundaries of identity. Kimi's state of madness denotes a heightened sensitivity, a wealth of knowledge, and subtle perception. It is the condition of those who transcend boundaries in a world that insists on erecting more demarcation lines. Kimi's decision not to be confined to the dictates of her gendered national identity and to challenge territorialized belongings places her on the margin, outside the national social imaginary. Her multiple identities are inscribed through intertextuality in an amalgam of East and West: James Joyce, W. B. Yeats, Shakespeare, Salah Jahin, and Arab and Western folktales. Madness becomes the fate of intellectual nomadism, when faced with material conditions of living in the world, or material nomadism. It is the fate of nomads who did not choose to be deterritorialized, but had deterritorialization imposed on them.

In an interview, in response to a question about Kimi's quest for identity, Ramadan insists that Kimi is not searching for an identity, nor does she need to choose one out of the possibilities available to her. However, "the whole world is telling her that you must have one. . . . She is the world in the future where visions and histories are all integrated inside her. Yet, despite this cultural richness and her long history, she seems to be in a weak position" (2001, 10). Kimi embodies what can be described as the paradox of the nomad, belonging everywhere and nowhere: "All nations are mine, and I am therefore without a nation. All languages are mine, and I am therefore without a language. An individual alone without a community. . . . This map is fit for the mad" (65).

Husam Fakhr (born in 1958) has lived since 1982 in New York, where he heads the Interpretation Service at the United Nations. Unlike other writers discussed here, Fakhr did not return to his country of origin after a short encounter with the West or after completing his studies. He settled in New York, which he came to regard as his second home, and identifies with the city and its inhabitants. Fakhr is not unique in his experience of writing from exile; there is an old and long tradition dating back to the end of the nineteenth century of Arab writers in the *mahjar* (exile) who have maintained their links with their "homes," both in their writing and in lived experience. His work is particularly interesting in its exploration of the experience of exile at the end of the twentieth century and beginning of the twenty-first, and its implications for the formulation of new Arab gendered identities.

Fakhr's first collection of short stories was *al-Busat laysa 'ahmadiyyan* (1985), which was introduced by Yusuf Idris, a renowned short-story writer in the Arab world. However, this first publication, as well as the subsequent one, *'Umm al-shu'ur* (1992), went unnoticed. Fakhr attracted critical attention with his work published in the new millennium by Dar merit: a collection of short stories, *Wujuh New York* (2004; Faces of New York); a novel, *Ya 'aziz 'ayni* (2006; O apple of my eyes);[4] a novel, *Hikayaat Amina* (2007; Amina's stories); and also *Hawadiyt al-'Akhar* (Tales of the other), a novel published by Dar al-'ayn in 2008. *Hikayaat Amina* won the Sawiris Prize for the best collection of short stories in 2009. It also propelled Fakhr into the

4. "Ya 'aziz 'ayni" is a term of endearment that means the apple of my eyes. It is the title of a famous song by Sayyid Darwish (1892–1923), the father of Egyptian popular music and composer of some of the most well-known songs of Egyptian nationalism. In this song, he criticized the forced conscription of Egyptian youth into the British army. Fakhr employs the song to accentuate the feeling of loss and abandonment in exile.

limelight, as it triggered interest in his writing, raising the possibility that he was the new Yusuf Idris or perhaps another Jahin (Sabri 2007).[5]

Fakhr's first work to be published in the new millennium, and after a long silence, was triggered by the events of 11 September, an event of massive scale and impact on international world politics in general, and certainly on the large population of migrants, especially in the West. The aftermath of 11 September was a radical increase in racial and religious prejudice directed against migrant communities, especially those of Muslim and Arab origin. Furthermore, and as the decade unfolded, questions about the relationship of migrants to their adopted homelands, the degree of their integration and loyalty, or lack of, occupied center stage in global political and cultural scenes. Fakhr's *Wujuh* is one attempt to address the meaning of exile and belonging, a theme that he develops in his subsequent work.

Fakhr dedicates the stories of *Wujuh New York* to "New York, my beloved city which I lost" (2004, 5).[6] A characteristic of Fakhr's work is that although this is a collection of short stories, it is also a novel, as the stories together depict the experience of one protagonist, the narrator, from the day of his arrival in New York, through his self identification as a New Yorker, and his subsequent estrangement after 11 September. The protagonist's story is told through seventeen individual stories presenting different faces of New

5. The link between Fakhr on the one hand and Salah Jahin and Yusuf Idris on the other is worthy of note. Jahin, as previously mentioned, was a prominent Egyptian poet, playwright, and cartoonist whose songs and poems are an integral part of the Egyptian national memory. Yusuf Idris (1927–1991) is considered to be the master of the Arabic short story. Both Jahin and Idris figure strongly in Fakhr's life: Idris introduced his first collection of short stories and hailed him as a new upcoming writer; Jahin is his maternal uncle. The appellation of Fakhr as "a new Jahinian talent" was first suggested in an article by Jalal Amin, who expressed his joy at coming across the writings of Fakhr while serving as a judge in the Sawiris Prize for Literature in 2006 (2007).

6. All quotations are taken from this edition. All translations are mine. In a postscript to the book, Fakhr tells us that all the stories were written between 11 and 28 September 2003, exactly two years after the attack on the World Trade Center, except for the story entitled "*wajh tahta al-matar*" (A face in the rain), which was written in 1995 under a different title (2004, 98).

York.[7] The first one is about the protagonist's face in the mirror of the taxi taking him to his hotel on his first day in New York. It is the face of a typical poor newcomer to the city, worried about the taxi fare. We then encounter faces of inhabitants of the city, as he gradually adapts to its different rules and lifestyles. The first few stories highlight the features of the city, which strike the narrator as different from his own background. In *Wajh jarati* (My neighbor's face), his neighbor's colorful dress initially reminds him of his grandmother. She, however, is a lonely old woman who fends for herself and wears a dirty dress, unlike his grandmother, who always smelled of perfume and was taken care of by members of her family. Although the neighbor treats him with some aggression and suspicion, he nevertheless visits her and offers to buy her groceries when he finds out that she has been ill. This comparison between the life of the lonely elderly neighbor and his grandmother establishes New York as a tough city where the elderly can face a life of neglect and loneliness. In another story, *Wajh khalfa al-zujaj* (A face behind glass), he describes his daily encounters with the man who sells train tickets, who consistently does not look at the narrator or respond to his morning greetings. At the end, the narrator follows suit, is silent while buying his tickets, and is not sure whether to rejoice or grieve for becoming a true inhabitant of the city (18). The narrator continues to paint portraits of New Yorkers: a Vietnam veteran who has lost his sanity and lives in a carton box outside the building; a young woman with an angelic face he meets in an idyllic atmosphere, who turns out to be a striptease dancer; a beggar who refuses to take more money than is usual; and many more. The stories insightfully capture the small pleasures and pains that are the essence of human existence. The reader is able to follow the narrator as he becomes integrated into the city, while still being aware of its pitfalls. In *Barbara lam tufariq New York* (Barbara never left New York), he mourns the death of a friend who, for him, embodied the "spirit of New York" (31). She was loud, blunt, very tolerant, and humane, an avid reader and extremely knowledgeable about the inns and outs of the city. At her funeral, he is struck by the silence that envelops the rituals and is dismayed when a dog urinates on the

7. All the stories have the word "face" or "faces" in their titles, except for two.

tree where her ashes were laid. At that moment, he remembers her words whenever she heard him complain about the city: "This is New York. You either love it or leave it" (36). In another story, *Wajh khalfa al-zujaj 2* (A face behind glass 2), he is called by the police to identify the body of an acquaintance, a man from Peru, who although he lives a stringent life alone in the city, never thinks of going back: "I cannot live anywhere else, despite the harshness of my life and despite my loneliness. . . . I am addicted to New York's tolerance and its open arms" (58). The last five stories describe New York and the changes that befell the city after the events of 11 September. In *Wujuh New York 1* (Faces of New York 1), the narrator describes his reactions and thoughts on the day of the attack, his empathy with the victims, his horror at the scale of devastation and the loss of innocent lives, the utter sense of disbelief that marked the first few hours. He felt that the planes that "stabbed New York in the heart, stabbed me too in the heart" (74). He wondered: "What will happen to New York? What will happen to my city?" (77). In another story with the same title, *Wujuh New York 2,* the narrator makes an analogy between the pictures of those who were killed in the Twin Towers, which were plastered on the walls of buildings, and the Fayoum mummy portraits: "A few days after September 11, the walls of New York were transformed into the cover of a sarcophagus carrying thousands of pictures. Numerous faces upon faces covered the walls: white, dark, black, and yellow faces, lined up near the hospital door" (89–90). The Fayoum portraits are death masks, mummy portraits that were painted on wood and attached to the coffins of the dead during the Roman period in Egypt.[8] The narrator is haunted by the faces of the dead, as he feels their anger and rejection of him, branding him a terrorist and a criminal. In the last story, *Wajh fi al-zalam* (A face in the dark), he describes a moment of fear when there is a power outage in New York in 2003 that covered the city with utter darkness. The possibility of it being another terrorist attack on New York reminds him of a friend's theory, that they (all Arabs), will be put in concentration camps similar to what happened to the Japanese Americans during World War II.

8. The Fayoum portraits were discovered in Fayoum and give insight into the lives of local inhabitants during the Roman period in Egypt.

He sadly faces the fact that "New York, the city of lights, has lost its colors. Everything now is either black or white" (97).

The narrator's New York story is semiautobiographical, as it follows the life of Fakhr and his move to a new city. His relationship is vastly different from the earlier journeys of Eastern men to Western cities. His awareness of the differences between Cairo and New York does not stop him from identifying himself as a New Yorker and calling it his city. The stories constitute an exploration of a journey into a new place of exile that gradually becomes familiar, like home, and then strange again. It sheds light on an aspect of postcolonial nomadism, where the nomad is traveling towards a point that remains beyond his reach, as he is forced to continue moving.

In his novel *Ya 'aziz 'ayni* (2006)[9] Fakhr continues to explore the ramifications of exile and estrangement, particularly the impact they have on relationships between men and women. He dedicates it to all those who have been "burned with the enriching fire of exile/estrangement from one's homeland" (111). The novel consists of a story within a story, and both are about a love affair between an Egyptian man and a Mexican woman. In the frame story, Yusuf, a migrant settled in New York, falls in love with Esperanza, another migrant. The second story takes place in the middle of the nineteenth century and follows the fate of two Egyptian peasants, Ibrahim and Gharib, who are forcefully conscripted in the khedive's army, which sends Egyptian forces to support Napoleon's III campaign in Mexico. In Mexico, Ibrahim falls in love with Esperanza, a Mexican peasant. Unlike Yusuf, the twentieth-century migrant, Ibrahim and Gharib do not have a clue about what has happened to them. They arrive in Mexico with the French forces, are technically part of an occupation army, and are baffled by the hostility of Mexicans, who naturally perceive them as invaders.

The story within the story, set in the nineteenth century, is presented as a proposed project for writing either a historical novel, a play, or a film script. The author, Yusuf in the frame story, is self-conscious of his craft and shares with the reader his notes about the process of writing. The self-reflexive technique allows the author to be explicit about the thinking behind his choice

9. All quotations are taken from this edition. All translations are mine.

of subject matter, specific events as well as dialogue. More important, he acknowledges his inability to decide on the artistic genre most suited to his project—a film or a novel or a play—and voices his reservations about the imperfect use of historical knowledge, as well as the relationship between his ideological convictions and artistic expression. In fact, the novel is filled with the author's comments, which note gaps that need to be filled, or weak points that need correction and reconsideration. This oscillation in deciding on the more appropriate artistic genre, as well as the many revisionist notes and comments, illustrate or symbolize the extreme difficulty the author/Yusuf faces in his attempt to capture the experience of exile, especially as he moves beyond the conventional East/West binary opposition.

In both stories, the love relationship is between a man and a woman from the Third World, or countries with a colonial legacy. In the nineteenth-century story there is a further complication in the balance of power because Ibrahim, a victim of forced conscription in the service of a colonial oppressor, becomes himself a colonizer, as he is part of the occupying French forces in Mexico. This colonized/colonizer position undercuts the binarism implicit in migrant experiences, opening up new horizons for understanding. In Mexico, Ibrahim and his fellow Egyptian soldiers are distinguished from the French troops they are marching along with by their ragged and worn-out appearance. Conversely, Ibrahim looks at the Mexicans who are watching them march and remarks that they "look exactly like us" (55), even mistaking an old man for Haj Salim from his village. The similarity between Mexicans and Egyptians is stressed throughout. Ibrahim then meets Esperanza and helps her carry a heavy load back to her house. As he escorts her to her village, he observes that it is "almost an exact copy of his village beyond the sea, with the exception of the little pigs running all over the place" (69). Also, after he is introduced to her family and is given food to take back to his camp, and he subsequently returns the plates filled with food, Esperanza remarks: "You seem to be very much like us. If you take a plate of food, you return it full of food. Why then are you here fighting against us?" (81). The emphasis on the similarity between strangers in a cross-cultural/colonial encounter subverts the dichotomy of sameness and difference that underlies discussions of migrant experiences.

Fakhr attempts a parallel subversion of representations of migrant strangeness in his depiction of a contemporary love story in New York.

Yusuf's love affair with a Mexican woman, also called Esperanza, is narrated predominantly through Yusuf's eyes, but also through Esperanza's. This is not the typical Arab-migrant-to-the-West love affair with a Western woman who represents Western civilization that is complicated by colonial history and unequal power relations. Both are migrants from Third World countries, both are estranged from their land of origin, and both communicate in a language that is not their mother tongue. They talk about their countries, he becomes an expert in Mexican cuisine, and he calls her Amal, the Arabic version of Esperanza. Yusuf is convinced that he is fully integrated in his new home and that his romantic relationship is unmarred by conflict or tension on account of difference:

> I am a global citizen. I therefore cannot live anywhere except in New York, which combines in a nutshell the whole world. Also, one of the greatest philosophers of my country, called Juha, was asked "where is your homeland/country," and he said "it is where my wife lives." Now, I discovered that he was mistaken. He should have said "my homeland is my wife." You, Amal, the hope of my life, are my homeland. It no longer matters where I live, so long as we are together. (61)

Notwithstanding the above, we discover that Yusuf's alleged global identity is a figment of his imagination. He confronts the reality as he sees himself through Esperanza's eyes when she is in a fit of anger after coming back from a trip to Mexico, where her parents deny her. Yusuf's mask is ripped open. She rails at him for calling her Amal instead of Esperanza—"how would you feel if I called you José?"—for talking incessantly about Egypt, its beauty, its glorious past; for going to the museum and insisting on going to the Egyptian section, instead of going to a special exhibition of the Mexican artist Frida Kahlo, as she expected. She accuses him of never taking any real interest in Mexican history even though it is her country and a great one at that, that his interest stems from the fact that twelve hundred Egyptian soldiers were sent to Mexico 170 years ago. Her sharp words expose the sham identification between them based on equality and respect, especially Yusuf's numerous avowals of interest and knowledge of everything Mexican. Their love, based on excessive emphasis on their similarity and non-conflictual encounter, does not survive the tensions and residual pressures of dreams of the homeland.

The persistence of dreams of home constitutes a major dilemma for the postcolonial nomad and raises questions around the empowering dimension of nomadism. In the final analysis, the nineteenth-century Ibrahim yearns to go home, and the twenty-first century Yusuf is equally nostalgic for his nation.

The novel comprises another story of estrangement and pain, the story of Nadia, a twelve-year-old Romanian orphan adopted by an American couple, Robert and Janet. Although her new parents go to great lengths to provide her with comfort and love, Nadia is unable to communicate and misses the companionship and familiarity of her old orphanage. After a Christmas dinner with her adopted parents, as well as Yusuf and Esperanza, where Nadia is showered with presents and attention, she collapses into tears, becomes violent when her parents attempt to console her, and has a nervous breakdown. Her story acts as a commentary on the tenuous American dream shared by all the characters in the novel.

Alienation and loneliness become the fate of all the characters in the novel. Nadia is committed to a mental hospital, Janet and Esperanza leave their husbands, the French are defeated in Mexico and end the campaign, and Ibrahim is left behind with no hope of going back to his country. In the final scene, Robert and Yusuf are walking together in Central Park after a snowstorm. Robert asks Yusuf to remind him of the name of the hero of his historical novel, Ibrahim. Imitating the end of a film, the camera zooms out, and the music of the song "Ya 'aziz 'ayni" is heard. The song, written to criticize the forced conscription of Egyptian youth in a colonial army, accentuates the feeling of loss and abandonment in exile and the persistent burden of postcolonial subjects.

In another collection of short stories, *Hikayaat Amina* (2007)[10] Fakhr's love of New York is conflated with his love for his grandmother, Amina, who, is remembered as a formative figure in his childhood, adolescence, and adulthood. She was a storyteller whose stories opened up the world of the imagination for him. She was also the inspiration for his stories and his creativity, as she encouraged him to write and exercise his imagination. The protagonist, from his New York home, remembers his grandmother's wisdom, kindness,

10. All quotations are taken from this edition. All translations are mine.

and vivid imagination. She symbolizes the best of what home means—the smells, the colors, and the sounds of his earlier life. His grandmother's life is entwined in the history of Egypt as he remembers how as a young girl, she loved Sa'ad Zaghlul, the nationalist leader who challenged the British occupation, and also Gamal Abdel Nasser for introducing television to Egypt. His love for New York is presented as perfectly harmonious with his love for his grandmother: there is no conflict, no dilemma. In a story entitled "Hikayaat al-musiqa fi Grand Central" (The story of music in Grand Central), the narrator, addresses New York as his beloved: "How beautiful you are at all times. I adore you with all my heart, my darling city, all the months of the year. But your magic is revealed at its best near Christmas" (83). His grandmother was the first person with whom he shared his love for New York:

> when I was a child, you told me the story of the little boy who dreamed of going to London and imagined that its streets were paved with gold. Like him, I came to New York and found its streets paved with asphalt and diamonds. Grandmother, they grind glass and mix it with asphalt and then pave the roads. At night, the lights are reflected against the specks of glass and shine like the diamonds that caught the eyes of Sinbad when he was carried away by the roc. Grandmother, it is a scene of sheer beauty. (83)

He also receives the news of his grandmother's death in New York, and it is heralded by music, as she had always imagined. The music is a mixture of Arabic and English, verses from the Qur'an and the Bible, sung by a young nun "with a face that exudes peace" (85). A serene and harmonious peace marks the death of his grandmother, blessing the narrator's life in his new home.

Hikayaat Amina recalls Suhayr al-Qalamawi's *'Ahadith jaddati* (My grandmother's stories) published in 1935, which depicts the intimate and warm relationship between a young woman and her grandmother through stories and conversations. Like *One Thousand and One Nights,* there is a frame story in which several stories are embedded. The grandmother tells stories from the past that draw comparisons between past times and the present. Although she always sides with the past, its wisdom and traditions, she sometimes acknowledges the advantages of modern times and modern ways. The grandmother criticizes what she deems excessive freedom exercised by young women, which has compromised their virtue and honor.

Al-Qalamawi's treatment of the nationalist dilemma between modernity and tradition, embodied in the figures of the grandmother and granddaughter, is not rendered as a conflict, but more as a relationship filled with love and understanding. Al-Qalamawi is certainly clear that the two women from two different generations represent opposing points of view, and that their disagreements will only be resolved over time. She also suggests that the outcome will be in favor of the new generation and their modern visions. In his introduction to the stories, however, Taha Husayn foregrounds the conflict and lack of understanding between the two generations, arguing that there is not much to learn from the older generation. He insists on a complete and radical break with the past, with tradition, and an espousal of the modern as exemplified by Europe. According to him, we can only revisit past times with nostalgia, not to learn or evaluate with an eye on the future: "We are closer to the hearts and minds of Europeans than we are to the hearts and minds of the older generation of Egyptians. We talk to them in Arabic, but we need a translator" (1978, 13). Husayn is certainly reading his own ideological beliefs into al-Qalamawi's stories. For him, the generation gap is unbridgeable, and he advocates a radical break with the past and the older generation. Al-Qalamawi, on the other hand, acknowledges the gap but believes that the older generation can be won over to the more modern views. Both writers agree that the opposition between the old and the new is quite marked and difficult to surmount.

A comparison between al-Qalamawi's *'Ahadith* and Fakhr's *Hikayaat* suggests that it is likely that Fakhr had al-Qalamawi's text in mind when writing his and consciously engaged with its underlying assumptions and subverted its ideological premise. While al-Qalamawi espouse the modernist binarism of old and new, Fakhr emphasizes continuity and rootedness. The grandmother is revered and acknowledged as the primary source of knowledge about the world, about relationships, and about identity. She had much to offer, and he had much to learn. Her influence was so instrumental in shaping his worldview and beliefs as a young boy that the first time he discovers that some of her stories are not very accurate, he suffers from deep disillusionment. She is significantly called Amina (which means honest, trustworthy) and is entrusted with the task of safeguarding values and traditions for the new generation. Fakhr's worldview, unlike Husayn's and al-Qalamawi's, is not premised on a rupture with the past as a prerequisite for becoming modern; rather, he highlights continuities and explores possible venues for reciprocal exchange and communication.

Hawadit al-'akhar, Fakhr's latest novel, continues the exploration of the impact of exile and estrangement. It is divided into two parts; the first was written in the 1980s as a short story, and the second part was written twenty-three years later. In an interview, Fakhr reveals that he was particularly disappointed with the critical silence with which his first two collections of short stories were met, especially the story "Hawadit al-'akhar," because he particularly loved the story. He felt that it signaled a decisive moment in his development as a writer, as he moved away from the hold Yusuf Idris had on him and found his own voice and style. This style is characterized by a structure that depends on a frame story from which other stories sprout, constituting one work and one world (Fakhr 2008b). He was then encouraged to write the second part after a meeting with Gamal al-Ghitany (2008b).[11]

Hawadit al-'akhar is an allegorical tale of exile and loss. Fakhr draws upon the artistic conventions and stories in the *One Thousand and One Nights* to describe the pain and sense of alienation of a man who leaves his homeland and travels to the City of Brass. Struggling for survival in a place where people are measured by their material worth, he soon gets himself into trouble and is condemned by the king of the land to tell stories to save his life. Storytelling as survival is reminiscent of the plight of Shahrazad who was forced to entertain a king with stories to save her neck. The name of the destination of the traveler, the City of Brass, establishes an intertextual link with the "city of brass" in the *Thousand and One Nights,* which is one of the stories that have been described as early examples science fiction. Fakhr also employs a frame story: the protagonist, the exile, tells his story to the narrator, who narrates it to us, the readers. The man in exile is the "other," recounting stories to the self, the narrator. Throughout, the narrator

11. In the same interview, Fakhr recounts that after meeting Gamal al-Ghitany in New York in 2007, he sent the story to him. A few months later, and to his great surprise, he discovered that it was being published in *'Akhbar al-'adab* with a note saying that it was part of a collection of short stories that was forthcoming. This inspired him, and he finished his novel in a record five weeks.

carries the heavy load of the stories, literally—because the "other" has landed himself forcefully on his shoulders and refuses to let go until he finishes his stories—and metaphorically. The most compelling story of all is a symbolic tale about exilic existence. The protagonist makes another mistake and is given a prison sentence, which entails the surgical removal of his soul. He is not physically incarcerated, but his soul is held captive. He is allowed to pay periodic visits to his soul, but after a while he finds the visits tedious, so he stops. Upon the termination of his sentence, he undergoes another operation to reinsert his soul. He suffers from an unprecedented serious complication: his body rejects his soul "like a foreign body" (2008a, 38),[12] as it has gotten used to living without it. Part 1 of the novel ends here. In part 2, the narrator is compelled by an inner voice to search for the "other" to find out what befell him. He does find him and, once more, listens to his stories about his search for his soul. The "other" tells how he carried around his soul in a vial in a journey fraught with trials and danger, searching for a way of restoring it to his body. Finally, the "other" loses the vial with his soul after a momentous event that sowed havoc and panic in the City of Brass. His screams about his lost soul are met with sympathetic understanding of other inhabitants of the city, who have also lost their souls. We soon realize that the event in question is the catastrophic destruction that befell New York city on the 11 September 2001. The title of this story, "Kulluna fi al-hawa sawa," suggesting that we are all in the same boat, sums up the moral gist of the story. And, although the protagonist's pain is not relieved by the feeling of shared loss, life in the City of Brass has taught him to accept it for what it is and not how he had imagined it to be. This realization enables him to regain his life and his soul. The novel ends with a reconciliation between the narrator, the self, and the exile, the other.

Fakhr's imaginary world in *Hawadit al-'akhar* is also populated with parodies of easily recognizable figures, such as Gamal Abdel Nasser and George W. Bush: the first symbolizes failed hope and a lost dream; the second concretizes the prophet of doom and destruction. Through the construction of an imaginary world reminiscent of the *One Thousand and One Nights,* he

12. All quotations are taken from this edition. All translations are mine.

depicts a contemporary state of mind, exile, and an event of great magnitude in the twenty-first century. Asked about his reasons for doing so, he says: "Resorting to the imagination can be an escape from reality and can also be a reformulation of reality, an interpretation or a musical variation" (2008b).

Conclusion

In conclusion, I would like to refer to an earlier text that interrogated binary demarcations of national gendered identities, Radwa Ashour's *al-Rihla* (The journey), published in the 1980s. It is an autobiographical journey to the West by an Arab student to obtain a doctorate. The student in this case, and unlike the majority of Arab students of earlier decades, is a woman. From the outset, she positions herself within this tradition of Arab students in the West, starting with Rifa'a al-Tahtawi, while at the same time distinguishing herself from her predecessors: "Like Rifa'a, I was on my way to a land 'very far away from us' to acquire knowledge, but unlike him, I did not have the neutrality of someone who did not know what lay ahead. Neither was I like subsequent generations of students who came back besotted with the lights of imperialism" (Ashour 1983, 6).[13] Ashour's depiction of her relationship with the United States is not premised on a crude East/West divide. Rather, it is an informed and critical postcolonial point of view, conscious of the impact of colonialism on the Third World, but also acutely aware of the diversity and many contradictions at the heart of colonial centers. In Amherst, she joins forces with progressive students' groups: her choices of relationships are not based on racial or cultural origins, but on ideological and political standpoints. She recounts a multiplicity of experiences, encounters with Americans and strangers, all adding important strokes to the overall picture. Ashour's southern roommate, who is afraid of her because of her race and religion, is offset by her kind professor, and other students whom she befriends. On a trip to New York with her husband, Murid, Ashour notes the underlying contradictions in this complex city: the Statue of Liberty in a segregated city, with African Americans confined to Harlem and not to be seen in the center. On the Fourth of July, or Independence Day, she quotes almost in full the speech

13. All quotations are taken from this edition. All translations are mine.

delivered by Frederick Douglass on 5 July 1852 about slavery in America. The inherent contradictions in the ideals of freedom and equality for all that mark the American dream, are highlighted. Ashour is neither infatuated by Western civilization, nor does she reject it as the embodiment of the other,[14] the antithesis of the self. There are many dimensions of America that resonate with the self. Michelle Hartman has argued that Ashour has managed "to open up a contested space of tension that challenges her readers to think about Arab identity and subjectivity outside of binary terms" (2004, 26).[15] It is noteworthy, however, that her project, to better understand the relationship with the other outside binary opposites, is firmly grounded in her sense of identity and national belonging. She is in a hurry to finish her mission in the United States and return home, where she belongs. This is radically different from what Ramadan and Fakhr are attempting to accomplish.

Both Somaya Ramadan and Husam Fakhr have tried to go beyond the binarism at the heart of the East/West encounter, and the binarism of the self versus the other in colonial and national representations of gendered identities. They have also insisted on their location in between the sides, like nomads, belonging everywhere and nowhere. Both seek to represent spaces that are not bounded by binary logic and dominant stereotypes, and both have struggled to forge an alternative language and imaginary. Kimi's madness is a metaphor for this alternative space that does not operate according to established rules of representation and perception. Yusuf's indecision about the genre and content of his work set in the nineteenth century is an objective correlative of the difficulties and constraints that confront projects that attempt to chart new gendered identities that are not premised on the dichotomous binaries.

Moreover, both writers resist or challenge attempts to limit their work to either side of the East/West continuum. This is clearly demonstrated in their responses to questions in interviews, questions formulated according

14. See Rasheed el-Enany, who has argued that "the text's antipathy towards the US is undisguised" (2006, 180).

15. Hartman also maintains that Ashour was able to do so by "allowing New York to function on some level as an 'other' within the US" (2004, 26). I am arguing that Ashour's project to transcend the binarism is not restricted to the New York interlude in the text, but extends to her overall approach to her American experience.

to a logic that presupposes distinct polarities of identity. Both Ramadan and Fakhr resort to deconstructing the logic of the questions. Ramadan, for example, when asked about the implications of choosing a pharaonic name for her protagonist (*kemet* is a pharaonic word for Egypt) and the suggestion that Kimi symbolizes Egypt, says: "Kimi, Kemet, means Black Soil. It is a pharaonic word but is used as a nickname for children and adults in daily life. It is important to note that Kimi is not pharaonic, neither is she Islamic only, nor does she aspire to the north. She is made of flesh and blood and is very realistic. . . . I am very concerned about saying that Kimi is Egypt because the relationship is not that direct" (2001, 10).

In a similar vein, Fakhr is asked about whether his feeling of alienation and exile was behind his opting for a *Thousand and One Nights* style in his *Hawadit al-'akhar.* He responds by pointing out that some critics have also noted his use of the colloquial dialect in *Wujuh New York* and *Ya 'aziz 'ayni* and have suggested that this was an attempt to "regain the nation by making New York another Cairo." He insists that he has used the colloquial in much of his writing, sometimes to tell the whole story, and not just in dialogue, and that when he starts writing, "he does not make a conscious decision about which language or dialect to use." He then adds: "But now that you have asked me about alienation/estrangement, allow me to say that my acute sense of alienation in New York is only matched by my feeling of alienation in Cairo. I do not see that either feeling has anything to do with my employment of classical language or Egyptian vernacular" (2008b).

Both Ramadan and Fakhr resist pressures to take sides, to choose one place over the other, one identity over the other. However, their projects are ongoing, are in a state of flux, and have not reached a resolution. *'Awraq al-narjis* ends with Kimi gazing at herself in the mirror. Fakhr's *Ya 'aziz 'ayni* is strewn with quotes about nations, homeland, and belonging. The following quote is from his blog: "I had always thought that my heart is divided equally between my two hometowns until it dawned on me that my writing remains almost exclusively in Arabic. Maybe one of them still occupies a larger part after all!"[16] In her study of Francophone women writers of the

16. Fakhr, "Blog" at http://caironyman.blogspot.com.

Maghreb, Valerie Orlando distinguishes between nomadic and nationalists novels. While the nationalist novel is rooted in the history of nationalism and independence movements, the nomadic novel "posits identity in a third space of negotiation between past and present, in between French and Maghrebian cultures and beyond colonial and postcolonial binaries" (2006, 34). Examining the work of Francophone contemporary women novelists in the Maghreb, she finds that they fall in neither category, and concludes that they are situated "somewhere in between the nomadic and the revolutionary" (47). I have tried to show how the nomadic consciousness of both Ramadan and Fakhr does not preclude a nationalist commitment, nor does it automatically signify a position of empowerment.

The nomadic Arabic novel depicts a state of mind, an intellectual project, and a style of life not as ends in themselves, but as strategies to negotiate new, more liberating identities. It is not necessarily a happy story. Kimi's struggle against confinement to national and colonial representations of her identity as an Arab woman leads to her ostracism from the social order. Fakhr's variations on the theme of exile and belonging signal his constant movement as a nomad between points, without settlement, but with a desire to create an alternative, non-essentialized space where he can settle. As nomads, they have "no passport—or too many of them" (Braidotti 1994, 33). This condition is not necessarily empowering, or desirable. In an ideal world, they would probably choose to be both nationalists and nomads.

9

Liminal Spaces/Liminal Identities

Hamdi Abu Golayyel, Ahmed Alaidy, and Muhammad 'Ala' al-Din

The contemporary literary scene in Egypt is rich, vibrant, and very diverse. A wide and largely inclusive space for literary experimentation and new voices blossomed in the 1990s. The new millennium brought with it more innovation, more diversity, and much iconoclasm. Newcomers to the literary field challenge established norms and traditions and interrogate the canonical national imaginary. In this chapter I will examine three novels that explore new gendered identities occupying liminal spaces, physically, psychologically, and existentially. Hamdi Abu Golayyel's *Lusus mutaqa'idun* (2001; English translation, *Thieves in Retirement,* 2006) is the story of a marginalized community of men and women living in an informal urban settlement, one of the many *'ashwa'iyyat* that have sprouted on the edges of the city of Cairo. Ahmed Alaidy's *'An Takun 'Abbas al-'Abd* (2003; English translation, *Being Abbas El Abd,* 2006) is a psychological portrait of masculinities living a liminal existence on the threshold of the social order. Muhammad 'Ala' al-Din's *Injil Adam* (2006; The gospel according to Adam)[1] is an existential quest for understanding the self, amid uncertainty and loss of faith in grand narratives of nationhood, religion, and civilizations.

1. Humphrey Davies translated a section of the novel under the title *The Gospel According to Adam.* The translation is posted on 'Ala' al-Din's blog: http://alaaeldin.blogspot.com/2007/01/gospel-according-to-adam.html. Accessed 12 October 2009.

Hamdi Abu Golayyel was born in 1967, the son of an impoverished Bedouin family that joined a rural settlement in Fayoum and became farmers. While finding his way as a writer, he became a construction worker, a job that brought him to the city of Cairo and allowed him to experience different parts of the city, as he moved from one construction site to another. He was eventually employed by various state institutions, affiliated to the Ministry of Culture, and also worked as a journalist, writing articles for newspapers and cultural magazines.[2] The publication of his first novel, *Lusus mutaqa'idun* in 2002 brought him instant fame and recognition in literary circles.[3] It was translated into English, French, and Spanish.[4] His second novel, *al-Fa'il* (Construction worker), won the Naguib Mahfouz Medal for best novel in 2008.

Abu Golayyel's fame has not been devoid of controversy. His literary style—his flouting of conventional novelistic rules and perceived shocking use of language—has aggravated some literary tastes. In a report on the occasion of his winning the Naguib Mahfouz Medal for Literature for *al-Fa'il* in 2008, the reporter highlights the "mysterious reasons" that prompted the prize committee of judges to vote for "a text that falls outside the rules of novelistic writing." The reporter then ponders the possible reasons: "Is it the case that the committee and the board entrusted with the organization of the awards, according to the concerns of a large number of Egyptian writers, wishes to ensure that a particular writing style prevails? We also do not know when it came about that the vision of award committees was ahead of what can be called, public taste" (Musa 2008).

In *Lusus mutaqa'idun* all the characters are residents of the apartment building number 36 in Manshiyyat Nasir. All of them are migrants in one

2. Hamdi Abu Golayyel was editor of a literary series, *'Afaq al-Kitaba* (Horizons of writing), editor of *Dirasat Sha'biyya* (Popular culture studies), and affiliated with the *Hay'at qusur al-thaqafa* (Mass/public culture organisation) of the Ministry of Culture in Egypt.

3. He wrote two collections of short stories before the publication of his first novel: *'Asrab al-naml* (Hay'at qusur al-thaqafa, 1997); and *'Ashya' matwiyya bi 'inaya fa'iqa* (Things folded with extreme care; GBO, 2000).

4. The English translation, *Thieves in Retirement* (2006), won second place in the Sayf Ghobash-Banipal prize for Arabic literary translation in 2007.

way or another, from rural areas, from other poor districts, or from more affluent areas in Cairo. It is a relatively new district, and Abu Golayyel provides us with an interesting story of origin:

> The leader, Gamal Abdel Nasser, paid a surprise visit to one of the factories founded by his revolution in Helwan. He found an enormous number of workers spending the night in the factory. Overjoyed by their devotion to their work, he approached one of the workers, shook his hand with obvious enthusiasm, "Best of luck young man." The worker rose to kiss his hand saying: "God bless you Sir, [my name is] 'Abd al-Halim 'Abd al-Halim." "Are you working two shifts then?" Suspecting that he was being interrogated, the worker replied: "Well, Sir, only one shift, Sir." "Then why don't you go home?" "Go where, Sir?" The President was disconcerted, as he had thought that the workers were sleeping in the factory because of their desire to work day and night, and not simply because they had no place to live. To save his revolution, he waved his hand in the direction of an empty area that was accidentally within sight and said: "Let them live here." The workers rushed in revolutionary style toward the area, and within days, Manshiyyat Gamal Abdel Nasser was born. (2004, 79)[5]

'Abd al-Halim in the story of origin is also Abu Jamal, or the father of Jamal, and the owner of building 36. He belongs to the generation of workers who came to the city from rural areas to participate in the industrial revolution championed by the 1952 officers' coup. A true son of the revolution, he names his first-born son Jamal, after President Gamal Abdel Nasser. The story of Abu Jamal is an objective correlative of the ambivalence of revolutionary dreams and achievements, as well as their fate. At the age of twenty-two, he was appointed as a worker in a silk factory in Helwan and became one of the first beneficiaries of Nasser's nationalization project, which supported workers rights. At fifty-four, he was one of the first victims of forced redundancy caused by the new privatization laws heralded by Sadat's open-door policies and implemented throughout the Mubarak era. Undaunted by the paradoxical turn of events, he quickly adapted to his change of fortunes

5. All quotations are taken from this edition. All translations are mine.

and embarked on his lifelong project, "his quest for some kind of recognition and appreciation" (11). This project translated into setting up a place for himself in front of his building, a place he cleans diligently and in accordance with a set number of rituals, a place that allows him to intercept strangers who are passing by and invite them almost pleadingly to have tea or lunch, and "who, confronted with this ardent face, and these honest greetings, can only oblige, and articulate the recognition that Abu Jamal is searching for" (13). In line with his reinvention of himself, Abu Jamal has a different take on the story of origin of Manshiyyat Nasir:

> In all honesty, this *manshiyya* should have been named after me. I had just completed a month in the factory when Gamal Abdel Nasser paid us a visit. The manager was terrified. I, however, stood up to him like a lion and did not mince my words: "Sir, we have no place to sleep." So he pointed toward the *manshiyya*. It was a wasteland, by God, a wasteland. If you do not believe me, pictures do not lie. And he draws a crumbled photograph in which he stands tall, while the hand of the Leader is landed on the back of his head. (99)

The pathos in Abu Jamal's story is juxtaposed to his vulgar manners and mean temperament. His criteria for selecting tenants are that they are from the same region in the south of Egypt and that they are "inflicted with some error or failing" (52), so that he can blackmail them when need be, something he does not hesitate to do. He is emotionally cut off from his family and is entangled in a fierce power struggle with his son Jamal over the control of the building and its tenants.

The sons are all the children of the *'ashwa'iyyat,* and their identities are shaped by the place's paradoxes and incongruities. Jamal is a drug dealer, but also a mediocre writer. He is ready to sacrifice anything, even his own children, for the sake of his comfort: "Some people may be occupied with improving the world; I, however, am only occupied with my own little self" (35). 'Amir, another son, is handsome, elegant, and a leader of a "well-known" gang of marijuana-smoking youth. He is a failure in his job as a car mechanic but very successful as a *futuwwa,* feared and respected in his neighborhood. He is also a drug addict, a consequence of his work as a dealer with his brother Jamal. He funds his addiction by stealing, mainly from members of his family, because he considered "robbing strangers an insult to his manhood" (76). Sayf, the youngest son, is an actor and a singer. He is also gay, or rather, bisexual. He thinks of himself as "an actor rebelling against the reduction of his life to one role. He believes that his life is much more open to possibilities" (18). After being committed to an asylum by his father and brother Jamal, he returns with a certificate that testifies to the soundness of his mind and a note by his physician, advising the family to take care of him and arrange for him to be married. Salah, the fourth son, is the only member of the family who seems to be in tune with life in the big metropolis. His membership in the basketball team at the Zamalik sporting club allowed him to travel and acquire a certain lifestyle, which he maintains after he leaves the team. He spends two weeks a year on the beach in Alexandria on holiday. This annual excursion makes his apartment easy and logical prey to 'Amir's robbery plans: his urban-middle-class-inclined lifestyle renders him vulnerable to subversive encroachment from the margins.

The nonfamily tenants of the building present an array of characters who inhabit the *'ashwa'iyyat.* Not all of them were born there, but all ended up in the *manshiyya* for a discernible reason. Ramadan is a poet and storyteller. Like the narrator, he came to the *manshiyya* when he went through a phase of "retreat, boredom, and wisdom" (41). He left his father's elegant building in the Qubba Gardens, a more affluent but rundown neighborhood in Cairo, to escape his wife, the beauty queen of Bani Suwayf in Upper Egypt, and her endless fights with his brothers and sisters. Living on the outskirts of Cairo suits his search for peace and quiet. He is deeply infatuated with Zannuba, 'Amir's wife, but only from a distance. During his lifetime, his poetic talent is never quite established, though he does have a regular salon frequented by young poets. Another tenant, Sheikh Hassan from Upper Egypt, came to the *manshiyya* torn with guilt and remorse for committing the sin of sleeping with his mother-in-law. After establishing himself in the *manshiyya,* and thinking that he is secure enough to pass judgment, he makes the mistake of criticizing Jamal's moral conduct. Vilified in public by Abu Jamal, who reveals his secret sin in the mosque, he is driven out of the building and the *manshiyya.* To complete the array of marginalized characters, we meet 'Adil, a Copt, whose arrival to the building is welcomed by the narrator as someone he can feel sorry for. He is called *coftas* by Abu Jamal, which, the narrator explains, is a variant of Copt in English, or *Copte* in French, all meaning *qibti,* or ancient Egyptian. "For 'Adil, however, it meant something else, something beyond insult. When he hears the word, he recoils, like he was bit from a dark hole. And because our ears are usually good at picking up what hurts most, he was constantly recoiling." (90) 'Adil soon befriends 'Amir and joins his marijuana-smoking youth gang. He remains a mystery to the narrator however, who never really understands what he is all about.

Finally there is the *duktura,* the female nurse turned prostitute. Daughter of a worker who died by being crushed by a factory machine, she was thrown out of her sister's house because of the attention bestowed on her by her sister's husband and was accepted as a tenant by Abu Jamal because he knew he could exploit her. When she stands up for herself against Jamal, she is forcefully evicted by the father with the help of the sons. *Al-duktura* occupies a short space in the narrative, proportionate to her short interlude in the building. However, her working class origin, particularly the death of her father in a factory and the consequences of his loss on her life, render her, like Abu Jamal, another casualty of the ambivalent national project. On another level, her training as a nurse did not secure a decent life for her, forcing her to resort to the age-old occupation available to women.

The other female characters are not as developed as the male characters. This is not to say that they are less central. Like all the characters in the novel, they are portrayed through the eyes of the narrator, a tenant himself in the building, hence his portraits of his neighbors are largely guided by the knowledge he has of them and by his ability to form an opinion. We hear of Zannuba, wife of 'Amir, who flirts with Ramadan, and of the beauty queen of Bani Suwayf, his wife. Umm Jamal, wife of Abu Jamal, is the most puzzling to the narrator, though her story reminds him of his grandmother, making her story the Everywoman story. Umm Jamal spends all night praying to God to make her a man, but she wakes up early every morning to face her disappointment. This male envy is deeply rooted in societal prejudice that favors male over female offspring. Umm Jamal's mother, Naqawa (meaning purity), whose husband married seven more women after she bore him a female child, got rid of two more female children she bore. More, she regretted that she did not get rid of her daughter, Umm Jamal, in the same way when she was a child, hence contributing to her daughter's feeling of rejection. Her strategy to secure power in the household by getting rid of her female daughters reminds the narrator of his great-grandmother, also called Naqawa, who, after being presented with a second young wife who could bear more sons, exacted her revenge by making sure that the male children did not survive. Although victims of social violence and rejection, all the women internalize the violent ethos and reproduce it.

The narrator's depiction of the inhabitants of the building is satirical, teasing out the incongruities, the affectations, and the ridiculous in various situations. Ramadan, the poet, who goes to the *manshiyya* seeking a quiet environment where he can think and contemplate, has a "thinking gear" he took good care of: "more accurately he did nothing but take care of it: his thick eyeglasses with a black frame and silver chain, and his pipe" (41–42). The narrator tells us that his literary reputation was much better after his death than during his life, crowned with a publication that consisted of his important poems and an appropriate eulogy exalting his life and his achievement. This grandiose tribute, which stands in juxtaposition to what the reader already knows about Ramadan and his life circumstances, is deeply ironic, as it presents an alternative and very sobering view on the construction of literary reputations, as well as literary tastes. About Sheikh Hasan, his quest for redemption is presented in a new light, as it devolves into more of a business transaction than a spiritual journey: "he seized every opportunity to accumulate good deeds, an activity which according to him was similar to depositing money in a bank account that can only increase" (48).

The satirical tone that permeates Golayyel's novel has been interpreted to indicate a reformist vision of the writer and has earned him the appellation *islahi ladhi'*, "a sharp-tongued reformist" (Qurani 2002, 10). Muhammad Badawi maintains that "satire is an expression of oppression, in as much as it involves suppressed bitterness, but it goes beyond this when it views the world with suspicion" (2002, 16). Abu Golayyel's response to the interviewer who uses the phrase *islahi ladhi'* is worth quoting at length:

> One of the problems that face satirical writing in our Arab context and literature is that it is regarded as equivalent to criticism that seeks to change or reform . . . [however] the glory of satire, I believe, rests in the fact that it is a valid tool for understanding contradictions and for tackling them with

> extreme objectivity. To prove this point, it is sufficient to say that paradox is a key feature of satire. It is not always the case that satirizing someone means criticizing this person: it is more of an attempt to understand him and represent him in a manner that accommodates his contradictions . . .
>
> For me, satire has allowed me to distance myself a little from myself and from my characters and has saved me from emotional involvement. . . . Therefore, I am forced to relinquish the position of a "sharp-tongued reformist" *islahi ladhi'* that you have bestowed on me, not because I reject it, for who would sacrifice the prestige of being a reformist, but because I am not qualified to begin with. I envy your ability to discover this quality in me, especially that some people came to the conclusion that my novel beautifies ugliness, even promotes decadence. (quoted in Qurani 2002, 10)

Abu Golayyel's biting satire certainly comes across as an earnest attempt to understand the complexities of identities that have emerged in new nonnational spaces. He particularly explores the meanings of manhood as perceived and enacted by his characters. Introducing Sayf, the bisexual son of Abu Jamal for the first time, the narrator reflects on the limitations of prescribed social identities and roles and expresses a deep sympathy with Sayf's dilemma accordingly: "Somehow, deep inside each one of us is a poor actor who performs one role all his life. It is a role limited by circumstances of work, family, propriety, traditions, and our stern consciences" (Abu Golayyel 2004, 17). That is why we become harsh judges of people who do not conform to their prescribed roles and images, and why Sayf's family committed him to an asylum to treat his perceived abnormal behavior, but also to protect their social standing. It is not only Sayf who struggles to come to terms with his sexual identity. All of the male characters ponder the meaning of manhood, on what it means to be a man in society. Abu Golayyel explores some of the stereotypical characteristics associated with manhood and employs satire to understand their contradictions:

> 'Amir is a successful *futuwwa*. There is not a single person in Manshiyyat Nasir who is not terrified of him. He possesses a unique type of courage that can only be found in wild animals. For, despite his slender build, he is ready to wrestle with the entire street. First, he would take off his shirt,

> then beat his modest chest twice with his fists, two strikes that leave you trembling in your skin when he looks at you. He upholds a code of chivalry only to be found among professional criminals. He is always searching for the meaning of manhood, a mysterious concept, even for him. All he knows is that it denotes strength, and a crude sense of power that divides people into two groups: a group of valiant and victorious men, and a group of defeated emasculated men. (75)

Jamal's definition of manhood is also scrutinized. While forcefully evicting the nurse, *al-duktura* from the building, and as she struggled and almost won, "Jamal noticed that she was not wearing a bra. Hence he seized the opportunity to kill two birds with one stone, to have the family triumph and to defend his wasted manhood. He forcefully squeezed her breasts and did not let go until she declared her surrender and agreed to leave the building" (53) This depiction of how Jamal's violent aggressive act against the nurse is justified as support for his family and a defense of his "wasted" manly honor is deeply ironic, but also indicative of a perverse social phenomenon where strong women are perceived as threatening to male identity, leading to exaggerated male aggression against women, condoned as an expression of manhood.

The most well-rounded male figure in the novel is the narrator, who recounts events from his point of view, which is often omniscient as he reveals the inner workings of the characters' minds. The narrator is of Bedouin origin. He identifies with his nomadic roots, with his tribe. His father, like many other Bedouins who left the desert to live on the outskirts of the city, worked as a *ghafir,* a security guard. Bedouins often take this job because they are famous for their courage: "a nomadic life in the desert imposes a certain measure of courage . . . nomadism is similar to death" (23). The stereotypical fearless nomad however, is more of a legendary figure than a reality. He has left the desert and has been molded into the life of the city. The narrator, for example, belongs to the generation of Bedouins who, despite their dispossession, "were not ashamed to farm the remains of their land" (56). As nomad-cum-farmer, he acquired qualities that made him appear to be, in the eyes of his enemies among farmers, a poor man who minds his own business, but in the eyes of his tribesmen, a Bedouin "with angry fire in his eyes" (57). At the same time, the proverbial courage of Bedouins is undercut by the narrator's account of the survival tactics he adopted upon moving to the *manshiyya.* In short, good behavior, abstinence, and some idiocy became his tools for dealing with his fear: "fear is the safe haven for people in my condition. It is normal to be afraid when standing on the top of a steep cliff, or upon meeting a large group of strangers" (20). This fear is a far cry from nomadic courage, a frame of mind that comes with settlement in a particular place. Settlement, or the termination of a nomadic lifestyle, the transition to rural settings, and then urban places, has inevitably resulted in the transformation of the identity of the nomad, and the values and practices associated with nomadic manhood.

Asked why he abandoned the Bedouin environment celebrated in his early work, Abu Golayyel rejects confinement to an iconic status of an essential and limiting Bedouinness:

> This approach . . . actually contradicts the existential crisis experienced by the Bedouin now. On the realistic, material, and physical level, at least in Egypt, the Bedouin has actually left the desert, departed forever, and is now hovering around the edges of the city coveting what his ancestors recoiled from, that is, permanent settlement in a place. This does not mean that he went against or denied his Bedouinness or his memory, for, although he has left the desert physically, he, at the same time, preserves it as a sanctuary, without which he loses his identity. . . . *Thieves in Retirement* never left the Bedouin environment. It tried, I hope, to chart the double consciousness of the Bedouin, the desert inside him and the city, which he tries by all means to be accepted by, without noise or clash. (quoted in Qurani 2002)

Places in the novel are generally not set up in opposition to one another, but are more of a continuum in flux. Most of the inhabitants of the *manshiyya* have rural roots and bring to it rural values and practices. It "resembles a village. At the end of the day, its old inhabitants, like Abu Jamal, are like family members, and work-mates in the Helwan factory. Every house knows the secrets of other houses. They will safeguard those secrets and will never allow a stranger to expose them" (Abu Golayyel 2004, 49–50). Also, the narrator tells us that "*al-manshiyya* is a state of hybridity between the village and an informal settlement *hay 'ashwa'i*" (80).

Much has been written about how these informal settlements constitute ghettos that are isolated from the modern city, whose inhabitants are cut off from their roots and dominant social mores. Within this framework, Abu Golayyel's *manshiyya* has been described by Dina Hishmat as a ghettoized space where "the text establishes social rules that are totally different from the prevalent rules in society. In fact, it seeks to establish a counter value system" (2006, 151).[6] She bases her argument on the fact that most of the characters in the novel do not abide by the social moral code of behavior, but more significantly on the use of satire by the author, which allows him to describe his characters without judging them on moral grounds. She concludes by saying that "this kind of behavior and this kind of writing gives the impression that there is a world that functions in accordance to its own value system and is almost isolated from the outside world" (2006, 152).

Rather than a ghetto, Manshayyat Nasir is more of a liminal space, on the outskirts of the city but still part of it, in fact encroaching on its center. Abu Golayyel, of Bedouin origin himself, describes the place with a nomadic sensibility that is more in tune with mobility, indeterminacy, and openness. Perceptions of ideal manhood are queried, not to pass judgment, or to suggest a counter-system, but rather to transgress fixities and understand multiple possibilities. Abu Golayyel incorporates this indeterminacy in his narrative style. The very first word in the novel calls upon the reader to "assume," assume that he is living his life as a character in a novel. The narrator repeatedly interrupts the narrative to reflect on his role as a character, hence foregrounding the idea that his story has multiple possibilities, and that his character can potentially end up playing different roles. Multiple narratives are not restricted to the narrator. Places have multiple narratives of origin, as is demonstrated by the two stories about how the *manshiyya* was founded. The same technique is used to explain why 'Adil hated the appellation *coftas*. One account is a very dramatic moment in 'Adil's childhood:

6. Hishmat's book is a translation by the author of her PhD thesis, submitted in 2004 in French to the University of Paris III: Sorbonne Nouvelle.

other children in the village all drink from the sheik's pitcher; he, however, drops it on the sheikh's head and becomes the target of abuse, which marks him as the "other." Or maybe none of that happened, and the sheikh allowed him to have a drink like all the other children but looked at him in a way that 'Adil expected (90–93). In liminal spaces, identities are indeterminate, not fixed and potentially transgressive.

Born in 1974, Alaidy started his career as a graphic designer, then was a script writer for quiz shows and films. He then wrote stories for young people in a privately owned publishing company, Dar al-mubdi'un. He was commissioned to write for a series of comic books entitled *Majanin* (Mad people), which was meant to be a book version of the American magazine *Mad.* In fact, the first draft of *'Abbas al-'Abd* was written as a second installment in the magazine. The publisher did not approve the book, and after a number of rejections, the novel was published by Dar merit.[7]

The novel is about a generation of disaffected, disenfranchised youth who struggle to find meaning in a nightmarish world. The narrator is extremely critical and angry at the world and at people and announces his rebellion against the status quo, against all rules and social conventions. He embarks on a journey of self-discovery by literally throwing himself into the wilderness with no compass or map:

> Who am I
>
> I am who I am, and I have my own reasons. There is nothing at all that makes me indebted to you or to any one else. . . .
>
> Stop judging me.
>
> Accept me as I am, not as you would like me to be. (Alaidy 2003, 11–12)[8]

The narrator tells us about his friend 'Abbas al-'Abd, who shocks and fascinates him at the same time. He is depicted as a social misfit par excellence:

7. Hazim Abyad, "Review," http://www.arabworldbooks.com/authors/ahmed_elaidi.htm. Accessed Saturday 24 Nov. 2007.

8. All quotations are taken from this edition. All translations are mine.

dirty, disgusting, antisocial. Nevertheless, he expresses almost an instinctive wisdom or common sense attitude to the chaos around him. 'Abbas takes pity on his new friend when he discovers that he has no female acquaintances and sets him up with two prostitutes, both called Hind, at the same time. The narrator eventually tries to take revenge on 'Abbas by convincing one of the women to write 'Abbas's mobile number on the toilet walls of malls. The other male character is 'Awni, the narrator's uncle. He is a psychiatrist who decided to use his nephew as a guinea pig in a psychiatric experiment that ends in disaster. We discover at the end that the three male characters are one and the same, that our narrator is schizophrenic, and that 'Abbas is the narrator's alter ego.

At the beginning of the novel, Alaidy writes an unusual dedication to his "accomplices in crime in the order of the level of complicity." Starting with his father and mother, he then identifies the names of writers and friends. The first name on the list is Chuck Palahniuk, American writer and author of the famous novel *Fight Club,* published in 1996 and turned into a famous film in 1999 that eventually became a cult movie. The novel is about the crisis in American masculinity as a result of living in a society that has been taken over by consumerism and a hypocritical value system disseminated by the media. The protagonist belongs to Douglas Coupland's Generation X (a generation born in the 1980s in a society ruled by rabid consumerism depicted in his novel *Generation X: Tales for an Accelerated Culture,* 1991). In *Fight Club,* the protagonist draws attention to the feeling of betrayal experienced by "the middle children of history, raised by television to believe that someday we'll be millionaires a,nd movie stars and rock stars, but we won't" (Palahniuk 2005 166). In an attempt to salvage his lost masculinity, he first joins the "Remaining Men Together" group, then with his alter ego, Tyler, he establishes a fight club to help men, many of whom have white collar jobs, regain their masculinity through the exercise of unchecked violence. This leads to Project Mayhem, which initiates a series of acts of sabotage: "I wanted to destroy everything beautiful I'd never had . . . break up civilization so we can make something better out of the world" (2005, 123, 125).

Fight Club is clearly an important influence on Alaidy's novel, and there are clear parallels. In *'An Takun 'Abbas al-'Abd,* the narrator also suffers from insomnia; 'Abbas is his alter ego; 'Abbas is the side of him that takes action to resolve his crisis; acts of sabotage and antisocial behavior are also contemplated and practiced; the novel foregrounds the rampant consumerism that has taken over societal values; like Tyler, 'Abbas comes across as a legendary figure; at the level of structure, some sentences are repeated like refrains; and finally the novel is also about "injured masculinities."

On the other hand, the two novels are not by any means identical in the treatment of themes or emphasis. In *'Abbas al-'Abd,* the crisis in masculinity is not only a function of rampant consumerism and neo-liberal market logic: it is primarily a consequence of the crisis in postcolonial national projects, or the failed dreams of nationalism. Like many of the protagonists in Sonallah Ibrahim's novels, the narrator suffers from his acute awareness of the gap that separates the national dream of progress and prosperity from the sordid political and social reality around him. The novel is about new postcolonial identities and their relationship with national narratives. Alaidy's treatment of the theme of broken masculinities departs significantly from previous generations of writers, particularly the generation of the 1960s. On the one hand, we have the narrator, an angry, defeated man who suffers from all the known and unknown phobias imaginable. He distinguishes himself and his generation from the generation of the 1960s in this manner:

> In Egypt there was the defeated generation [*jil al-naksa*],
>
> We are the following generation, the "I have nothing to lose generation."
>
> We are the autistic generation, living under the same roof, with strangers with names that resemble ours. (41)

This is the voice of the protagonist, trying to put on a brave face, as if it does not matter. But it does matter. He recognizes that he is lying to himself when he claims that he has nothing to lose, as he continues to cling to old dreams. In this way, the narrator is still very much an heir to the 1960s, the "defeated generation" that mourns the decline of the dream. 'Abbas, on the other hand, is the prototype of a new type of man, representing a postnational masculinity. His whole manner and behavior exists literally outside the nationalist value system that has been celebrated, remembered with nostalgia, or mourned by previous writers. In a conversation with 'Abbas, the narrator says:

> I told him that we will never progress so long as we have people like him among us, people whose hobby is to kill time and collect lizards and so on. The gap between us and the West will continue so long as we are too lax with our history, like students without guardians.
>
> The West and the East.
>
> Here and There. (39)

And ʻAbbas responds angrily:

> Do you want to progress?
>
> Then burn history books, and forget your dead and precious civilization.
>
> Stop suckling the past.
>
> Destroy your Pharaonic history. (39)

In another conversation about the meaning of life and happiness, ʻAbbas says:

> We are not searching for money for its sake as we imagine. We are searching for more *'ubshans* [the English word, options, is given an Arabic pronunciation].
>
> Isn't hell, to use a reductive statement, the taking away of one's *'ubshans?*
>
> . . . Happiness is not equated with money or health or beauty or power.
>
> Happiness is having *'ubshans.* Tell me what your *'ubshans* are and I will tell you who you are. (99)

ʻAbbas is the product of the *ʻashwa'iyyat,* the new informal urban spaces that sprang up with minimal or no links with the nation-state apparatuses and structures. He represents a generation of marginalized subjects that have never been integrated in the national imaginary, of progress, of building a modern nation. He embodies a postnational masculinity that exists at odds with old precepts and values. He is fascinating from the point of view of the narrator because he has found a way of stepping outside the nationalist dilemma that persists in oppositional logic: us versus them, tradition versus modernity, East and West. Like Tyler, ʻAbbas is proactive in addressing the problem. Unlike Tyler, however, his solution is not to embark on a destructive rampage of the society he shuns. His solution is in finding a different way of being that does not answer to preconceived norms about ideal masculinities.

Muhammad 'Ala' al-Din (born 1979) gained critical acclaim upon the publication of his first novel, *'Injil 'Adam* (The gospel according to Adam) in 2006. Like Alaidy, 'Ala' al-Din started his career in 2000 writing for the comic magazine *Majanin,* published by Dar mubdi'un. He is a freelance script writer, writes comic books, and participates in creative writing workshops for children. In 2002, he contributed to an international workshop on the creation of comic books, which led to the publication of *The Adventures of Prince Sayf Ibn Zi Yazan* in Arabic, English, and French.[9] *'Injil 'Adam* belongs to a new generation of writing by young writers who embark on bold experiments to break literary conventions as well as social and political taboos. The novel immediately elicited enthusiastic reviews, which described it as constituting "a shift at the level of genre and experimentation in the contemporary narrative text in Egypt" (Farghali 2006b). Conversely, the novel has been described as "a hallucinating text that takes place inside the mind of a madman" (Hannah 2005). These two polarized responses testify to the novelty and experimental style of the novel, as well as the sheer shocking effect it has had on the literary scene. The reader is warned at the beginning that he will be taken on a strenuous journey with the characters, under the penetrating eye of the sun, which will expose and scorch: "The piercing eye of the sun glares at the street. Its lashes scorch the heads and backs of passers-by. Sticky sweat slides over my forehead, as I walk slowly, seeking shelter in the shade of buildings on my right. A few steps away, the wide square is opened up. Its face is also shining with sweat. I do not know the sin it committed, to have the sun scald it with its gaze so" ('Ala' al-Din 2006, 9).[10] The narrator then

9. 'Ala' al-Din's first literary venture was a collection of short stories, *al-Daffa al-'ukhra* (The other bank) published in 2003 by Hay'at qusur al-thaqafa, a state-owned publishing house. In 2004, his unpublished novel *al-Dawa'ir* (Circles) won the third prize in a national competition organized by the Hay'at qusur al-thaqafa. He wrote two more novels, *al-Yawm al-thani wa al-'ishrun* (The twenty-second day; Cairo: Dar al-'Ayn, 2007); *al-Sanam* (The idol; Cairo: Dar al-'Ayn, 2008); and a collection of short stories, *al-Hayat al-siriyya li al-muwatin mim* (The secret life of citizen M; Cairo: Mizan, 2008).

10. All quotations are taken from this edition. All translations are mine.

notices "a protruding breast under a tight blouse" (9). Wanting to approach the young woman, but not knowing how, and not feeling confident enough about who he is, how she will respond to him, or what she is all about, he sets out on an imaginary journey exploring multiple identities, triggered by the phrase: "if I were someone else . . ." This hypothetical "if" initiates an avalanche of hypothetical personae and situations, all in the mind of the narrator and all envisaged as possible manifestations of his identity. The personae draw on stereotypical expressions of masculinity that have been reduced to single-minded mental attitudes, modern versions of the "humours" that were the subject of Menippean satire: the Brash Moron, the Sensitive Painter, the Brutal Bohemian Artist, the Bald and Ugly Mechanic, the Respected Old Man, the Stern Policeman, the Brash and Vulgar Chief Inspector. Their basic animal instincts, mostly the dark sides of their personalities, are exaggerated, creating a carnivalesque parade of grotesque types and bodies. 'Ala' al-Din succeeds in creating a hypothetical scenario populated by one-dimensional types, whose temperaments are manifested in their language as well as in their physical attributes. The novel is carnivalesque in the Bakhtinian sense. It subverts established structures and social systems through the use of satire, parody, and hyperbole. All truths are interrogated and contested; accepted logic is turned upside down; and in the place of order, continuity, and linearity, we have disruption and chaos.

The novel has two female figures. They, too, are one-dimensional, depicting types rather than rounded characters. But unlike the male characters, they are introduced through the eyes of a patriarchal social order that reduces women to their sexual role. The first female figure is the woman who triggers the action, and who is referred to repeatedly, in a refrainlike style, as "the girl with protruding breasts and yielding backside." The second woman is older and is therefore called the "woman in her forties." Again, emphasis is placed on her physical/sexual attributes, "her white legs." Her age is consistently foregrounded, signaling the prevalent decline in the social capital of older women as sex objects. All references to the women are profane and degrading, an indication of the debased relationships that are sought and exist between the various personae.

All the male personae covet one or the other of the two women, and their attributes are revealed as they contemplate ways of approaching them or relating to them. Thinking about "the young girl with protruding breasts," the Brutal Bohemian Artist imagines "slapping and kicking her, and sticking [his] finger painfully inside her" (11). Assuming the persona of The Sensitive Painter however, results in a different scenario altogether:

> I will savor her gently, as I do French wine. And maybe she will not like it because she wants someone who forces himself inside her like a bull and treats her like a piece of meat that must be stabbed and sliced so that it is cooked more quickly and successfully. I shall not condone this because my French education and my living abroad have made me see women as sweets with a heavenly taste, that must be nibbled at, one centimeter at a time. (11)

The Sensitive Painter is particularly interesting, as he develops, or rather mutates, into other types. His transformation is instigated by a typical artistic listlessness, a sort of dissatisfaction with his limitations, coupled with a deep desire for recognition and fame. The Sensitive Painter also wishes to pursue the Woman in Her Forties because she owns an art gallery where he wants to hold an exhibition of his work. However, his artistic quest for inspiration makes him give up the financial privileges and comfort he had: he leaves his house in Zamalik and moves to a popular low-income area. He then contemplates the life of a monk or a sufi as "a haven and a last resort for his life journey" (31). He recognizes that he still yearns for recognition and fame. The Sensitive Painter then becomes a monk, a son of the desert, a dreamy piper. His eyes fall on the "young woman with protruding breasts and yielding backside," and he is able to look at her for the first time not as a sex object, but as a human being. He is overwhelmed by "her beauty and her clear eyes," and he becomes "part of a whole" (32). Hence, a new persona emerges: the Sensitive Painter-cum-Prophet.

Multiple types of masculinity are paraded in the novel. Most types are signaled as mental attitudes, reflected in the adjectives used to describe them, such as the Sensitive Painter or the Brutal Bohemian Artist. In some cases, their physical attributes reflect their temperaments, creating an array of grotesque embodiments. The Bald and Ugly Mechanic's approach to women is vulgar and crude, but he also enjoys sex with young boys, especially the young apprentices in his workshop. Rebuffed by the Woman in Her Forties, he thinks that if he had not been bald, he might have appealed to women. His reflections on the type of hair he fancies, thick, black, straight hair, rather than light hair, "which is disgusting" (19), borders on the grotesque. He then decides that baldness is a sign of manhood because the Pasha, the Stern Policeman, was also bald. This Stern Police Officer and Master of Creativity gained his title because he excelled in terrorizing and torturing suspects in his custody: in other words, he was creative in inventing new torture techniques. The Stern Officer uses foul, vulgar, and abusive language consistently: "Now as Chief Intelligence Officer, who is brash and vulgar, I do not find vulgarity something to be ashamed of. Rather, it is an authentic expression of true manhood" (22). He then reveals that he is the elder brother of the Brash Moron, also a junior police officer. He is aware of his younger brother's hatred of him because of the stern upbringing to which he subjected him. The Stern Policeman looks at his brother with disdain: "I taught him to be a man, but he turned out to be a chicken" (24).

In the second half of the novel, and as the Sensitive Painter-cum-Prophet emerges as the main persona who guides the narrative, the author raises major existential and philosophical questions about gendered identities, life and death, good and evil, the role of religion, the nature of divine justice. This is done very cleverly, as different types react to the advent of the Prophet as well as define themselves in relation to him. The Respected Old Man "could never understand Prophets and religious leaders" (32). For him, they offered people imaginary visions of a nonexistent world, or "castles in the sand" (32). However, because he has no absolute certainty in any one position, he concedes the possibility that the Prophet is right after all. The Cruel Police Officer, however, understands the Prophet because for him it is all about control and power: he controls men through fear, while the Prophet controls them through faith. One day he screams in his face:

> "Prophet, what is behind your alleged prophecy? What is your aim?" He answered with the famous smile on his face: "I am only here for the sake of the sheep of our misguided city." I knew that behind his alleged luminosity was the mind of a wolf. I was a master only because people are sheep. And since he knew that too, he will lead them, like a shepherd leads his stray herd, with his pipe and stick. (36)

Also, and in relation to the Prophet, the two women find their voices, a development in the narrative whereby they express how they feel, as opposed to being consistently the objects of the male gaze. The Woman in Her Forties is the Prophet's mother. Her story is a mixture of the religious and the profane: she does not know who the father is and does not dare admit it. So, like the Virgin Mary, she says that she woke up one day to find herself with child: "How did it happen, while the room was closed, and no human entered or touched me all night?" (37). The Woman in Her Forties, the mother, the Virgin Mary, also desires the young woman "with protruding breasts," who is in love with the Prophet. She hates her son, the Prophet, for becoming a man who will judge her, and she joins the plot to kill him. Her declaration of rebellion against the stereotyping of her identity as a woman is declared as she rejects the qualities associated with femininity: "All men treat me like a whore, and I am tired of it all. . . . Why can't I do what I want? . . . I will be the lover of the whore [the young woman] and will fear nothing. . . . For the first time, I will be who I want to be. . . . At last, I am all men. Farewell fear and confusion and blaming oneself without having committed a sin" (39–40). The Young Woman with Protruding Breasts and Yielding Backside who recognizes that she is "a whore in the eyes of everyone" (41) becomes a devoted follower/beloved of the Prophet, a modern Mary Magdalene, who worships the Prophet and washes his feet, especially when he challenges his disciples: "let he whose repentance is greater than hers throw a stone at her" (40). Her new persona as a repentant sinner makes her unforgiving and unmerciful toward other sinners, who will become "the fodder/fuel of the holy fire" (42).

In typical carnivalesque fashion, the appearance of the Prophet toward the end of the novel, and the plot to kill him, elicits an interrogation and contestation of the various religious narratives. 'Ala' al-Din weaves the stories of Moses, Jesus, and Mohamed together, creating a story of all prophets who have been persecuted or challenged. Biblical and Qur'anic echoes permeate the text: the plot to kill the Prophet will be executed by the twelve heads of families in the city; the Prophet will be denied by his cousin thrice; he has a last dinner with his disciples; his cousin will sleep in the Prophet's bed to mislead his assassins; the Prophet's body rises to heaven; the Prophet will return from death after three days; Adam and Eve are expelled from paradise; Cain kills Abel. The murder triggers a heated discussion between Eve and Adam about divine justice—why all the children of Adam are made responsible for the sin of Cain; why, if everyone's destiny is preordained, must human beings go through the trials of life—and a discussion about free will and choice. These are just a few examples, as the text is replete with such references and echoes. What is striking and interesting is that all the religious echoes, words, and incidents are variations on the original, not identical replications, a characteristic feature of the novel as it undermines the stability and fixity and foregrounds indeterminacy, diversity, and shifting points of view. Major historical and religious narratives, like identities, are not fixed. The polyphony of voices is matched by the multitudinous narratives, the twists and turns to age-old stories about prophets, about good and evil, and right and wrong.

In line with the liminal indeterminacy of identities and narratives in the novel, the structure of the text is circular: the text develops according to a logic of incremental variation that is nonlinear, allowing for major shifts and revisions. The plot unravels at a breathtaking pace, almost nonstop, not allowing for pauses or breaks. The novel is short, approximately sixty pages long, and is not divided into paragraphs or sections. This unrelenting pace and progression mirrors the development of the plot according to an association of ideas with abrupt shifts in mood and voices. The hypothetical "If I were . . ." at the beginning of the novel has certainly opened up floodgates that sweep the reader. The question is, are they the floodgates of heaven or hell? Ibrahim Farghali described the narrator as cunning, as he does not reveal anything about himself, and finds his hypothetical identities and journeys hellish.[11] In the last few lines, the plot reaches full circle, as the narrator is back at the point where he started, though now he is more secure in his own identity. The sun is still burning people and scorching the square with its lashes, but the narrator does not notice or does not care: "I was many other people/selves but I still did not win the young woman with protruding breasts and yielding backside. I will talk to her, and I will not be either strong or weak. And

11. Farghali (2006b) used the phrase *jahim al-ihtimalat* (The hell of hypothetical suppositions).

she will not be either a virgin or a whore. I walked briskly back to where she was. I said to myself that I must be myself, and no one else. And she must be herself and no one else" (60). One possible answer to the question posed above is that the hypothetical "If I were . . ." leads neither to heaven nor to hell. It does allow the narrator to transcend binary logic in defining identities, the world, and our narratives of the world. "If" ushers in a liminal state with all its possibilities, opportunities, and restrictions. It is a space disjointed from rigid ideas about communities or institutions or relationships. It is also a space that forces the reader out of his/her comfort zone and follows a circular progression, from one voice to another, one identity to another, constantly breaking taboos, contesting established truths. It is a new gospel according to Adam. His hypothetical experiment/journey/explorations of potential lead him to address existential and philosophical issues about life and death, good and evil, the place of man on earth, the meaning of the divine, religious issues about the place of evil, choice, destiny. It does not lead to hell, but to an attempt to understand the self and divine truth.

Conclusion

Alaidy's novel creates an alternate space that enables new expressions of being. He uses the language used in chat rooms, word processing idioms such as cut and paste, English words either arabized or simply inserted in the text, a language that is disconnected, automated, and very close to the dialect spoken by the young. The structures of the sentences and the abbreviations mirror those used in Internet chat rooms and SMS messaging, especially among the young. *'An Takun 'Abbas al-'Abd* has been described as "outrageous, wild, outlandish, weird and zany" (Kaaki 2006). This is unfamiliar terrain, as yet unexplored or perhaps marginalized in the dominant national imaginary. It is a space for being that falls outside national structures and state apparatuses. Its inhabitants are creating new rules and social norms. It is the space currently available for generations who lie outside of, or parallel to, the national social order.

In chapter 7, I referred to Sabry Hafez's thesis that many of the writers of the 1990s are sons of the *'ashwa'iyyat*, or the third city, as he describes it, even if they were not born there. The *'ashwa'iyyat*, as the modern ghettos for the poor, the underprivileged, the forgotten citizens of the modern nation-state, evoke a host of negative images as breeding grounds of delinquent youth and extremist factions that threaten the national social order. In a study of life in Bulaq, an informal settlement on the outskirts of the city of Cairo, Salwa Ismail argues that these negative representations arise "in relation to a wider system of representation in which the conceptualization of urban planning projects is based on modern visions of order, progress, and civilization" (2006, 4). The *'ashwa'iyyat* become physical testimonies to the failure of the national dream of progress and prosperity. However, a trip to Cairo in the new millennium reveals that the *'ashwa'iyyat* are not self-contained spaces on the peripheries of the city: they have penetrated the city or, rather, are an integral part of the urban center and its life. *'Ashwa'i,* the adjective of *'ashwa'iyyat,* meaning chaotic, unplanned, nonconformist, unruly, has become a characteristic feature of the modern postcolonial city. *'Ashwa'i,* in a metaphoric sense, is a liminal space on the threshold of cities, narratives, identities. It is not exclusive to the inhabitants of the physical *'ashwa'iyyat.*

Liminal spaces allow for the exploration of potential, of multiple possibilities, indeterminacy, and transgressive identities. These new spaces have enabled the emergence of new subjects that are antithetical or exist in contradistinction to the earlier expressions of idealized womanhood and manhood in the national imaginary. These new identities are not necessarily confined to the borderlands of the nation but have become, and in reality are, part of the national fabric, though seemingly unrecognized and unaccounted for.

Postscript

After Tahrir: Imagining Otherwise

The guiding questions for this book have been: what are the implications of rethinking the history of the Arabic novel, taking into consideration gender as a category of analysis? What processes of inclusion and exclusion were in place owing to the dominance of normative representations of gendered roles by national elites? How were these dominant representations contested and negotiated by men and women writers? How have literary imaginings of a gendered nationhood shaped debates about national identity throughout the twentieth century and into the twenty-first? And finally, how has the shift to a transnational condition in the twenty-first century affected the very idea of a national canon, let alone the problematics associated with it, where a young generation of authors interrogate and redefine the meaning of nationhood and belonging?

Writing this postscript in the aftermath of the 25 January revolution in Egypt, it is almost impossible not to acknowledge the role of the new generations in the Arab world, the young men and women who dared to imagine new futures that were not conceivable, or deemed irrational or unattainable, by established centers of power and authority. The achievement of the Tahrir revolutionaries in toppling a dictator in eighteen days, regardless of outcomes, has undoubtedly initiated a whole new range of possibilities, new empowered subjects, new imaginings, and new realities. Arab writers throughout the modern period have played a key role in fashioning the imaginary of the nation. A decade into the new millennium, new forces and new variables are at play posing new challenges and opportunities.

A new generation of writers who are engaging critically with representations of the national self and the definition of the national canon from within a transnational context emerged in the 1990s. For the first time, there are as many women writers as there are male writers trying to raise new questions and experiment with new paradigms of thought. More important, for the first time, new media technologies have enabled the formation of diverse and multiple spaces for communication and interaction—political and social, as well as literary, spaces. Literary forums on websites, blogs, and Facebook run parallel to conventional literary gatherings in salons, cafés, or more structured seminars, inspiring new audiences and new imaginaries. The end of the first decade of the twenty-first century saw the creation of a new literary genre, the *mudawwana* (blog), texts originally appearing on the Internet in blogs published and sold in print form alongside collections of short stories and novels.[1] New communication and interactive tools that characterize the new millennium, inasmuch as they have empowered and inspired the new generation of politically active youth of the revolution and enabled them to forge new realities, have opened up new possibilities for literary voices to imagine otherwise.

1. I discuss the impact of blogging on the canon of Arabic literature in my article "Arab Women Bloggers: The Emergence of Literary Counterpublics" (Elsadda 2010).

References

Index

References

'Abd al-Halim, Ahmed Zaki. 1982. "Bahithat al-badiya zalamaha al-tarikh" [The searcher in the desert wronged by history]. *al-Hilal,* November.

'Abd al-Majid, Ibrahim. 1996. "Latifa al-Zayyat sahibat al-watan." In *Latifa al-Zayyat: al-'adab wa al-watan,* edited by Sayyid al-Bahrawi. Cairo: Nur, dar al-mar'a al-'arabiyya li al-nashr wa markaz al-buhuth al-'arabiyya li al-nashr.

'Abd al-Rahman, 'A'isha. 1962. *al-Sha'ira al-'arabiyya al-mu'asira* [The contemporary Arab woman poet]. Cairo: Matba'at lajnat al-ta'lif wa al-tarjama wa al-nashr.

Abdel Messih, Marie Therese. 2006. "Debunking the Heroic Self." *Banipal* 25 (Spring): 22–23.

Abu Golayyel, Hamdi. 2004. *Lusus mutaqa'idun.* 2d ed. Cairo: Dar merit.

———. 2006. *Thieves in Retirement.* Translated by Marilyn Booth. Syracuse: Syracuse Univ. Press.

Abu-Lughod, Lila, ed. 1998. *Remaking Women: Feminism and Modernity in the Middle East.* Princeton, New Jersey: Princeton Univ. Press, 126–70.

Accad, Evelyne. 1978. *Veil of Shame: The Role of Women in the Contemporary Fiction of North Africa and the Arab World.* Quebec: Naaman.

———. 1990. *Sexuality and War: Literary Masks of the Middle East.* New York: New York Univ. Press.

Aghacy, Samira. 2009. *Masculine Identity in the Fiction of the Arab East since 1967.* Syracuse: Syracuse Univ. Press.

Ahmad, Aijaz. 1987. "Jameson's Rhetoric of Otherness and the 'National Allegory.'" *Social Text,* no. 17 (Autumn): 3–25.

Ahmed, Leila. 1992. *Women and Gender in Islam.* New Haven and London: Yale Univ. Press.

'Ala' al-Din, Muhammad. 2006. *'Injil 'adam.* Cairo: Dar merit.

Alaidy, Ahmed. 2003. *'An Takun 'Abbas al-'Abd.* Cairo: Dar merit.

———. 2006. *Being Abbas El Abd.* Translated by Humphrey Davies. Cairo: American Univ. Press.

al-Ali, Nadje. 1994. *Gender Writing/Writing Gender: The Representation of Women in a Selection of Modern Egyptian Literature.* Cairo: American Univ. in Cairo Press.

Allen, Roger. 1995. *The Arabic Novel: An Historical and Critical Introduction.* 2d ed. Syracuse: Syracuse Univ. Press.

al-Amin, Anicee et al. 2007. *Tafkik mafhum al-dhukura al-muhaymina: al-rujula wa al-'ubuwwa al-yawm* [Deconstruction of the concept of masculinity and patriarchy in contemporary society]. Beirut: Tajamu' al-bahithat al-lubnaniyyat; printed and distributed by al-Markaz al-thaqafi al-'arabi.

Amin, Jalal. 2007. "Husam Fakhr, mawhiba 'Jahiniyya' jadida." *al-Masry al-Yawm,* no. 1080 (29 May).

Amin, Nura. 1997. *Qamis wardi farigh* [An empty pink shirt]. Cairo: Dar sharqiyyat.

———. 2004. "Struggling Like an Immigrant," interview with Adrian Grima, *Sunday Times,* 19 September, http://www.inizjamed.org/nora_amin_settembru04.htm. Accessed 1 February 2010.

Amin, Qasim. (1894) 1989. *al-Misriyyun.* In *Qasim Amin: al-'a'mal al-kamila,* edited by Muhammad 'Imara. Cairo: Dar al-shorouq.

———. (1899) 1989. *Tahrir al-mar'a.* In *Qasim Amin: al-'a'mal al-kamila,* edited by Muhammad 'Imara. Cairo: Dar al-shorouq.

———. (1900) 1989. *al-Mar'a al-jadida.* In *Qasim Amin: al-'a'mal al-kamila,* edited by Muhammad 'Imara. Cairo: Dar al-shorouq.

———. 1992. *The Liberation of Woman.* Translated by Samiha Sidhom Peterson. Cairo: The American Univ. Press.

———. 1995. *The New Woman.* Translated by Samiha Sidhom Peterson. Cairo: American Univ. Press.

Amireh, Amal. 1996. "Publishing in the West: Problems and Prospects for Arab Women Writers." *Aljadid: A Record of Arab Culture and the Arts* 2, no. 10 (August), http://www.aljadid.com/content/publishing-west-problems-and-prospects-arab-women-writers. Accessed 12 July 2009.

Anderson, Benedict. 1991. *Imagined Communities: Reflections on the Origin and Spread of Nationalism.* Rev. ed. London and New York: Verso.

al-'Aqqad, 'Abbas. 1965. *Shu'ara' misr wa bi'atuhum fi al-jil al-madi* [Egypt's poets and their environment in the previous generation]. 3d ed. Cairo: maktabat al-nahda.

Arebi, Saddeka. 1994. *Women and Words in Saudi Arabia: The Politics of Literary Discourse.* New York: Columbia Univ. Press.

al-'Aryan, Mohammed Sayyid. 1939. *Hayat al-Rafi'i* [al-Rafi'i's life]. Cairo: Maktabat al-Risala.

'Asfur, Jabir. 1996. "Introduction." In *Mohamed Hussein Haikal fi 'uyun mu'asirih* [Mohamed Hussein Haikal through the eyes of his contemporaries], edited by Nabil Faraj. Cairo: Matba'at dar al-kutub al-misriyya.

———. 1999. *Zaman al-riwaya.* Cairo: Maktabat al-'usra.

Ashour, Radwa. 1983. *al-Rihla: 'ayyam taliba misriyya fi 'amrika* [The journey: days of an Egyptian student in America]. Beirut: dar al-'adab.

———. 2009. *al-Hadatha al-mumkina: al-Shidyaq wa al-saq 'ala al-saq: al-riwaya al-'ula fi al-'adab al-'arabi al-hadith* [A possible modernity in al-Shidyaq's *Leg Over Leg:* the first novel in modern Arabic literature]. Cairo: Dar al-shorouq.

'Awadayn, Ahmed al-Sayyid. 1998. *Al-Mazini ba'da nisf qarn* [al-Mazini after half a century]. Cairo: Dar al-hilal.

'Ayyad, Shukri. 1971. *al-'Adab fi 'alam mutaghayyir.* Cairo: al-Hay'a al-misriyya al-'amma li al-ta'lif wa al-nashr.

Badawi, M. M. 1993. *A Short History of Modern Arabic Literature.* Oxford: Clarendon Press.

Badawi, Muhammad. 1999. "Interview." In *Kalam 'an al-kitaba* [Words about writing]. Documentary directed by 'Aliyya al-Biyali.

———. 2002. "Lusus mutaqa'idun li al-masri Hamdi Abu Golayyel: kitaba riwa'iyya mukhtalifa li mawdu' taqlidi" [*Thieves in Retirement* by the Egyptian writer Hamdi Abu Gollayel: Writing a different narrative on a traditional topic]. *al-Hayat,* no. 14250 (26 March): 16.

Badr, 'Abd al-Muhsin Taha. 1968. *Tatawwur al-riwaya al-'arabiyya al-haditha fi misr 1870–1938* [The development of the modern Arabic novel]. Cairo: Dar al-ma'arif.

Badran, Margot. 1995. *Feminists, Islam and Nation: Gender and the Making of Modern Egypt.* Princeton: Princeton University Press.

Badran, Margot, and Miriam Cooke, eds. 1990. *Opening the Gates: A Century of Arab Feminist Writing.* Bloomington: Indiana Univ. Press.

al-Badri, Hala. 1996. "Latifa al-Zayyat al-'insan wa al-ramz." In *Latifa al-Zayyat: al-'adab wa al-watan,* edited by Sayyid al-Bahrawi. Cairo: Nur, dar al-mar'a al-'arabiyya li al-nashr wa markaz al-buhuth al-'arabiyya li al-nashr.

al-Bahrawi, Sayyid. 1996a. "al-Adab wa al-watan." *Nur* 6 (Winter): 31–33.

———. 1996b. *Muhtawa al-shakl fi al-riwaya al-'arabiyya.* Vol. 1, *al-Nusus al-misriyya al-'ula* [Form in the Arabic novel, vol. 1, Early Egyptian texts]. Cairo: al-Hay'a al-'amma li al-kitab.

Barakat, Halim. 1975. "Arabic Novels and Social Transformation." In *Studies in Modern Arabic Literature,* edited by R. C. Ostle, 126–37. Warminster, UK: Aris and Philips.

al-Bardi, Mohammed. 2001. "Al-Mazini saridan wa 'as'ilat al-tajnis" [al-Mazini the narrator and questions of genre]. In *Ibrahim al-Mazini: 'ibda' wa tajdid* [Ibrahim al-Mazini: innovation and creativity]. Proceedings of a conference held in Cairo in June 1999. Cairo: al-Majlis al-'ala li al-thaqafa.

Baron, Beth. 1994. *The Women's Awakening in Egypt.* New Haven and London: Yale Univ. Press.

———. 2005. *Egypt as a Woman: Nationalism, Gender, and Politics.* Cairo: American Univ. in Cairo Press.

Barrada, Muhammad. 1996. "Hamlat taftish 'awraq shakhsiyya." In *Latifa al-Zayyat al-'adab wa al-watan,* edited by Sayyid al-Bahrawi, 175–78. Cairo: Nur, dar al-mar'a al-'arabiyya li al-nashr wa markaz al-buhuth al-'arabiyya li al-nashr.

Baydun, 'Azza Sharara. 2007. *al-Rujula wa taghayyur 'ahwal al-nisa'* [Manhood and the changes in women's conditions: an empirical study]. Beirut: al-Markaz al-thaqafi al-'arabi.

Beard, Michael, and Adnan Haydar eds. 1993. *Naguib Mahfouz: From Regional Fame to Global Recognition.* Syracuse: Syracuse Univ. Press.

Bhabha, Homi. 1990. "Dissemination: Time, Narrative, and the Margins of the Modern Nation." In *Nation and Narration,* ed. Homi Bhabha, 291–322. London and New York: Routledge.

Birayri, Muhammad. 2002. "Fi'l al-kitaba wa su'al al-wujud: qira'a fi 'awraq Somaya Ramadan al-narjisiyya," [Writing and being: a reading of Somaya Ramadan's *Leaves of Narcissus*]. *Alif: Journal of Comparative Poetics. The Language of the Self: Autobiographies and Testimonies* 22:94–113.

Booth, Marilyn. 1991. "Biography and Feminist Rhetoric in Twentieth-Century Egypt: Mayy Ziyada's Studies of Three Women's Lives." In *Journal of Women's History* 3, no. 1 (Spring): 38–64.

———. 1995. "Exemplary Lives, Feminist Aspirations: Zaynab Fawwaz and the Arabic Biographical Tradition." *Journal of Arabic Studies* 26, no. 2: 120–46.

———. 2001a. "'Amthila min al-bina' al-adabi li hayat Malak Hifni Nasif." In *Min ra'idat al-qarn al-'ishriyn: shakhsiyyat wa qadaya,* edited and introduced by Hoda Elsadda, 61–71. Cairo: Multaqa al-mar'a wa al-dhakira.

———. 2001b. *May Her Likes Be Multiplied: Biography and Gender Politics in Egypt.* Berkeley, Los Angeles, and London: Univ. of California Press.

———. 2001c. "Woman in Islam: Men and the 'Woman's Press' in Turn-of-the-Century Egypt." *International Journal of Middle East Studies* 33, no. 2:171–201.

Braidotti, Rosi. 1994. *Nomadic Subjects: Embodiment and Sexual Difference in Contemporary Feminist Theory.* New York: Columbia Univ. Press.

———. 1996. "Nomadism with a Difference: Deleuze's Legacy in a Feminist Perspective." *Man and World* 29:305–4.

Brennan, Timothy. 1990. "The National Longing for Form." In *Nation and Narration,* edited by Homi Bhabha, 44–70. London and New York: Routledge.

Cachia, Pierre. 1990. *An Overview of Modern Arabic Literature.* Islamic Surveys 17. Edinburgh: Edinburgh University Press.

Caiani, Fabio. 2007. *Contemporary Arab Fiction: Innovation from Rama to Yalu.* London and New York: Routledge.

Chatterjee, Partha. 1996. "Whose Imagined Community?" In *Mapping the Nation,* edited by Gopal Balakrishnan, with an introduction by Benedict Anderson, 214–45. London and New York: Verso.

Cixous, Hélène. 1976. "The Laugh of the Medusa." Translated by Keith Cohen and Paula Cohen. *Signs* 1, no. 4 (Summer): 875–93.

Cole, Juan R. I. 1993. *Colonialism and Revolution in the Middle East: Social and Cultural Origins of Egypt's 'Urabi Movement.* Princeton, NJ: Princeton Univ. Press.

Colla, Elliot. 2009. "How Zaynab Became the First Arabic Novel." *History Compass* 7, no. 1:214–25.

Connell, R. W. 1987. *Gender and Power: Society, the Person and Sexual Politics.* Oxford: Polity Press in association with Basil Blackwell.

———. 2002. "The History of Masculinity." In *The Masculinity Studies Reader,* ed. Rachel Adams and David Savran. Oxford: Blackwell.

———. 2005. "Hegemonic Masculinity: Rethinking the Concept." *Gender and Society* 19, no. 6:829–59.

Cooke, Miriam. 1988. *War's Other Voices: Women Writers on the Lebanese Civil War.* Cambridge: Cambridge Univ. Press.

———. 1994. "Naguib Mahfouz, Men, and the Egyptian Underworld." In *Fictions of Masculinity: Crossing Cultures, Crossing Sexualities,* edited by Peter F. Murphy, 96–120. New York and London: New York Univ. Press.

Corse, Sarah M. 1995. "Nations and Novels: Cultural Politics and Literary Use." *Social Forces* 73, no. 4 (June): 1279–1308.

Coupland, Douglas. 1991. *Generation X: Tales for an Accelerated Culture.* London: Abacus Book.

Cromer, Evelyn Baring. 1908. *Modern Egypt.* New York: Macmillan.

Darraj, Faysal. 1996. "Hamlat Taftish 'aw 'ahzan al-mutamarrid." In *Latifa al-Zayyat: al-adab wa al-watan,* edited by Sayyid al-Bahrawi, 183–84. Cairo: Nur, dar al-mar'a al-'arabiyya li al-nashr wa markaz al-buhuth al-'arabiyya li al-nashr.

Dawson, Graham. 1994. *Soldier Heroes: British Adventure, Empire, and the Imaginary of Masculinities.* London and New York: Routledge.

Deleuze, Gilles, and Felix Guattari. (1980) 2004. *A Thousand Plateaus: Capitalism and Schizophrenia.* Translated by Brian Massumi. London: Continuum.

Derne, Steve. 2000. "Men's Sexuality and Women's Subordination in Indian Nationalisms." In *Gender Ironies of Nationalism: Sexing the Nation,* edited by Tamar Mayer, 237–60. London and New York: Routledge.

Doss, Madiha. 1997. "al-'Amiyya al-misriyya 'inda 'Abdallah al-Nadim" [Egyptian colloquial Arabic in the writings of Abdallah al-Nadim]. In *Buhuth nadwat al-'ihtifal bi thikra murur mi'at 'am 'ala wafat 'Abdallah al-Nadim,* 291–92. Cairo: al-Majlis al-'a'la li al-thaqafa.

Du Bois, W. E. B. (1903) 1968. "The Souls of Black Folk." In *Black Voices: An Anthology of Afro-American Literature,* edited by Abraham Chapman. New York: New American Library.

Duma, Khayri. n.d. "Riwayat al-sira al-dhatiyya al-jadida: qira'a fi ba'd 'riwayat al-banat' fi misr al-tis'inat" [The new autobiographical novel: a reading of selected 'novels by young women' in the 1990s in Egypt]. *Nizwa,* 27 July 2009. http://www.nizwa.com/articles.php?id=2885. Accessed 25 November 2009.

Eagleton, Terry. 1983. "The Rise of English." In *Literary Theory: An Introduction.* London: Basil Blackwell.

Elsadda, Hoda. 1993. "al-Mar'a mantiqat muharramat: qira'a fi 'a'mal Qasim Amin" [Woman, a taboo area: a reading of the work of Qasim Amin].In *Hajar,* edited by Hoda Elsadda and Salwa Bakr, 144–60. Cairo: Dar sina.

———. 1994. "Malak Hifni Nasif: sawt mafqud fi ta'rikh al-nahda al-misriyya" [Malak Hifni Nassef: a missing voice in the history of the Egyptian enlightenment]. In *Hajar,* edited by Hoda Elsadda and Salwa Bakr, 109–19. Cairo: Dar sina.

———. 1995. "Latifa al-Zayyat's *Sahib al-bayt.*" In *Cairo Studies in English: Essays in Honour of Angele B. Samaan,* 25–47. Cairo: Cairo Univ.

———. 1998. "Muqaddima" [Introduction]. In *Nisa'iyyat,* by Malak Hifni Nasif, 6–33. Cairo: Multaqa al-mar'a wa al-dhakira.

———. 2000. "Ru'yat al-rajul li dhatihi fi maraya tasawuratihi al-tamthiliyya 'an al-mar'a" [Male perceptions of their selves through the mirror of their representations of women]. In *'A'mal mu'tamar mi'at 'am 'ala tahrir al-mar'a* [Proceedings of a conference entitled A Hundred Years since the Liberation of Women], 349–65. Cairo: al-Majlis al-'a'la li al-thaqafa.

———. 2004. "al-Kitaba al-'ibda'iyya li al-nisa' fi misr" [Women's creative writing in Egypt]. In *Dhakira li al-mustaqbal: mawsu'at al-mar'a al-'arabiyya* [The memory of the future: an encyclopedia of Arab women's writings], 7–59. Cairo: Nur and al-majlis al-'a'la li al-thaqafa.

———. 2006. "Gendered Citizenship: Discourses on Domesticity in the Second Half of the Nineteenth Century." *Hawwa: Journal of Women of the Middle East and the Islamic World* 4, no. 1:1–28.

———. 2007. "Imaging the 'New Man': Gender and Nation in Arab Literary Narratives in the Early Twentieth Century." *JMEWS: Journal of Middle East Women's Studies* 3, no. 2 (Spring): 31–55.

———. 2008. "Egypt." In *Arab Women Writers: A Critical Reference Guide 1873–1999,* edited by Radwa Ashour, Ferial Ghazoul, and Hasna Mekdashi; translated by Mandy McClure, 98–161. Cairo and New York: American Univ. Press.

———. 2010. "Arab Women Bloggers: The Emergence of Literary Counterpublics." *Middle East Journal of Culture and Communication* 3, no. 3:312–32.

El-Enany, Rasheed. 1993. *Naguib Mahfouz: The Pursuit of Meaning.* London and New York: Routledge.

———. 2006. *Arab Representations of the Occident: East-West Encounters in Arabic Fiction.* London and New York: Routledge.

Enloe, Cynthia. 1989. *Bananas, Beaches, and Bases: Making Feminist Sense of International Politics.* Berkeley: Univ. of California Press.

Ez Eldin, Mansoura. 2006. "An Awkward Situation." *Banipal* 25 (Spring): 52.

Fakhr, Husam. 1985. *al-Busat laysa 'ahmadiyyan.* With an introduction by Yusuf Idris. Cairo: al-Ahram.

———. 1992. *'Umm al-shu'ur.* Cairo: Mukhtarat fusul, al-hay'a al-'ama li al-kitab.

———. 2004. *Wujuh New York* [Faces of New York]. Cairo: Dar merit.

———. 2006. Ya 'aziz 'ayni [O apple of my eyes]. Cairo: Dar merit.

———. 2007. *Hikayaat Amina* [Amina's stories]. Cairo: Dar merit.

———. 2008a. *Hawadit al-'akhar* [Tales of the other]. Cairo: dar al-'ayn.

———. 2008b. Interview with Ahmad Wa'il on *Hawadit al-'akhar. 'Akhbar al-'adab,* 22 June.

Fanon, Frantz. (1961) 1967. *The Wretched of the Earth.* Translated by Constance Farrington, with a preface by Jean-Paul Sartre. London: Penguin Books.

———. (1975) 1986. *Black Skin, White Masks.* Translated by Charles Lam Markmann. London: Pluto.

Faqir, Fadia. 1995. "Introduction." In *The Golden Chariot,* by Salwa Bakr, translated by Dinah Manisty, v–ix. Reading: Garnett.

Farghali, Ibrahim. 2006a. "The Disconcerted Individual." *Banipal* 25 (Spring): 89.

———. 2006b. "Injil 'Adam li Muhammad 'Ala' al-Din: shayatin al-kitaba wa al-hayah." *al-Nahar* (Lebanese newspaper), 22 July. http://alaaeldin.blogspot.com/2006/09/2_10.html. Accessed 1 November.

Fawwaz, Zaynab. (1893) 1984. *al-Hawa wa al-wafa'* [Love and fidelity]. Cairo: al-Matba'a al-hindiyya; Beirut: al-Majlis al-thaqafi li janub Lubnan.

———. 1894. *Kitab al-durr al-manthur fi tabaqat rabbat al-khudur* [Scattered pearls in the biographies of hidden women]. Cairo: Bulaq, al-matba'a al-kubra al-'amiriyya.

———. (1899) 1984. *Husn al-'awaqib: Ghada al-Zahra'* [Good consequences or Ghada the Radiant]. Cairo: al-Matba'a al-hindiyya; Beirut: al-Majlis al-thaqafi li janub Lubnan.

———. 1905. *al-Malik Qurush* [King Qurush]. Cairo.

———. 1906. *al-Rasa'il al-zaynabiyya* [Zaynab's epistles]. Cairo: al-Matba'a al-mutawassitiyya.

Fawzi, Fatima. 2000. "Qamis wardi farigh: al-kitaba 'abra dawa'ir mughlaqa." *'Adab wa naqd,* November, 118–25.

Friedman, Susan Stanford. 1998. "Women's Autobiographical Selves: Theory and Practice." In *Women, Autobiography, Theory: A Reader,* edited by Sidonie Smith and Julia Watson, 72–82. Madison: Univ. of Wisconsin Press.

Fu'ad, Ni'mat. 1953. *Dirasa fi Adab al-Rafi'i* [A study of the literary work of al-Rafi'i]. Cairo: Dar al-fikr al-'Arabi.

———. 1978. *Ibrahim Abdel Qadir al-Mazini.* Cairo: Al-Hay'a al-'amma li al-kitab.

Gauch, Suzanne. 2007. *Liberating Shahrazad: Feminism, Postcolonialism, and Islam.* Minneapolis: Univ. of Minnesota Press.

Gerami, Shahin. 2005. "Islamist Masculinity and Muslim Masculinities." In *Handbook of Studies on Men and Masculinities,* edited by Michael S. Kimmel et al., 448–57. London and New Delhi: Sage Publications.

Ghazoul, Ferial. 1996. "al-Muqawamah 'abra al-mufaraqah" [Resistance via paradox]. In *Latifa al-Zayyat: al-adab wa al-watan,* edited by Sayyid al-Bahrawi, 197–200. Cairo: Nur, dar al-mar'a al-'arabiyya li al-nashr wa markaz al-buhuth al-'arabiyya li al-nashr.

Ghoussoub, May, and Emma Sinclair-Webb, eds. 2000. *Imagined Masculinities: Male Identity and Culture in the Modern Middle East.* London: Saqi Books.

Gordimer, Nadine. 1997. "Foreword: The Dialogue of Late Afternoon." In *Echoes of an Autobiography,* by Naguib Mahfouz, translated by Denys Johnson Davies. Cairo: American Univ. in Cairo Press.

Grace, Daphne. 2004. *The Woman in the Muslin Mask: Veiling and Identity in Post-colonial Literature.* London: Pluto Press.

Grewal, Inderpal, and Kaplan, Caren eds. 1997. *Scattered Hegemonies: Postmodernity and Transnational Feminist Practices.* Minneapolis and London: Univ. of Minnesota Press.

al-Hadari, Ihab. 2007. "al-Lugha al-jadida: 'akhtar wa muta': 'intaqalat min al-shari' wa dahaliz al-internet ila al-riwayat" [The new language: dangers and pleasures which moved from the street and the corridors of the Internet to novels]. *al-Sharq al-'awsat,* 9 May. http://www.aawsat.com/details.asp?section=19&issueno=10389&article=418428&feature=1. Accessed on 1 May 2008.

Hafez, Sabry. 1976. "The Egyptian Novel in the Sixties." *Journal of Arabic Literature* 7:68–84.

———. 1993. *The Genesis of Arabic Narrative Discourse: A Study in the Sociology of Modern Arabic Literature.* London: Saqi Books.

———. 2001. "Jamaliyyat al-riwaya al-jadida: al-qati'a al-ma'rifiyya wa al-naz'a al-mudadda li al-ghina'iyya" [Poetics of the new novel] *Alif: Journal of Comparative Poetics. The Lyrical Phenomenon* 21:184–246.

———. 2002. "Torture, Imprisonment, and Political Assassination in the Arab Novel." Translated from Arabic by Basil Samara. *Al Jadid* 8, no. 38 (Winter), http://www.aljadid.com/content/torture-imprisonment-and-political-assassination-arab-novel. Accessed 12 May 2009

al-Hafiz, Yasir 'Abd. 1996. "Vito 'ala kitabat al-banat" [A veto on girls' writing]. *'Akhbar al-'adab* (22 December): 8.

———. 1997a. "Sab'at 'ashar kawkaban fi sama' kitabat 1997" [Seventeen planets in the sky of literature written in the 1997s] *'Akhbar al-'adab* (28 September): 15

———. 1997b. "Wahdati tadfa'uni li kitaba tanshud al-kamal" [Interview with Nura Amin: my loneliness pushes me to a writing that seeks completion]. *'Akhbar al-'adab* (8 June): 9.

Haikal, Mohammed Hussein. (1914) 1992. *Zaynab.* 5th ed. Cairo: Dar al-ma'arif.

———. 1990. *Zainab.* Translated by J. M. Grinsted. Darf Publishers.

al-Hakim, Tawfiq. (1933) 2005. *'Awdat al-ruh.* Cairo: Dar al-shorouq.

———. 1938a. *Tahta shams al-fikr.* Cairo: Maktabat al-'adab wa matba'atuha.

———. 1938b. *'Usfur min al-sharq.* Cairo: Lajnat al-ta'lif.

———. (1943) 1975. *Zahrat al-'umr.* Cairo: Dar al-hilal.

———. (1944) 1972. *al-Ribat al-muqaddas.* Cairo: Maktabat al-'adab.

———. 1964. *Sijn al-'umr.* Cairo: al-Matba'a al-namuthajiyya.

———. 1966. *Bird of the East.* Translated by R. Bayly Winder. Beirut: Khayyats.

———. 1976. *Himar al-Hakim,* Cairo: al-Matba'a al-namuthajiyya.

———. 1990. *The Return of the Spirit.* Translated by William M. Hutchins. Three Continents Press.

Halim, 'Asma. 1977. *Hikayat 'Abdu 'Abd al-Rahman* [The story of Abdu Abd al-Rahman]. Cairo: Dar al-thaqafa al-jadida.

Hannah, Michelle. 2005. "*'Injil 'Adam.*" *Boswtol* online magazine, no. 70 (8 November); no longer available.

Haqqi, Yahya. (1944) 1984. *Qindil 'Umm Hashim.* Cairo: Dar al-ma'arif.

———. 1973. *The Saint's Lamp and Other Stories.* Translated by M. M. Badawi. Leiden: E. J. Brill.

———. 1986. *Fajr al-qissa al-misriyya.* Cairo: al-Hay'a al-'amma li al-kitab.

Hartman, Michelle. 2004. "'Besotted with the Bright Lights of Imperialism'? Arab Subjectivity Constructed Against New York's Many Faces." *Journal of Arabic Literature* 35, no. 3:270–96.

Hashim, Labiba. 1899. "Hasanat al-hub." *al-Diya',* 30 June, 634.

———. (1904) 2002. *Qalb al-rajul* [The heart of man]. With an introduction by Yumna al-'Id. Damascus: Dar al-mada.

———. 1906. "Introduction." *Fatat al-sharq,* no. 1.

Hassan, Wail S. 2003. "Gender (and) Imperialism: Structures of Masculinity in Tayeb Salih's *Season of Migration to the North.*" *Men and Masculinities* 5, no. 3:309–24.

Hatem, Mervat. 1994. "Egyptian Discourses on Gender and Political Liberalization: Do Secularist and Islamist Views Really Differ?" *Middle East Journal* 48, no. 4 (Autumn): 661–76.

———. 1998. "Dumu' 'A'isha Taymur wa naqd khatabay al-hadatha wa al-niswi 'an misr fi al-qarn al-tasi' 'ashar" [The tears of Aisha Taymur: a critique of modernist and feminist discourses on Egypt in the nineteenth century]. In *Zaman al-nisa' wa al-dhakira al-badila* [Women's time and alternate memory], edited by Hoda Elsadda et al., 245–74. Cairo: Multaqa al-mar'a wa al-dhakira.

———. 2001a. "A Discursive Study of the Debate on the Changing Roles of Women in Late Nineteenth Century Egypt and the Development of a Social-Sexual Contract." Paper presented at the Second Mediterranean Social and Political Research Meeting, Mediterranean Programme, Robert Schuman Centre for Advanced Studies, European Univ. Institute, Florence. March.

———. 2001b. "Malak Hifni Nasif bayna ru'a qadima wa jadida." In *Min ra'idat al-qarn al-'ishriyn: shakhsiyyat wa qadaya,* edited and introduced by Hoda Elsadda, 23–37. Cairo: Multaqa al-mar'a wa al-dhakira.

———. 2003. "Introduction." In *Nata'ij al-'ahwal fi al-'aqwal wa al-'af'al.* 2d ed. Cairo: al-Majlis al-qawmi li al-mar'a.

———. 2008. "Writing About Life Through Loss: 'A'isha Taymur's Elegies and the Subversion of the Arabic Canon." In *Transforming Loss into Beauty: Essays on Arabic Literature and Culture in Honor of Magda al-Nowaihi,* edited by Marle Hammond and Dana Sajdi, 229–52. Cairo and New York: American Univ. in Cairo Press.

———. 2011. *Literature, Gender and Nation-Building in Nineteenth-Century Egypt: The Life and Works of 'Aisha Taymur.* New York: Palgrave Macmillan.

Hawwas, Abd al-Hamid. 1997. "'Abdallah al-Nadim wa'y al-tahrir min al-fulklur ila al-thaqafa al-wataniyya" ['Abdallah al-Nadim—Liberation consciousness: from folklore to national culture]. In *Buhuth nadwat al-'ihtifal bi dhikra murur mi'at 'am 'ala wafat 'Abdallah al-Nadim,* 129–33. Cairo: al-Majlis al-'a'la li al-thaqafa.

Haydar, Adnan, and Michael Beard. 1993. "Mapping the World of Naguib Mahfouz." In *Naguib Mahfouz: From Regional Fame to Global Recognition,* edited by Michael Beard and Adnan Haydar, 1–9. Syracuse: Syracuse Univ. Press.

Helie-Lucas, Marie-Aimee. 1990. "Women, Nationalism, and Religion in the Algerian Liberation Struggle." In *Opening the Gates: A Century of Arab Feminist Writing,* edited by Margot Badran and Miriam Cooke, 105–14. London: Virago.

Herrera, Linda. 2002. "'The Soul of a Nation'–'Abdallah al-Nadim and Educational Reform in Egypt (1845–1896)." *Mediterranean Journal of Educational Studies* 7, no. 1:1–24.

Hishmat, Dina. 2006. *al-Qahira fi al-adab al-misri al-hadith wa al-mu'asir: min hilm al-madina al-kabira ila 'uzlat al-dawahi.* Cairo: al-Majlis al-'a'la li al-thaqafa.

Hrock, Miroslav. 1996. "From National Movement to the Fully-formed Nation: The Nation-building Process in Europe." *Mapping the Nation,* ed. Gopal Balakrishnan. London and New York: Verso.

Hunter, J. Paul. 1990. *Before Novels: The Cultural Contexts of Eighteen Century English Fiction.* New York and London: W. W. Norton and Company.

Husayn, Taha. 1978. "Introduction." In *'Ahadith jiddatti,* by Suhayr al-Qalamawi 9–19. Cairo: Dar al-hilal.

Ibrahim, Sonallah. (1966) 2003. *Tilka al-ra'iha.* Minya: Dar al-huda.

———. 1971. *The Smell of It.* Translated by Denys Johnson-Davies. London: Heinemann.

———. (1981) 1991. *al-Lajna.* 6th ed. Cairo: Dar sharqiyyat.

———. (1992) 2003. *Dhat.* Cairo: Dar al-mustaqbal al-'arabi.

———. 1997. *Sharaf.* Cairo: Dar al-hilal.

———. 2001a. *The Committee.* Translated by Mary St. Germain and Charlene Constable, with an afterword by Roger Allen. Syracuse: Syracuse Univ. Press.

———. 2001b. *Zaat.* Translated by Anthony Calderbank. Cairo: American Univ. in Cairo Press.

———. 2003. "Interview with Youssef Rakha." *al-Ahram Weekly* no. 666 (27 November–3 December). http://weekly.ahram.org.eg/2003/666/cu1.htm.

———. 2004. *'Amrikanli* [The American way]. 2d ed. Cairo: Dar al-mustaqbal al-'arabi.

———. 2008. *al-Qanun al-faransi* [The French law]. Cairo: Dar al-mustaqbal al-'arabi.

al-'Id, Yumna. 2002a. "Interview." *'Akhbar al-'adab,* 3 November, 8.

———. 2002b. "Muqaddima" [Introduction]. *Qalb al-rajul* by Labiba Hashim. Damascus: dar al-mada.

Ismail, Salwa. 2006. *Political Life in Cairo's New Quarters: Encountering the Everyday State.* Minneapolis: Univ. of Minnesota Press.

al-Jabiri, 'Abd al-Mit'al. 1976. *al-Muslima al-'asriya 'inda Bahithat al-Badiya Malak Hifni Nasif.* [The modern Muslim woman in the writings of the searcher in the desert]. Cairo: Dar al-bayan.

Jacob, Wilson Chacko. 2004. "The Turban, the Tarbush, and the Top Hat: Masculinity, Modernity, and National Identity in Interwar Egypt." *al-Raida* 21, no. 104–5 (Winter/Spring): 23–37.

———. 2007. "Eventful Transformations: al-Futuwwa Between History and the Everyday." *Comparative Studies in Society and History* 49, no. 3:689– 712.

Jacquemond, Richard. 2004. "The Shifting Limits of the Sayable in Egyptian Fiction." *The MIT Electronic Journal of Middle East Studies* 4 (Fall): 41–52.

———. 2008. *Conscience of the Nation: Writers, State, and Society in Modern Egypt.* Cairo and New York: American Univ. in Cairo Press.

Jameson, Frederic. 1986. "Third-World Literature in the Era of Multinational Capitalism." *Social Text* 15 (Autumn): 65–88.

JanMohamed, Abdul R. 1983. *Manichean Aesthetics: The Politics of Literature in Colonial Africa.* Amherst: Univ. of Massachusetts Press.

Jayyusi, Salma Khadra. 1992. “Introduction: Palestinian Literature in Modern Times.” In *Anthology of Modern Palestinian Literature,* edited and introduced by Salma Khadra Jayyusi, 1–80. New York: Columbia Univ.

———. 1993. “The Arab Laureate and the Road to Nobel.” In *Naguib Mahfouz: From Regional Fame to Global Recognition,* edited by Michael Beard and Adnan Haydar, 10–20. Syracuse: Syracuse Univ. Press.

al-Jindi, Anwar. 1966. *al-Ma‘arik al-’adabiyya fi al-shi‘r wa al-nathr wa al-thaqafa wa al-lugha wa al-qawmiyya al-‘arabiyya* [Literary battles over poetry, prose, culture, language and Arab nationalism]. Cairo: Matba‘at al-risala.

al-Jimi‘i, ‘Abd al-Mon‘im Ibrahim. 1994. “An Analytical Study.” In *al-Tankit wa al-tabkit,* by ‘Abdallah al-Nadim, with an introduction by ‘Abd al-‘Azim Ramadan. Cairo: al-Hay’a al-‘amma li al-kitab.

Kaaki, Lisa. 2006. “Ahmed Alaidy’s Mad Mad World.” *Arab News,* 2 November. http://archive.arabnews.com/?page=21&section=0&article=84718&d=6&m=11&y=2006. Accessed 28 April 2008.

Kahf, Mohja. 2000. “Packaging ‘Huda’: Sha‘rawi’s Memoirs in the United States Reception Environment.” In *Going Global: The Transnational Reception of Third World Women Writers,* edited by Amal Amireh and Lisa Suhair Majaj, 148–72. New York and London: Garland.

Kamal, Hala. 2001. “’Awraq al-narjis: al-junun muqawamat al-samt bil kitaba” [Leaves of narcissus: madness and resisting silence in writing]. *’Adab wa naqd* 132.

Kamal, Therese Fabi. 1988. “Riwayat al-ribat al-muqaddas li Tawfiq al-Hakim wa ‘alaqatuha bi riwayat tayyis li Anatole France.” In *Tawfiq al-Hakim: al-’adib, al- mufakkir, al-’insan: al-kitab al-tidhkari.* Vol. 1. Introduced by ‘Abd al-‘Aziz al-Dissuqi. Cairo: al-Markaz al-qawmi li al-’adab, wizarat al-thaqafa.

Kandiyoti, Deniz. 1991. “Identity and Its Discontents: Women and the Nation.” *Millenium: Journal of International Studies* 20, no. 3:429–43.

———. 1994. “Paradoxes of Masculinity: Some Thoughts on Segregated Societies.” In *Dislocating Masculinity: Comparative Ethnographies,* edited by Andrea Cornwall and Nancy Lindisfarne, 196–212. London and New York: Routledge.

Kaplan, Caren. 1990. “Deterritorializations: The Rewriting of Home and Exile in Western Feminist Discourse.” In *The Nature and Context of Minority Discourse,* edited by Abdul R. JanMohamed and David Lloyd, 357–68. New York and Oxford: Oxford Univ. Press.

Kendall, Elisabeth. 2003. “The Theoretical Roots of the Literary Avant-garde in 1960s Egypt.” *Edebiyat* 14, no. 1–2:39–56.

———. 2006. *Literature, Journalism, and the Avant-Garde: Intersection in Egypt.* London: Routledge.

Khalaf, Samir, and John Gagnon, eds. 2006. *Sexuality in the Arab World.* London, San Francisco, and Beirut: Saqi.

Khalifa, 'Ijlal. 1973. *al-Haraka al-nisa'iyya al-haditha.* Cairo: al-Matba'a al-haditha.

Kholoussy, Hanan. 2010. *For Better, For Worse: The Marriage Crisis that Made Modern Egypt.* Stanford, CA: Stanford Univ. Press.

Khulayf, Yusuf. 1993. *al-Adab wa al-Haya al-Misriyya: Mohammed Hussein Haikal* [Literature and life in Egypt]. Cairo: Dar al-hilal.

Kilpatrick, Hilary. 1992. "The Egyptian Novel from *Zaynab* to 1980." In *Modern Arabic Literature,* edited by M. M. Badawi, 223–69. Cambridge: Cambridge Univ. Press.

Kimmel, Michael S., et al., eds. 2005. *Handbook of Studies on Men and Masculinities.* London and New Delhi: Sage Publications.

Krishnaswamy, Revathi. 1998. *Effeminism: The Economy of Colonial Desire.* Ann Arbor: Univ. of Michigan Press.

Leeuwen, Richard van. 1995. "Love and the Mechanisms of Power: Kamal Abd al-Jawwad and Sa'id al-Juhayni." In *Love and Sexuality in Modern Arabic Literature,* edited by Roger Allen, Hilary Kilpatrick, and Ed de Moor, 91–117. London: Saqi Books.

Lionnet, Francoise. 1995. *Postcolonial Representations: Women, Literature, Identity.* Ithaca: Cornell Univ. Press.

Mahfouz, Naguib. (1947) 1982. *Zuqaq al-midaq.* Cairo: Maktabat misr.

———. (1956) 1983. *Bayn al-qasrayn.* Cairo: Maktabat misr.

———. (1957) 1984a. *Qasr al-shawq.* Cairo: Maktabat misr.

———. (1957) 1984b. *al-Sukkariyyah.* Cairo: Maktabat misr.

———. 1967. *'Awlad haritna.* Beirut: Dar al-'adab al-lubnaniyya.

———. 1969. *Hams al-junun.* Cairo: Maktabat misr.

———. 1977. *al-Harafish.* Cairo: Maktabat misr.

———. 1990. *Palace Walk.* Translated by William Maynard Hutchins and Olive E. Kenny. New York: Anchor Books and Doubleday.

———. 1991. *Palace of Desire* Translated by William Maynard Hutchins, Olive E. Kenny, and Lorne M. Kenny. New York: Doubleday.

———. 1992a. *Midaq Alley.* Translated by Trevor Le Gassick. New York: Anchor.

———. 1992b. *Sugar Street.* Translated by William Maynard Hutchins and Angele Botros Samaan. New York: Anchor Books.

Majaj, Lisa Suhair, Paula Sunderman, and Therese Saliba, eds. 2002. *Intersections: Gender, Nation, and Community in Arab Women's Novels.* Syracuse: Syracuse Univ. Press.

Malti-Douglas, Fedwa. 1991. *Woman's Body, Woman's Word: Gender and Discourse in Arabo-Islamic Writing.* Princeton, NJ: Princeton Univ. Press.

Mandour, Mohamed. 1954. *Ibrahim al-Mazini.* Cairo: Maktabat nahdat Misr.

Massad, Joseph A. 2007. *Desiring Arabs.* Chicago: Univ. of Chicago Press.

Mayer, Tamar, ed. 2000. *Gender Ironies of Nationalism: Sexing the Nation.* London and New York: Routledge.

al-Mazini, Ibrahim ʿAbd al-Qadir. 1931. *Ibrahim al-katib.* Cairo: Matbaʿat maktabat misr.

———. 1976. *Ibrahim the Writer.* Translated by Magdi Wahba. Cairo: al-Hay'a al-ʿamma li al-kitab.

McClintock, Anne. 1995. *Imperial Leather: Race, Gender, and Sexuality in the Colonial Contest.* London and New York: Routledge.

Mehrez, Samia. 1994. *Egyptian Writers Between History and Fiction: Essays on Naguib Mahfouz, Sonallah Ibrahim, and Gamal al-Ghitani.* Cairo: American Univ. in Cairo Press.

———. 2001–2. "Where Have All the Families Gone? Egyptian Literary Texts of the 1990s." *Arab Studies Journal* 10, no. 1 (Fall/Spring): 31–49.

———. 2008. *Egypt's Culture Wars: Politics and Practice.* London and New York: Routledge.

Mehta, Brinda. 2007. *Rituals of Memory in Contemporary Arab Women's Writing.* Syracuse: Syracuse Univ. Press.

Metcalf, Barbara, ed. 1984. *Moral Conduct and Authority: The Place of Adab in South Asian Literature.* Berkeley: Univ. of California Press.

Meyer, Stefan. 2001. *The Experimental Arabic Novel: Postcolonial Literary Modernism in the Levant.* New York: State Univ. of New York Press.

Mikhail, Mona. 1978. *Images of Arab Women: Fact and Fiction.* Washington, DC: Three Continents Press.

Miller, Christopher L. 1998. *Nationalists and Nomads: Essays on Francophone African Literature and Culture.* Chicago and London: Univ. of Chicago Press.

Mitchell, Timothy. 1989. *Colonizing Egypt.* Cairo: American Univ. Press.

Mondal, Anshuman. 1999. "Naguib Mahfouz and His Women: The Cairo Trilogy," *SOAS Literary Review* 1 (November). http://www.soas.ac.uk/soaslit/issue1/MONDAL.PDF. Accessed 13 May 2009.

Moore, Lindsey. 2008. *Arab, Muslim, Woman: Voice and Vision in Postcolonial Literature.* London and New York: Routledge.

Murray, Stephen O., and Will Roscoe, eds. 1997. *Islamic Homosexualities: Culture, History, and Literature.* New York: New York Univ. Press.

Musa, Subhi. 2008. "Gamal al-Ghitani 'alqa muhadara fi 'ihtifal ja'izat Naguib Mahfouz li al-riwaya . . . Hamdi Abu Golayyel yantasir li al-'adab al-hamishi." *al-Hayat,* 18 December. http://international.daralhayat.com/archivearticle/289581. Accessed 10 November 2009.

al-Musawi, Muhsin Jassim. 2003. *The Postcolonial Arabic Novel: Debating Ambivalence.* Leiden and Boston: Brill.

———. 2007. "Engaging Globalization in Modern Arabic Literature: Appropriation and Resistance." In *Modern Language Quarterly* 68, no. 2 (June): 305–29.

Naaman, Mara. 2006. "America Undone: Sonallah Ibrahim's Intra-Imperial Investigations." *Alif: Journal of Comparative Poetics. Wanderlust: Travel Literature of Egypt and the Middle East* 26:71–93.

al-Nadim, 'Abdallah. (1881) 1994. *al-Tankit wa al-tabkit.* With an introduction by 'Abd al-'Azim Ramadan. Cairo: al-hay'a al-'amma li al-kitab.

———. (1892–93) 1994. *Al-Ustadh.* With an introduction by 'Abd al-'Azim Ramadan. Cairo: al-Hay'a al-'amma li al-kitab.

Naji, Sawsan. 1989. *al-Mar'a fi al-mir'at: dirasa naqdiyya li al-riwaya al-nisa'iyya fi misr, 1888–1985* [Woman in the mirror: a critical study of women's novels in Egypt, 1888–1985]. Cairo: al-Ra'i.

———. 2006. *Surat al-rajul fi al-qassas al-nisa'i* [The image of man in short stories by women]. Cairo: al-Majlis al-'a'la li al-thaqafa.

al-Najjar, Safa'. 2006. "Literature of the 'Ghetto'." *Banipal* 25 (Spring): 100.

Najmabadi, Afsaneh. 1991. "The Hazards of Modernity and Morality: Women, State, and Ideology in Contemporary Iran." In *Women, Islam, and the State,* edited by Deniz Kandiyoti, 48–76. Philadelphia: Temple Univ. Press.

Nandy, Ashis. 1983. *The Intimate Enemy: Loss and Recovery of Self under Colonialism.* New Delhi: Oxford Univ. Press.

al-Naqqash, Raja'. 1998. *Naguib Mahfouz: safahat min mudhakiratihi wa 'adwa' jadida 'ala 'adabihi wa hayatihi* [Naguib Mahfouz: pages from his memoirs and new insights into his art and life]. Cairo: al-Markaz al-ahram li al-tarjama wa al-nashr.

Nasif, Malak Hifni. (1910) 1998. *al-Nisa'iyyat.* With an introduction by Hoda Elsadda. Cairo: Multaqa al-mar'a wa al-dhakira.

———. 1962. *'Athar Bahithat al-Badiya Malak Hifni Nasif 1886–1918.* Cairo: Wizarat al-thaqafa wa al-'irshad al-qawmi.

Nawfal, Hind. (1892–93) 2007. *Al-Fatah* [The young woman]. Republished with an introduction by Hoda Elsadda. Cairo: al-mar'a wa al-thakira.

Nestrovski, Arthur. 1988. "Blindness and Inwit: James Joyce and the Sirens: A Reading of Chapter 11 of *Ulysses.*" *Iowa Review* 18, no. 1 (Winter): 18–26.

al-Nowaihi, Magda. 2000. "The 'Middle East'? Or . . . /Arabic Literature and the Postcolonial Predicament." In *A Companion to Postcolonial Studies,* edited by Henry Schwarz and Sangeeta Ray, 282–303. Oxford: Blackwell.

———. 2001. "Resisting Silence in Arab Women's Autobiographies." *International Journal of Middle East Studies* 33, no. 4:477–502.

Noyes, John K. 2004. "Nomadism, Nomadology, Postcolonialism." *Interventions* 6, no. 2: 159–68.

Orlando, Valerie. 1999. *Nomadic Voices of Exile: Feminine Identity in Francophone Literature of the Maghreb.* Athens: Ohio Univ. Press.

———. 2006. "To Be Singularly Nomadic or a Territorialized National: At the Crossroads of Francophone Women's Writing of the Maghreb." *Meridians: Feminism, Race, Transnationalism* 6, no. 2:33–53.

Ouzgane, Lahoucine. 2003. "Islamic Masculinities: Introduction." *Men and Masculinities* 5, no. 3:231–35.

———, ed. 2006. *Islamic Masculinities.* London: Zed Books.

Ouzgane, Lahoucine, and Robert Morrell, eds. 2005. *African Masculinities: Men in Africa from the Late Nineteenth Century to the Present.* New York: Palgrave MacMillan; Scottsville: Univ. of KwaZulu-Natal Press.

Palahniuk, Chuck. 2005. *Fight Club.* With a new afterword, London: Vintage.

Parker, Andrew, et al., eds. 1992. *Nationalisms and Sexualities.* London and New York: Routledge.

Pierson, Ruth Roach, and Nupur Chaudhuri, eds. 1998. *Nation, Empire, Colony: Historicizing Gender and Race.* Bloomington and Indianapolis: Indiana Univ. Press.

Pollard, Lisa. 2005. *Nurturing the Nation: The Family Politics of Modernizing, Colonizing, and Liberating Egypt, 1805–1923.* Berkeley, Los Angeles, and London: Univ. of California Press.

al-Qalamawi, Suhayr. (1935) 1978. *'Ahadith jaddati* [My grandmother's stories]. Cairo: Dar al-hilal.

———. 1962. "Muqaddima" [Introduction]. In *'Athar Bahithat al-Badiya Malak Hifni Nasif 1886–1918,* by Malak Hifni Nasif. Collected and edited by Majd al-Din Hifni Nasif. Cairo: Wizarat al-thaqafa wa al-'irshad al-qawmi.

Qurani, Mahmoud. 2002. "al-Riwa'i wa al-qas Hamdi Abu Golayyel yahtafi bilususihi al-mutaqa'idin" [Interview: novelist and short story writer Hamdi Golayyel celebrates his *Thieves in Retirement*]. *al-Quds al-'Arabi,* 3 April, 10.

al-Qutt, 'Abd al-Qadir. 1982. *Bina' al-riwaya fi al-'adab al-misri al-hadith.* Cairo: Dar al-ma'arif.

Radhakrishnan, R. 1992. "Nationalism, Gender, and the Narrative of Identity." In *Nationalisms and Sexualities,* edited by Andrew Parker et al., 77–95. London and New York: Routledge

Radwan, Noha. 2008. "A Place for Fiction in the Historical Archive." *Critique: Critical Middle Eastern Studies* 17, no. 1 (Spring): 79–95.

al-Rafi'i, Mustafa Sadiq. 1931. *Awraq al-ward: rasa'iluha wa rasa'iluhu* [Rose petals: her epistles and his epistles]. Cairo: al-Matba'a al-salafiyya.

———. 1934a. "Armalat al-hukuma" [Widow of the nation]. *al-Risala* 2, no. 66 (8 October): 1643, 1644, 1679.

———. 1934b. "Fi al-lahab wa la tahtariq" [In the flames and she does not burn]. *al-Risala* 2, no. 57 (6 August): 1283–85.

———. 1934c. "Istanwaqa al-jamal" [He mistook the he-camel for a she-camel]. *al-Risala* 2, no. 64 (24 September):1563–65.

———. 1934d. "Zawjat imam" [Wife of an imam]. *al-Risala* 3, no. 88:243–47, 283–86.

———. 1935. "al-Ta'isha" [A reckless woman]. *al-Risala* 3, no. 96:963–67, 1003–6.

———. 1936a. "al-Qalb al-miskiyn 1" [The wretched heart]. *al-Risala* 4, no. 173 (26 October): 1723–25.

———. 1936b. "al-Qalb al-miskiyn 2." *al-Risala* 4, no. 175 (9 November): 1823–25.

———. 1936c. "al-Qalb al-miskiyn 3." *al-Risala* 4, no. 176 (16 November): 1863–65.

———. 1936d. "al-Qalb al-miskiyn 4." *al-Risala* 4, no. 177 (23 November): 1903–4.

———. 1936e. "al-Qalb al-miskiyn 5." *al-Risala* 4:179 (7 December): 1983–85.

———. 1936f. "al-Qalb al-miskiyn 6." *al-Risala* 4: 180 (14 December): 2023–25.

———. 1936g. "al-Qalb al-miskiyn 7." *al-Risala* 4: 182 (28 December): 2104–5.

———. 1937h. "al-Qalb al-miskiyn 8." *al-Risala* 5: 184 (11 January): 45–47.

al-Ra'i, 'Ali. 1964. *Dirasat fi al-riwaya al-misriyya* [Studies of the Egyptian novel]. Cairo: al-Mu'assasa al-misriyya al-'amma li al-ta'lif wa al-tarjama wa al-tiba'a wa al-nashr.

Ramadan, Somaya. 1995a. "'Adinu laha biwa'yi." *'Akhbar al-'adab,* 28 July, 12.

———. 1995b. *Khashab wa nuhas* [Wood and brass]. Cairo: Dar sharqiyyat.

———. 1996. "Hawla malaff al-banat yaktubna 'ajsadahunna: lisan wa shafatan." *'Ibda'*, 10 September, 35–39.

———. 2000. *'Awraq al-narjis.* Cairo: Dar sharqiyyat.

———. 2001. "Interview with Yasir 'Abd al-Hafiz." *'Akhbar al-'Adab* 189, (27 May): 10.

———. 2002. *Leaves of Narcissus.* Translated by Marilyn Booth. Cairo: American Univ. Press.

Rashid, Amina. 1995. "Latifa al-Zayyat." *Nur* 5 (Autumn).

Rastegar, Kamran. 2007. *Literary Modernity Between the Middle East and Europe: Textual Transactions in Nineteenth Century Arabic, English, and Persian Literature.* London and New York: Routledge.

Robertson, Roland. 1995. "Glocalization: Time-Space and Homogeneity-Heterogeneity." In *Global Modernities,* edited by Mike Featherstone, Scott Lash, and Roland Robertson, 25–44. London: Sage.

Rowbotham, Sheila. 1973. *Woman's Consciousness, Man's World.* London: Penguin.

al-Rubi, 'Ulfat. 1999. "Mayy Ziyada wa al-naqd al-nisa'i: qira'a fi kitabiha 'an 'A'isha Taymur" [Mayy Ziyada and feminist criticism: a reading of her book on 'A'isha Taymur]. *'Alif: al-junusa wa al-ma'rifa: siyaghat al-ma'arif bayna al-ta'nith wa al-tadhkir* [*Alif: Journal of Comparative Poetics. Gender and Knowledge: Contribution of Gender Perspectives to Intellectual Formations*] 19:144–69.

———. 2001. "Kitabat al-nisa' 'ala kitabat al-nisa': Mayy Ziyada wa bahithat al-badiya." In *Min ra'idat al-qarn al-'ishriyn: shakhsiyyat wa qadaya,* edited and introduced by Hoda Elsadda, 39–59. Cairo: Multaqa al-mar'a wa al-dhakira.

Russell, Mona L. 2004. *Creating the New Egyptian Woman: Consumerism, Education, and National Identity, 1863–1922.* New York: Palgrave Macmillan.

Ryzova, Lucie. 2005. "Egyptianizing Modernity: The 'New Effendiyya' Social and Cultural Constructions of the Middle Class in Egypt under the Monarchy." In *Re-Envisioning the Egyptian Monarchy,* edited by Arthur Goldschmidt et al., 124–63. Cairo: American Univ. in Cairo Press.

Sabri, Lubna. 2007. "Husam Fakhr: Yusuf Idris 'akhar 'am mawhiba jahiniyya jadida?" *Elaph,* 23 June. http://www.elaph.com/Web/Culture/2007/6/242741.htm?sectionarchive=Culture. Accessed 2 December 2009.

Safran, Nadav. 1961. *Egypt in Search of Political Community: An Analysis of the Intellectual and Political Evolution of Egypt, 1804–1952.* Cambridge: Harvard Univ. Press.

Said, Edward. (1978) 1979. *Orientalism.* New York: Vintage Books.

———. (1993) 1994. *Culture and Imperialism*. London: Vintage.

Sarkis, Hanna Afandi. 1904. "Qalb al-rajul." *'Anis al-jalis,* 1794.

al-Sayyid, Ahmed Lutfi. (1908) 1937. "Banatuna wa 'abna'una." In *al-Muntakhabat* [Selected pieces]. Cairo: Dar al-nashr al-hadith.

Selim, Samah. 2003. "The Narrative Craft: Realism and Fiction in the Arabic Canon." *Edebiyat* 14, no. 1/2:109–28.

———. 2004a. "The Nahdah, Popular Fiction, and the Politics of Translation." *MIT-EJMES* 4 (Fall): 71–90.

———. 2004b. *The Novel and the Rural Imaginary in Egypt, 1880–1985.* New York and London: Routledge Curzon.

Scott, Joan W. 1986. "Gender: A Useful Category of Analysis." *American Historical Review* 91, no. 5, 1053–75.

Shakry, Omnia. 1998. "Schooled Mothers and Structured Play: Child Rearing in Turn-of-the-Century Egypt." In *Remaking Women: Feminism and Modernity in the Middle East,* ed. Lila Abu-Lughod. Princeton, New Jersey: Princeton University Press, pp. 126–70.

Shaaban, Bouthaina. 2009. *Voices Revealed: Arab Women Novelists, 1898–2000.* Boulder and London: Lynne Rienner Publishers.

Shalan, Jeff. 2002. "Writing the Nation: The Emergence of Egypt in the Modern Arabic Novel." *Journal of Arabic Literature* 33, no. 3:211–47.

Shalash, Ali. 1988. *Al-majallat al-'adabiyya fi misr* [Literary magazines in Egypt]. Cairo: al-Ha'a al-'amma li al-kitab.

al-Sharif, Ahmed. 1998. "Qamis wardi farigh: al-hayat 'abra al-kitaba." *'Adab wa naqd* 151 (March): 97–104.

Sharif, Hiba. 1993. "Hal li al-nass al-nisa'i khususiyya? Dirasa li riwayat *al-Bab al-maftuh*" [What are the specificities of a feminist text? A study of *al-Bab al-Maftuh*]. In *Hajar* 1, edited by Hoda Elsadda and Salwa Bakr. Cairo: Dar sina li al-nashr.

el-Sheik, Ibrahim. 1991. "Egyptian Women as Portrayed in the Social Novels of Najib Mahfuz." In *Critical Perspectives on Naguib Mahfouz,* edited Trevor Le Gassick, 85–100. Washington, DC: Three Continents Press.

Shukri, Ghali. 1964. *al-Muntami: dirasa fi 'adab Naguib Mahfouz.* Cairo: Maktabat al-zanari.

———. 1966. *Thawrat al-mu'tazil: dirasah fi 'adab Tawfiq al-Hakim.* Cairo: Maktabat al-Anglo.

Siddiq, Muhammad. 2007. *Arab Culture and the Novel: Genre, Identity, and Agency in Egyptian Fiction.* London and New York: Routledge.

Sinha, Mrinalini. 1995. *The Manly Englishman and the Effeminate Bengali in the Late Nineteenth Century.* Manchester and New York: Manchester Univ. Press; St. Martin's.

Starkey, Paul. 1987. *From the Ivory Tower: A Critical Study of Tawfiq al-Hakim.* London: Ithaca Press, The Middle East Centre, St. Antony's College Oxford.

———. 1998. "Modern Egyptian Culture in the Arab World." In *The Cambridge History of Egypt.* Vol. 2, *Modern Egypt, from 1517 to the End of the Twentieth Century,* edited by M. W. Daly, 394–426. Cambridge: Cambridge Univ. Press.

———. 2006. *Modern Arabic Literature.* Edinburgh: Edinburgh Univ. Press.

Stehli-Werbeck, Ulrike. 2006. "The Question of Identity and the Narrative Concept of *Tilka al-ra'iha* by Sun'allah Ibrahım." *Middle Eastern Literatures* 9, no. 2 (August): 137–46.

al-Subki, Amal. 1986. *al-Haraka al-nisa'iyya fi misr ma bayna al-thawratayn 1919–1952.* Cairo: al-Hay'a al-misriyya al-'amma li al-kitab.

Tahir, Baha'. 2009. "Tawasul al-'ajyal fi al-'adab al-misri al-hadith: May Telmissany ka namudhaj." *Nizwa,* 14 July.

Tarabishi, George. (1977) 1997. *Sharq wa gharb, rujula wa 'unutha: dirasah fi 'azmat al-jins wa al-hadara fi al-riwaya al-'arabiyya.* Beirut: Dar al-tali'ah.

Taymur, 'A'isha. (1888) 2003. *Nata'ij al-'ahwal fi al-'aqwal wa al-'af'al* [The consequences of circumstances in words and deeds]. With an introduction by Mervat Hatem. Cairo: al-Majlis al-qawmi li al-mar'a.

———. (1892) 2002. *Mir'at al ta'amul fi al-'umur* [Mirror for reflection on affairs]. With an introduction by Mervat Hatem. Cairo: Multaqa la-mar'a wa al-dhakira.

Telmissany, May. 1996. "al-Kitaba 'ala hamish al-tarikh: misr al-ghiyab" [Writing on the margin of history: Egypt as absence]. In *Latifa al-Zayyat: al-'adab wa al-watan,* edited by Sayyid al-Bahrawi, 97–106. Cairo: Nur, dar al-mar'a al-'arabiyya li al-nashr wa markaz al-buhuth al-'arabiyya li al-nashr.

———. (1997) 2002. *Dunyazad.* Beirut: Dar al-'adab.

———. 2000. *Dunyazad.* Translated by Roger Allen. London: Saqi.

Tucker, Judith. 1985. *Women in Nineteenth-Century Egypt.* Cambridge: Cambridge Univ. Press.

Valassopoulos, Anastasia. 2007. *Contemporary Arab Women Writers: Cultural Expression in Context.* London and New York: Routledge.

Viswanathan, Guari. 1989. *Masks of Conquest: Literary Study and British Rule in India.* New York: Columbia Univ. Press.

Waugh, Patricia. 1984. *Metafiction: The Theory and Practice of Self-Conscious Fiction.* London and New York: Routledge.

West, Russell, and Frank Lay, eds. 2000. *Subverting Masculinity: Hegemonic and Alternative Versions of Masculinity in Contemporary Culture.* Amsterdam: Rodopi.

What About Masculinity. 2004. Special issue, *al-Raida* 21 (Winter/Spring): 104–5.

Wright, J. W., Jr., and Everett K. Rowson, eds. 1997. *Homoeroticism in Classical Arabic Literature.* New York: Columbia Univ. Press.

Yuval-Davis, Nira, and Flora Anthias, eds. 1989. *Woman-Nation-State.* London: Macmillan.

Yuval-Davis, Nira. 1997. *Gender and Nation.* London: Sage.

al-Zayyat, Latifa. (1960) 1989. *al-Bab al-maftuh.* Cairo: al-Hay'a al-misriyya al-'amma li al-kitab.

———. 1986. *al-Shaykhukha wa qisas 'ukhra.* Cairo: dar al-Mustaqbal al-'arabi.

———. 1989. *Min suwar al-mar'a fi al-riwaya wa al-qisas al-'arabiyya* [Images of women in Arabic novels and short stories]. Cairo: Dar al-thaqafa al-jadida.

———. 1990. "Hawla al-'iltizam al-siyasi wa al-kitaba al-nisa'iyya: muqabala m'a Latifa al-Zayyat" [Political commitment and feminist writing: interview with Latifa al-Zayyat]. *Alif* 10:134–50.

———. 1992a. *Hamlat taftish: 'awraq shakhsiyya.* Cairo: Dar al-hilal.

———. 1992b. "al-Katib wa al-huriyya" [The writer and freedom]. *Fusul* 11, no. 3 (Autumn): 237–39. Reprinted in *Latifa al-Zayyat: al-'adab wa al-watan,* edited by Sayyid al-Bahrawi. Cairo: Nur, dar al-mar'a al-'arabiyya li al-nashr wa markaz al-buhuth al-'arabiyya li al-nashr, 1996.

———. 1993. "Latifa al-Zayyat fi mir'at Latifa al-Zayyat." *'Ibda'* (1 January): 54–58.

———. 1994a. *Bay' wa shira'* [Selling and buying]. Cairo: al-Hay'a al-'amma li al-kitab.

———. 1994b. "Muqabala." *'Adab wa naqd* 106 (June).

———. 1994c. *Sahib al-bayt.* Cairo: Dar al-hilal.

———. 1994d. "Tajrubati fi al-kitaba" [My experience in writing]. In *Sahib al-bayt,* 117–29. Cairo: Dar al-hilal.

———. 1995. *al-Rajul al-ladhi 'arafa tuhmatahu.* Cairo: Dar sharqiyyat.

———. 1996. "shahadat mubdi'a" [Testimony of a woman creative writer]. *'Adab wa naqd* 135:17–20.

———. 1997a. *The Owner of the House.* Translated by Sophie Bennett. London: Quartet Books.

———. 1997b. *The Search: Personal Papers.* Translated by Sophie Bennett. London: Quartet.

———. 2000. *The Open Door.* Translated by Marilyn Booth. Cairo: American Univ. in Cairo Press.

Zeidan, Joseph T. 1995. *Arab Women Novelists: The Formative Years and Beyond.* New York: State Univ. of New York Press.

Zikri, Mustafa. 2006. "No More Big Issues." *Banipal* 25 (Spring): 82.

Zimmerman, Nadya. 2002. "Musical Form as Narrator: The Fugue of the Sirens in Joyce's Ulysses." In *Journal of Modern Literature* 26 (Fall): 108–18.

Ziyada, Mayy. 1920. *Bahithat al-badiya: bahth 'intiqadi.* Cairo: Matba'at al-muqtataf.

———. (1926) 1975. *'A'isha Taymur, sha'irat al-tali'a.* Beirut: Mu'assasat Nawfal.

Index